Truth and Objectivity

PHILOSOPHICAL THEORY

SERIES EDITORS

John McDowell, Philip Pettit and Crispin Wright

For Truth in Semantics
Anthony Appiah

Abstract Particulars
Keith Campbell

Tractarian Semantics
Finding Sense in Wittgenstein's Tractatus
Peter Carruthers

Truth and Objectivity
Brian Ellis

The Dynamics of Belief: A Normative Logic
Peter Forrest

Abstract Objects
Bob Hale

Fact and Meaning
Quine and Wittgenstein on
Philosophy of Language
Jane Heal

Conditionals
Frank Jackson

Reality and Representation
David Papineau

Facts and the Function of Truth
Huw Price

Moral Dilemmas
Walter Sinnott-Armstrong

Truth and Objectivity

BRIAN ELLIS

Basil Blackwell

1990

Copyright © Brian Ellis 1990

First published 1990

Basil Blackwell Ltd
108 Cowley Road, Oxford, OX4, 1JF, UK

Basil Blackwell, Inc.
3 Cambridge Center
Cambridge, Massachusetts 02142, USA

British Library Cataloguing in Publication Data

A CIP catalogue record for this book is available from the British Library.

Library of Congress Cataloging in Publication Data

Ellis, B. D. (Brian David), 1929–
    Truth and objectivity / Brian Ellis.
        p.   cm.
    Includes bibliographical references.
    ISBN 0–631–15397–7
    1. Truth.   2. Objectivity.   3. Ontology.   4. Knowledge, Theory of.
    5. Value.   6. Realism.   7. Science–Philosophy.   I. Title.
BD171.E44 1990
121–dc20   89–27798
                                                                        CIP

Typeset in 11 on 13 pt Baskerville
by Vera-Reyes Inc.
Printed in Great Britain by
T.J. Press (Padstow) Ltd, Padstow, Cornwall.

Contents

PART III   EPISTEMOLOGY

Preface

This book is part of a research programme on which I have been working for many years. The first stage of the programme was to naturalize logic by arguing that the laws of logic are laws of thought. They are, as I argued in *Rational Belief Systems* (1979), laws governing the structure of *ideally* rational belief systems. In that book, I argued that the status of the laws of logic is similar to that of most other scientific laws. Like other laws, they apply strictly only to idealized systems. Unlike other laws, however, they have normative force; they tell us how we *ought* rationally to structure our belief systems. To explain this, I argued that the normativeness of the laws of logic derives from the fact that the system of epistemic values needed to define the rational ideal must be just natural human epistemic values; hence the ideal must be one to which we naturally aspire.

The aim of this book is to naturalize our theories of truth and knowledge in the same kind of way, and to show how these theories can be used to justify a scientific ontology. The normativeness of the naturalized epistemology, and hence of the inductive strategies it endorses, will be shown to derive from the same source as that of the laws of logic. It is a values-based epistemology, and the values it depends on are natural human epistemic values.

In writing this book, I have been greatly helped by the comments and criticisms of colleagues and students in the Philosophy Department at La Trobe University. I am particularly grateful to John Bigelow, John Fox and Robert Pargetter for many good discussions of the main issues covered in the book. I am also grateful to Huw Price who read the first draft of the manuscript, and commented thoroughly and helpfully on it. In response to his comments I have made a number of significant changes to the text. John Clendinnen,

William Newton-Smith, Harvey Brown and Hugh Mellor also made helpful comments on some parts of the work when I was on leave in 1986.

In compiling the text, I have sometimes drawn quite heavily upon work I have published elsewhere. In particular, chapter 2 is based largely on my paper 'The Ontology of Scientific Realism', published in P. Pettit, R. Sylvan and J. Norman (eds) *Metaphysics and Morality: Essays in Honour of J. J. C. Smart*, Oxford, Blackwell, 1987; chapter 3 makes extensive use of material from my paper 'What Science Aims to Do', published in P. M. Churchland and C. A. Hooker (eds) *Images of Science*, Chicago University Press, 1985; and chapter 8 is heavily dependent on my paper 'Solving the Problem of Induction Using a Values-based Epistemology', published in the *British Journal for the Philosophy of Science* 39, 1988. In addition, excerpts from 'Internal Realism', published in *Synthese* 76, 1988 are to be found in several places in the text, and a modified version of 'Truth as a Mode of Evaluation', published in the *Pacific Philosophical Quarterly* 1, 1980, is included in chapter 7. I particularly wish to thank the editors and publishers of these books and journals for permission to use this material here.

My thanks are also due to John Wright and Janet Moyle who assisted me in preparing the bibliography. They are especially due to Mary Mulroney and Gai Dunn who prepared the manuscript for the publisher.

Brian Ellis
La Trobe University

Introduction

Our theories of truth and reality should be complementary. The theory of reality (i.e. our ontology) should permit the entities we need for our truth theory. The truth theory should be one on which we can justify our ontology. However, our theories of truth and reality often lack such nice coherence. In particular, the truth theories most commonly accepted by scientific realists appear to be incompatible with their ontologies. The correspondence theory of truth, for example, makes truth a relationship between eternal truth bearers and facts. But scientific realists have trouble identifying the entities required for this relationship to hold, even in the most elementary cases. In the more complex ones the task seems hopeless. The semantic theory of truth is better. For some elementary idealized languages, truth is definable in ways which are acceptable to some scientific realists. The truth bearers are the eternal sentences of these languages, and the truth makers are the objects which may satisfy them. However, many of the things we count as true do not appear to be expressible in a language of the required kind, and the programme of analysis which seeks to overcome this difficulty is now in some disarray. In particular, the existence of modal and conditional truths presents a major problem. The problem can be overcome by postulating that there is more to reality than scientific realism normally allows, viz. infinitely many worlds other than the actual world. I find this solution unacceptable, however, because the only reason we could have to believe in other possible worlds is that we need them to save the theory of truth which gives rise to them.

Part of the trouble may lie with the absolutist conception of truth which we inherited from the Greeks. On this conception, whatever is true is so timelessly, and independently of human language, thought and reasoning – a view which is naturally suggested by the propositions of mathematics. But such a conception of truth seems to require timeless truth bearers, and that we should have the capacities to comprehend and compare these entities with reality – a conclusion which Frege willingly acknowledged. But plausibly, such a conception of truth is more appropriate to a Platonic world-view than a scientific one. Therefore, it may be more in keeping with a scientific outlook to reject the classical concept of truth altogether, and replace it by an epistemic concept which is not absolute in this sense – a course which I suggested some years ago. However, it turns out that there is no need for conceptual revision. A theory of truth which preserves the classical properties of truth, and coheres with scientific realism, can be constructed.

This book traces an argument from a scientific ontology to such a theory of truth, and outlines an epistemology which will take us back to the ontology. The argument is circular, but none the worse for that, since its aim is to establish coherence. The ontology is the kind of theory of reality one would expect a scientific realist to hold, for it is constructed on the assumption that currently accepted scientific accounts of the nature of reality are the best theories available. It admits no more entities than appear to be necessary for these accounts to be viable. In contrast, the theory of truth I propose to defend is not one that is widely accepted by scientific realists. It is an evaluative theory in the sense that it identifies truth with what it is right to believe, and it is a naturalistic theory in that it is embedded in a naturalistic epistemology. I shall refer to it simply as 'the naturalistic theory of truth', since its most characteristic feature is its naturalism.

As a truth theory, it belongs to the pragmatic tradition. But it is sufficiently different from other theories in this tradition to require distinction. Roughly, the idea behind any pragmatic theory, or any other kind of evaluative theory, is that 'truth' is a term like 'rightness'; it has a role in epistemology like 'rightness' has in ethics, but is concerned with the evaluation of beliefs rather than actions. In other words, by the criteria appropriate to the epistemic evaluation of beliefs, the truth is what it is right to believe. What distinguishes the naturalistic evaluative theory I wish to defend is the kind of epistemology in which it is embedded. First, it is a values-based epistemology, as opposed to a rules-based system. Rules in this epistemology have only the status of epistemic strategies or rules of thumb for maximizing epistemic value. Secondly, the value system, with respect to which judgements of truth and falsity must be made, is assumed to be an autonomous system of natural epistemic values. Natural epistemic values thus have a key role in defining the naturalistic concept of truth. Other theories in the pragmatic tradition are less clear in distinguishing between epistemic and other kinds of values and less specific about the identity and status of these values. Moreover, the kind of epistemology, whether rules-based or values-based, required to define the concept of truth is rarely specified, and the epistemology itself is almost never worked out in detail.

The real work of defining the naturalistic concept of truth lies in expounding the complex system of basic epistemic values in terms of which epistemic rightness has to be defined. This task will occupy us towards the end of the book (in chapters 7 and 8). The exposition of this system of values has a good deal of independent interest; for to expound it, it is necessary to show how the value system works to structure and develop our belief systems. In many epistemologies it is assumed that knowledge grows by a process which involves following rules. This is true, for example, of all inductivist epistemologies. In other epistemologies, e.g. Popper's falsificationism, it is supposed that knowledge grows by a process akin to evolution by natural selection. Theories are invented and tested; those that fail the tests are eliminated, leaving only the fittest to survive. But what is needed here is a new kind of epistemology, in spirit more like inductivism than falsificationism, but based on values rather than rules. It should be like an ethical system, such as ideal utilitarianism, in which the aim is to maximize value, although, of course, the value to be maximized will be epistemic. Consequently, in the required epistemology, values will be supreme, and rules will have the status of rules of thumb, or general strategies for maximizing value, rather than synthetic *a priori* principles.

There is an important spin-off benefit from this. By changing the status of rules of inference, an evaluative epistemology changes the nature of the problem of induction. The apparently hopeless task of formulating an adequate inductive logic which reduces non-deductive reasoning to rule following can be abandoned without embracing the irrationalism of falsificationism. For inductive rules now take on the character of strategies, useful for promoting what we value epistemically, but not to be used indiscriminately – an attitude to induction which, I imagine, is likely to be shared by many people. The problem of induction, then, becomes that of justifying these strategies in relationship to the natural epistemic values they are supposed to promote. Of course, this problem is different from the traditional problem of induction. It is also much easier to solve, because there is no question of whether promoting these values promotes knowledge of the truth. For the truth, according to the naturalistic evaluative theory, is just what it is right to believe in relationship to these values.

The argument begins with an examination of the scientific point of view, and of its implications for the theory of human nature. It is argued that, from this point of view, dualism is untenable. The thoughts and experiences people have, and the emotions they feel, are just neurophysiological responses. It is also wrong for us to think of ourselves as agents freely constructing our belief systems on the basis of theory-neutral data given to us by perception. The data are not theory-neutral, and our constructions upon it are determined by physical causal processes. Many scientifically minded philosophers, who would accept this physicalist position, nevertheless continue to think of themselves dualistically. For they identify themselves with their faculties of reason and decision, and so think of themselves as rational agents, using the information they obtain by perception to construct their belief systems, and making decisions according to their beliefs. To construct their belief systems, they imagine that they have access to a set of *a priori* principles of reasoning, which they are free to use as they wish. It is argued that this kind of physical dualism is also a mistake. The processes involved in constructing our belief systems, viz. perceiving, reasoning, explaining, deliberating and deciding, are all physical causal processes. A belief system is not like a building, built by an agent; it is more like a landscape, formed and shaped by the external forces acting on it, and by the ecological balance of forces acting within it.

In chapter 2, the ontology which goes with accepting the scientific point of view is elaborated. I call it the ontology of scientific realism, because the chief argument for deriving the ontology is the main argument for scientific realism. The ontology includes categories of physical entities, physical events and physical properties, as well as various kinds of physical relationships, including causal, spatio-temporal and numerical relationships. The category of physical entities includes everything that has mass or energy; so, fundamentally, it includes such things as particles, fields and waves. The category of physical events includes all changes of energy distribution in the universe, and hence all causal interactions. There are, however, physical events which are not causal interactions. The class of physical properties includes all properties which influence causal interactions; the fundamental items in this category are presumably properties like mass, charge and spin.

The basic kinds of causal relationships which exist in nature are the fundamental forces, of which there would appear to be just four, viz. strong, weak, electromagnetic, and gravitational. All causal interactions involve one or more of these forces, or whatever the ultimate forces of nature are.[1] Spatio-temporal relationships between physical entities do not, at present, seem to have any atomic structure (unlike the items in the other categories), and appear to be irreducible. Numerical relationships between groups of physical entities also appear to be primitive.

The ontology does not admit abstract entities like propositions and sets, unless these can somehow be reduced to entities of other kinds. For such entities have no causes or effects, have no location in space or time, and cannot influence any causal processes. It is argued that while such entities may have a role in model theoretic explanations, acceptance of such explanations carries no ontological commitments; only the acceptance of causal explanations carries any such commitment to the entities involved. The entities occurring in our model theories should generally be regarded as fictions. The status of numbers is doubtful. For, while numbers are not themselves involved in causal explanations, numbers of specified kinds of things are. So it may be correct to think of numbers as second order properties, as has John Bigelow (1988) has recently suggested; i.e. one might regard the number two as the property of being doubly instantiated. Even so, there could only be a finite number of numbers in this sense; so that the number system, and its various extensions, would have to be regarded as fictitious.

The main challenge to scientific realism comes from empiricism, and this challenge is taken up in chapter 3. Empiricists argue that theories must always be empirically underdetermined, and that, consequently, we can never know which of the many theories compatible with the evidence is true. This argument derives from what is known as the empirical underdetermination thesis. It is admitted by nearly everyone that theories go beyond the evidence on which they are based, and hence that all theories are inductively underdetermined. Emeralds could, after all, turn out to be grue (Goodman 1954). The contentious issue is whether there are genuine, logically incompatible, theories which are empirically equivalent, in the *strong* sense that no evidence could possibly distinguish between them. It is argued that this thesis is essentially sceptical. It cannot be demonstrated by cases, because there is an openness of the field of evidence for a theory which makes it impossible to define the empirical content of a theory, and hence to show that any two genuine, logically incompatible, theories are ever empirically equivalent. The only way that alternative, empirically equivalent, theories can ever be defined is by building their empirical equivalence into their specifications, e.g. by saying such things as: 'Although the world behaves as if theory T were true, it is actually T' that is true, and God, or Nature, or some Evil Demon has conspired to forever conceal this fact from us.' That is, the strong empirical equivalence thesis can only be demonstrated by fiat.

To accept an Evil Demon argument of this kind, one has to be an absolutist about truth, and accept that truth is independent of what it could ever be right epistemically to believe – even if our theories were based on the best possible evidence, and were theoretically integrated in the best possible way. For the argument is not based on the claim that the Evil Demon variant of the best possible theory is as good as the original. It is just that the Evil Demon variant could just be true, despite the totality of evidence to the contrary. There are good reasons, however, why scientific realists should not accept a theory of truth of the kind that would be needed to make sense of this claim. They should not be absolutists about truth.

The main absolutist theories of truth are the correspondence theories, i.e. theories according to which truth is an objective relationship of correspondence between a truth bearer and reality – a relationship which holds, or fails to hold, independently of human beings, except that they happen to be the speakers of the languages with reference to which the truth bearers are normally defined. Of these, the most defensible is the semantic theory of truth, according to which truth is a complex relationship between words and the world, analysable in terms of two primitive semantic relationships, viz. those of denotation and satisfaction.

The semantic theory of truth, like every other correspondence theory, gives rise to a programme of analysis. In the case of the semantic theory, it is the programme of semantic analysis. The programme is needed, because it has to be shown how the theory applies to truths other than the simplest ones, where its application seems not to be problematic. The problem is to spell out realistically acceptable truth conditions for all of the various kinds of propositions which we consider to be true or false, or else to explain why we were wrong in thinking that they are either true or false.

However, from the point of view of a scientific realist, it appears that the programme has been a lamentable failure, as I show in detail in chapter 4. Realistically interpretable truth conditions for laws, theories, modals and conditionals, and hence for most of the propositions of science, cannot be specified, unless one is prepared to countenance an infinity of possible worlds other than the actual world; and, even then, there would be trouble in specifying adequate truth conditions for theories, arising from the openness of their fields of evidence. But belief in other possible worlds is incompatible with scientific realism, because: (a) it is contrary to the causal theory of knowledge to suppose that we could know anything at all about them; and (b) we are not required to believe in them as theoretical entities, because 'possible worlds' theories are not causal process theories. The only reason we could possibly have to believe in other possible worlds is that we need them to save the semantic theory of truth. Without possible worlds, there is not enough reality for all of the truths we believe in to correspond to.

Correspondence theories of truth are in trouble for a number of other reasons, as I argue in chapter 5. First there is a problem about the bearers of truth. Since nothing can be true at one time and false at another, a bearer of truth must be either an eternal entity, like a proposition or an eternal sentence, a temporally circumscribed entity, like an event of utterance, or a timeless entity, like a state of belief. For a scientific realist, a truth bearer cannot be an eternal entity, because there are no such things. It cannot be an event of utterance, because the same utterance may be intended or understood in many different ways, and whether it is true or false may depend on how it is intended or understood. It is argued that, from the point of view of a scientific realist, a truth bearer would have to be what someone thinks or believes, and any genuine correspondence relationship would have to be one between such a propositional attitude, or its neurophysiological object, and the world. Presumably, it is some kind of mapping relationship.

There are implications of thus psychologizing the bearers of truth, which many scientific realists may find disturbing. For the bearers of truth, whatever they may be, must also be the relata of logical relationships, and the subject-matter of logic must therefore by psychological. Moreover, since the number of beliefs is finite, the number of true beliefs, and hence truths, must also be finite. But these conclusions should be acceptable to scientific realists. Indeed, scientific realists should welcome a decent physicalist theory of what logic is all about.

There is, however, a crucial difficulty about taking truth to be a kind of mapping of the world on to the brain. For if truth is just such a mapping, it is hard to see why the truth should matter so much. Why, rationally, must I believe what I know to be true in this sense? And why, rationally, must I believe that whatever I am certain of, on ordinary evidential grounds, maps reality in this kind of way? If there is a connection between what maps reality in this sort of way, and what we should judge to be true on ordinary evidential grounds, then the connection would seem to be a contingent one. Therefore, on such a theory of truth, it cannot be a necessary proposition that we ought rationally to believe (on ordinary evidential grounds) what we know to be true (in the sense that it maps reality in the right sort of way), unless it is also the case that, in order to establish that the mapping relationship holds, we first have to establish, on ordinary evidential grounds, that the belief in question is true. But, in that case, it is irrelevant how the belief, considered as a neurophysiological state, maps reality. For a mapping will be considered to be a true mapping, iff the belief in question is known to be true.

Thus, it is argued that a physical correspondence theory of truth, which seeks to identify truth with some kind of mapping of the world on to the brain, cannot account for the *value* of truth. It cannot explain why this kind of mapping matters. To explain the value of truth, we need a relationship which somehow incorporates our epistemic values. For, we have to be able to derive what we *ought* rationally to believe from what we know *is true*, i.e. an epistemic 'ought' from an 'is'. But if 'is true' is a genuine predicate, then this will be impossible, unless it is an epistemic value-laden predicate meaning something like 'is the epistemically right thing to believe'.

If this is right, then it follows that a scientific realist cannot consistently hold a correspondence theory of truth, unless it be one in which the correspondence relationship somehow incorporates our epistemic values (as a concept of epistemic rightness would). But perhaps the truth predicate is not an attributive predicate at all, but is a grammatical device of another kind, e.g. one which is needed to increase the expressive power of the language. It has been said, for example, that the truth predicate is just a device for indirect assertion, or for semantic ascent, or for generating pro-sentences. It has also been claimed that 'It is true that' is just the default mode of assertion in a family of modes of assertion which includes, for example, 'It is probable that' and 'It is possible that'; for the assumption that it is the default mode would readily explain its normal redundancy. The truth predicate is normally redundant, on this theory, because any assertion which is not flagged as being something other than a truth claim, e.g. a probability, or possibility claim, is assumed, by default, to be a truth claim.

These possibilities are discussed in some detail in chapter 6, where it is shown that, quite apart from any technical difficulties there may be with redundancy theories like these, none of them is able to account for the *value* of truth. If the truth predicate is not an attributive predicate, but a grammatical device of some other kind, then presumably this would be a fact of some interest to linguists. But it hardly accounts for the concerns of philosophers and scientists to discover the truth.

The argument thus leads to the conclusion that the only kind of theory of truth compatible with scientific realism is a kind of pragmatic theory, in which truth is identified with what it is right epistemically to believe. Such a theory of truth is elaborated in chapter 7. According to this theory, truth has a role in epistemology analogous to that of rightness in ethics. The analogy between these two concepts can be shown to be a very close one, and to reflect basically similar patterns of thought and reasoning concerning beliefs and actions. Indeed, it is argued, the two concepts of rightness have a common origin – in a value of objectivity which is needed for co-operative action. Therefore, we should expect our theories of truth and morality to be structurally similar to each other. Our concept of moral rightness depends on our moral theory. If it is a values-based theory, then what is right will be what maximizes moral value. If it is a rules-based theory, then the right thing to do will be to act according to the rules. Analogously, therefore, our concept of truth, or epistemic rightness, should depend on our epistemology, and we should expect to find that there are two kinds of epistemologies, rules-based and values-based theories. Moreover, we should expect our moral and epistemological theories to be structurally similar, i.e. either both should be rules-based, or both should be values-based.

In the past, most epistemologists have tried to construct rules-based theories. They have supposed that the task of epistemology is to construct a system of inductive rules, and to show that their use to expand our knowledge of what is true is always rationally justified. However, this conception of epistemology has not been a fruitful one; for there is still no agreement on what the correct inductive logic is, and there is no generally acceptable solution to the problem of justifying induction. To solve the problem of induction, it is argued, we need a values-based epistemology in which inductive rules are not assumed to be rationally binding, but to have only the status of epistemic strategies, or rules of thumb, for maximizing epistemic value, i.e. a status like that of moral rules in values-based ethical systems. The task of developing the required kind of epistemology is the main burden of chapter 8.

In general, to understand a concept of rightness, we need to understand the system of rules, or the value system, with respect to which judgements of right and wrong are made. Therefore, it is argued, to know what truth is, we must have an understanding of the value system with respect to which judgements of truth and falsity are made. For truth is not itself a value, but is a mode of evaluation, just as moral rightness is. We may judge something to be true for many different kinds of reasons, e.g. because it has been empirically certified, or well corroborated, or because it is the best explanation, or the simplest and most conservative inductive projection of the data. We may judge something to be false, because it is inconsistent, or contradicts something we accept as true, or because it is not the best or simplest explanation. These, then, are some of the epistemic values with respect to which judgements of truth and falsity are made. The truth, I argue, is what it is ultimately right for anyone to believe, given this system of values.

With such a concept of truth, there is no difficulty, in principle, in solving the problem of induction. For, to justify our scientific inductive practices, we only have to show that they are good strategies for maximizing epistemic value. I do not claim to have done this in chapter 8; but, to the extent that these practices may be characterized as choosing or maintaining the best theory or hypothesis to account for the evidence, where what is epistemically the best is to be decided by appeal to our epistemic values, our scientific inductive practices are not in need of further justification. If truth is what would maximize epistemic value, given total evidence, then it is rational to maximize epistemic value on the evidence we have, and to seek further evidence where necessary, if knowledge of the truth is our aim.

In chapter 9, I return to reality. If 'naturalistic realism' is the theory of reality which is derivable from a naturalistic theory of truth, what are the ontological implications of this form of realism? Naturalistic realism is not metaphysical realism, because metaphysical realism derives from the correspondence theory of truth, a theory which drives a sharp wedge between what is true, and so presumably what exists, and what is ultimately knowable. By contrast, naturalistic realism must be derived from a theory of truth which specifically links what is true to what is ultimately knowable. Naturalistic realism must also be distinct from the kind of idealism which would go with a coherence theory of truth, such as F. H. Bradley's, because the systemic virtues of coherence and comprehensiveness are not the only epistemic virtues which are recognized. Nor will it be the kind of internal realism which conventionalists, and other neo-empiricists, have defended. The naturalistic epistemology in which the theory of truth is embedded is thoroughly anti-conventionalist (cf. chapter 3), and the claim that truth and reality are theory-relative is explicitly rejected. The theory of reality which corresponds to the naturalistic theory of truth might appropriately be said to be a form of Peircean realism, if this is the kind of theory of reality which goes with ideal pragmatism (i.e. with the kind of theory of truth defended by C. S. Peirce). For the naturalistic theory of truth is clearly an ideal pragmatic theory of a sort. The question is what kind of theory of reality does go with such a theory of truth.

The concept of truth which derives from the naturalistic theory is objective in the intersubjective sense in which any naturalistic ethical theory may be objective. That is, the theory makes truth and falsity relative to human nature. For, presumably, human beings have a certain epistemic perspective – an epistemic point of view, characterized by that specific system of human epistemic values used to construct our belief systems. I argue that it is reasonable to suppose that such a unique perspective exists, at least as a theoretically attainable ideal, since any individual or cultural differences of emphasis on epistemic values, which may exist in practice, can in principle be overcome by appeal to what I call our primary epistemic values, viz. those of consistency, empirical certification and corroboration. For these values are intrinsically dominant, and so may be used to monitor our secondary epistemic values. The naturalistic conception of truth is therefore an objective one, as far as human beings are concerned. But this argument for the existence of a unique human epistemic perspective, with reference to which an objective concept of truth might be defined, would not automatically apply to members of alien species. Therefore, it seemed to me that a scientific realist must be committed to accepting a form of species-relativism about truth, and hence reality. And, for a long time, I accepted this conclusion.

However, the argument for species-relativism concerning the nature of reality is inconclusive. For while it is possible to imagine species which operate with different systems of epistemic values, and have concepts of epistemic rightness similar to, but different from ours, we should not regard them as yielding rival conceptions of reality, unless the value systems on which they depended were more or less the same as ours. If they lacked one or more of our primary epistemic values, we should not regard their systems as belief systems in our sense, but, for example, as works of the imagination, making no claim to represent reality. If they lacked any of our secondary epistemic values, then we should need to be convinced that they were, nevertheless, fully rational. If they had all of our epistemic values, but just weighted them differently, then we should want to reason with them as we should with a human being who stressed some kinds of considerations more or less than we thought they should. If they appealed to values we did not recognize as epistemic, we should need to be convinced that satisfaction of these values would contribute to our knowledge and understanding of reality, if we were to adopt them ourselves.

And we should be right about all this. For the basic concepts we use to describe and evaluate belief systems, including our concepts of belief, rationality, epistemic value and truth, are classificatory or evaluative concepts, reflecting human values and interests. They are not natural kinds. If aliens are operating with different concepts, or have radically different ways of processing information, then it is not that they are giving different answers to the questions we are asking about nature: they are asking different questions, or they are doing something different altogether.

The ontological categories are, in this respect, different from the epistemic ones. For the various categories in the ontology of science are all natural kinds; and in many cases we can even say what their essences are. Hence, there is a fundamental difference between questions of truth and reality. 'What is true?' is ultimately an epistemic question. 'What exists in reality?' is an ontological question. The first is a matter of what it is right to believe. The second is a matter of explaining why it is so. To answer the first question, we must investigate nature in all the sorts of ways that scientists and historians do. To answer the second, we must try to identify the fundamental categories of things in existence, and seek to discover their essences. The two kinds of investigations come together in physical science. For, at its most fundamental level, the search for truth becomes the attempt to discover what exists in reality. Therefore, the ontology it is right for us to believe in is the ontology of science with which we began.

For the convenience of readers I have divided the book into three parts. Part I, which consists of the first three chapters, is concerned with the scientific view of man and the world, and the ontology that this implies. In chapter 1, a physicalist view of human nature is defended, and the question of what kind of epistemology is compatible with this position is considered. Chapter 2 elaborates on the ontology which is implied by science, and on the nature of scientific theory. In chapter 3, the aims of different kinds of scientific theories are distinguished, and a form of scientific realism is defended against the criticisms of neo-empiricists. The aims of Part I are to say, (a) what view of human nature we should take if we accept a scientific world-view, (b) what a theory of human knowledge, truth and rationality should be like, (c) what sorts of theoretical entities scientific realists should believe in, and hence (d) what sorts of entities postulated in theories of human rationality should be treated with ontological seriousness. The most important points to emerge are: (1) there is no good reason to believe in the sorts of abstract particulars postulated in model theories in science; (2) a theory of human rationality is likely to be a model theory of some kind in which the theoretical concept of an ideally rational agent having and maintaining an ideally rational belief system has a central role.

Part II includes a discussion of various correspondence theories of truth, and of the programmes of analysis to which they give rise. This is the subject matter of chapters 4 and 5, where it is argued that, quite apart from any internal difficulties with these theories of truth, and the evident failure of the programmes of logical empiricist and semantic analysis which they have generated, they are all incompatible with scientific realism. For a scientific realist, there are no adequate truth bearers, and if, as a scientific realist, one does not believe in possible worlds other than the actual world, then there is not enough reality for modal and conditional truths to correspond to. Moreover, there is a fundamental flaw in all correspondence theories of truth, a flaw which they have in common with redundancy theories (see chapter 6): they fail to account for the *value* of truth. For a satisfactory analysis of truth, and explanation of why truth matters, the evaluative nature of the concept of truth must be recognized, and epistemic value must be built into its analysis right from the start.

Part III begins in chapter 7 with the development of a naturalized epistemology and theory of truth – theories which in principle, if not in detail, should be acceptable to cognitive psychologists working in the area. The epistemology is a values-based epistemology, and the truth theory is an evaluative theory which depends on this epistemology. The epistemology requires an epistemic value system, which we may assume to be, at least approximately, the system of epistemic values which governs our scientific inductive practices. An ideally rational agent will then be one whose epistemic strategies are optimal with respect to this system of values, and the ideal of truth will be what it is right ultimately for an ideally rational agent to believe. The value system required for this epistemology is further developed and elaborated in chapter 8, where it is shown how the theory of rationality it yields might be used to solve the problem of induction. Chapter 9, which concludes Part III, takes us back on the path from epistemology to realism. It shows us how the epistemology on which the evaluative theory of truth depends leads us back to the ontology of science elaborated in Part I.

... with a chapter), the ones (see chapter 6), they fail to provide, for instance: for example, for a quantitative analysis of truth, and explanations about truth entities. The qualitative nature of the theory of truth once developed and properties value can be felt, not to be given back from the text.

Part III begins in chapter 7 with the description of a naturalized epistemology, and theory of truth theories, which in chapter 8 are developed around to ascending to a genuine psychological setting in the brain. The epistemology is a values-based epistemology, and the truth theory is an evaluative theory, which depends on the requirement. The epistemology requires an ... and evaluation, which will allow us to set a clear distinction: say, the system of particular value which coerces our scientific inductive practices. An ideally rational agent will face face a choice system that is the equivalent with respect to a truth system of value, and the wish of truth will be so, but it is right. Intuitively, so in a mediby setting, one to believe. The value system required for this epistemology is further developed and elaborated in chapter 9, where it is shown how the theory of coherent inductive claims be fixed to solve the problem of induction from Chapter 8, which, more like Part III, takes us back on the path to a philosophy to reconnect. It shows us how the epistemology we can arrive the evaluative theory of truth depends, takes us back to the philosophy of the particular state kinds to ...

Part I

Ontology

1

The Scientific Point of View

The argument to be presented in this book proceeds from the assumption that the current scientific view of the nature of reality is the best guide to what there is. The reasons for accepting this value judgement are that there is no other body of knowledge which is as well supported or attested, as thoroughly checked, as precise and detailed in its predictions, as comprehensive and systematic in its explanations, or as satisfying intellectually. Moreover, the practice of science, and the body of knowledge it has yielded, are the products of a long history of inquiry by many thousands of dedicated men and women, operating with a code of honesty and objectivity, or reporting designed precisely to yield objective knowledge of the world, i.e. knowledge which is independent of creed, political interest and authority. One would have to have very good reasons indeed, or be very arrogant, not to accept the scientific viewpoint on questions of ontology as the best there is.

1.1 THE PHYSICAL WORLD

The world-view one obtains from a study of physical science is a curious mixture of atomism and holism. On the one hand, it posits the existence of fundamental particles, with certain primary properties, e.g. spin, which are intrinsic to their nature, and certain basic forces which are the source of all interactions between them. Given this picture, we may see all matter as being composed ultimately of fundamental particles, all properties as being dependent upon the intrinsic primary properties of these particles, and upon whatever accidental spatio-temporal relationships may hold between them, and all causal interactions as more or less complex interactions brought about by the basic forces of nature. So all matter may be reduced to fundamental particles, all properties to a few primitive properties of fundamental particles (and some spatio-temporal relationships), and all causal connections to a few primitive kinds of causal interactions.

On the other hand, the fundamental particles may themselves be products of much more basic cosmic processes. For it is commonly supposed that the fundamental particles were brought into existence by the processes which produced the Big Bang, and so are not the ultimate constituents of the universe. What is ultimate, according to J. A. Wheeler, is space itself:

> The enormous factor from nuclear densities, 10^{14} g/cm^3, to the density of field fluctuation energy in the vacuum, 10^{94} g/cm^3, argues that elementary particles represent a percentage-wise almost completely negligible change in the locally violent conditions that characterize the vacuum ... In other words, elementary particles do not form a really basic starting point for the description of nature. Instead, they represent a first order correction to vacuum physics. That vacuum, the zero-order state of affairs, with its enormous densities of virtual photons and virtual positive–negative pairs and virtual wormholes, has to be described properly before one has a fundamental starting point for a proper perturbation theoretic analysis. (Misner, Thorne and Wheeler 1973, p. 1202)

Hence, philosophers who take their ontology from science need not, in any ordinary sense, be atomists, or even materialists. If Wheeler is right, the energy represented by the material constituents of the universe is just a tiny fraction of its total energy.

The ontological reduction of the physical world to its most fundamental constituents will be examined in detail in the next chapter, where it will be shown that an atomistic ontology of the kind envisaged is comprehensive, highly reductive in each basic category of existence, and of considerable explanatory power. That being so, this is the ontology we should accept, at least for the time being. We should admit that science may one day require a different ontology, but, for reasons to be explained, we should not abandon the ontology it gives us just to accommodate psychological, logical or mathematical entities, unless we really have to.

Anyone who takes the view that the kind of ontology which is needed for the physical sciences is adequate as a general theory of what there is is called 'a physicalist', and this is the sense in which the term will be used here. There is a weaker physicalist thesis which admits *qualia*, i.e. the qualities of sense experience, to an ontological category of their own, but insists that the experiences which have qualia are physical events or processes which are ultimately describable in physico-chemical terms. This thesis, otherwise known as *emergent physicalism*, will be discussed in section 1.3 below.

There are at least two quite distinct kinds of physical theory. One kind describes the processes which may be supposed to underlie physical phenomena. It refers to various physical entities (later to be identified as things with mass or energy) interacting in various ways to produce manifest effects. When tracks appear in a bubble chamber, for example, we may explain their appearance by the ionizing effects of certain fundamental particles. In doing so, we are offering a *causal process explanation* of what has evidently occurred in the chamber. The theory, if it is any good, explains the appearance of the tracks in considerable detail – their thickness, curvature, and sudden deviations of direction – all in a manner which is compatible with some very general conservation and symmetry principles which we suppose to govern the behaviour of the fundamental particles. Such an explanation as this undoubtedly carries an ontological commitment. To accept the theory is to accept that the particles in question exist, that they have the properties which are ascribed to them, and that they interact with each other in the ways they are said to.

The second kind of physical theory is quite different. The entities it apparently refers to are ideal types of one kind or another, and often the properties attributed to them are ones which no ordinary physical system does, or even could, possess. Far from there being any commitment to the existence of these entities, there may even be a commitment to their non-existence. The laws of mechanics, for example, are formulated with respect to closed and isolated systems, those of fluid mechanics refer to incompressible fluids and to fluids in free flow, those of special relativity refer to inertial systems, and of course we speak of such things as perfectly reversible heat engines, black body radiators, perfect gases and empty space. But probably no such things as these exist; and in some cases there are good theoretical reasons to believe that they *could not* exist. So it would be absurd to insist that science is committed to their existence. Ontological commitment can derive only from causal process explanations, not from *model-theoretic explanations* involving entities like these.[1]

Many of the most fundamental laws of nature are formulated with respect to abstract ideals. According to the special theory of relativity, for example, the laws of nature are the same with respect to all inertial systems. But inertial systems are not to be equated with any actual physical systems. They are just abstractly considered frames of reference of a kind which we now think could not exist in reality. An inertial system would, for example, have to be gravity-free. But we know that there are no such systems. Of course, some physical systems can, for the purposes of applying the theory, be considered to be more or less good approximations to the abstract ideal. But no actual frame of reference could be strictly inertial. The concept of an inertial frame is, nevertheless, a key one in special relativity theory; without it we could not even state the basic principle of the theory, or formulate *any* of its laws.

Some naive scientific realists take the view that these very fundamental laws of nature which are formulated with reference to abstract ideals are really only *approximately true*, because to *be true* they would have to be true of actual physical systems. They take this view because this is what their theories of laws, of truth, and of explanation, require them to say. A law, for those I have in mind, is a statement like 'All crows are black'. Indeed, this has served, in some realist circles, as a paradigm of a scientific law since J. S. Mill first used the example about a hundred years ago. The example is congenial to them because it has readily specifiable truth conditions, it can be used in conjunction with 'This is a crow' to deduce 'This is black', and hence to give an explanation of this fact which conforms to Hempel's nomological-deductive model, and it is clearly empirical – if not verifiable, then at least falsifiable observationally. If all laws were like this, then we should know what their truth conditions were, and we could accept a Hempelian account of scientific explanation. However, as N. R. Campbell once remarked, 'Mill's examples . . . are all taken from obscure and unimportant parts of science and show the usual lack of appreciation of the true nature of a law' (Campbell 1957, p. 117n). To take 'All crows are black' as an example of a scientific law is comparable to taking the wheel as an example of modern technology.

At least some, if not all, of the most fundamental laws of nature make essential reference to abstract ideals of one kind or another – things which either do not, or could not, exist in nature. These laws specify how certain idealized systems would behave in certain limiting circumstances. To consider fundamental laws to be universal generalizations like 'All crows are black' is to miss one of their most significant features. Crows exist, but inertial systems, for example, do not. So if we would offer an extensional analysis of laws, we should have to say that at least these most fundamental ones are only vacuously true.

Laws which refer to abstract ideals are what I call *framework principles*. The aptness of the name will, I hope, become clearer as we proceed. Framework principles have a role – a very important role – in scientific explanation, but it is not that of a law under which individual facts may be subsumed. What a framework principle does, within the context of a model theory, is say how an ideal system would behave. It provides a basis or framework for comparison with actual behaviour. We know in advance that actual physical systems will not satisfy the requirements on the model. Hence we do not expect them to behave as they would if they were ideal. We *expect* them to be different. So explanations on a model are not achieved by subsumption under the laws postulated for the model, as in a Hempelian explanation. They could not be, because the laws in question are extensionally vacuous.

For a model theory to have a role in scientific explanation it must have an intended interpretation. It must be possible to identify certain elements in the model with certain elements of those physical systems of which it is the model. In N. R. Campbell's terminology we require a *dictionary* linking the model-theoretic objects and variables with their physical counterparts. Given such a dictionary, the system whose behaviour or properties are to be explained can be treated theoretically, and predictions can be made on the basis of the theoretical model. But these predictions will not normally be fulfilled. So we have not yet explained the actual behaviour of the system. We may, however, have made some advance towards providing such an explanation. For now what remains to be explained is only the *difference* between the actual and the theoretically ideal behaviour. To explain this, we might propose some additional constraints or requirements on the model, and enlarge the dictionary appropriately to provide an interpretation for them. If successful, the theoretical behaviour will now more closely approximate to the actual behaviour. But still, we should expect the actual behaviour to differ somewhat from the new theoretical ideal. If it does so, then we should have some new differences to account for.

A difference between an actual state of affairs and a theoretically ideal one is what we should normally regard as an effect – as something requiring causal explanation. In so far as something does not behave as it would if it were theoretically ideal, there is something to be explained. For the assumption we make must be that the system *would* behave in this way if it weren't for something. To explain such a difference, it is never enough just to say that the system violates the requirements on the model, since we know that anyway. What we must do is pick out some factors, the presence or absence of which violates these requirements, show that these factors are indeed present or absent, as the case may be, and argue that they are *sufficient* to account for the difference to be explained.

A lot of what T. S. Kuhn calls normal science (Kuhn 1962) consists in checking the predictions of a model theory, constructing causal explanations of what appear to be anomalous results, checking on whether the proposed causal influences are present or absent, and using whatever other theories we may have concerning these influences to check whether they are at least of an order of magnitude sufficient to account for the original anomalies. The viability of a given model theory depends on the availability of such causal explanations, and on whether they check out sufficiently well for the theory to be maintained. So long as such explanations are forthcoming, and are reasonably well confirmed, i.e. as well as can be expected given our limited investigative resources, the model theory may continue to be accepted as an adequate foundation for further research.

A model-theoretic explanation has a structure and function which are quite different from the causal process explanations from which I would derive my ontology. The abstract ideals of our model theories provide only the *frameworks* for our causal explanations, for it is against them that our requests for causal explanation are set; *but they are not themselves ingredients of these explanations. Hence there is no ontological commitment to the existence of these ideals.* They do not themselves take part in the causal processes of nature. The postulation of such ideals may be necessary for us to gain an *understanding* of nature, and obviously some theoretical ideals serve this purpose better than others. But our need of them does not entail that they exist. On the contrary, our assumption is always that they do not exist, or even that it is physically impossible for them to exist. It is true that we often generalize over abstract ideals, and that we are quite happy to speak of the properties of inertial systems, Hilbert spaces, Euclidean spaces, numbers, sets, propositions and the like, just as though these were real existences. But these assertions should be understood counterfactually if what I have been saying here is correct. To say that the speed of light is constant with respect to all inertial systems is just to say that if A and B were any two inertial systems the speed of light with respect to A would be equal to its speed with respect to B.

To illustrate the concept of a model-theoretic explanation, consider Euclidean geometry. At least in its initial conception, this geometry was a theory of spatial relationships. It was, and still is, used to explain various facts about how things are related to each other spatially. We can use it to explain why this angle is equal to that one, why this distance is twice as great as that one, or why this volume is greater than that. But the points, lines and planes of Euclidean geometry have properties which no physical systems could have. Consequently, there is no question of there being such entities in nature. There are certain things which we can *represent theoretically* as points, lines or planes in a Euclidean space. Therefore, we can use the theory to make predictions about the spatial relationships which ought to hold between such things. But so far there are no references to any physical causal processes. And none would be required at all if the predictions made using the theory proved to be sufficiently accurate. A causal explanation would only be required if the predictions were significantly different from the

results obtained by measurement. And such an explanation would
have to be adequate to explain this difference.

Formally, the general relativistic explanations of the advance of
the perihelion of Mercury, of the failure of the Michelson–Morley
experiment, and of the clock paradox are similar. They do not
reveal any causal processes which might be supposed to underlie
these phenomena. In this respect they are like the explanations
provided by Euclidean geometry. That the clock of the returning
twin is retarded relative to his stay-at-home brother's is a fact
about the geometry of space-time – or rather, we can use a
geometry of space-time to explain it in much the same way as we
might use Euclidean geometry to explain some purely spatial
relationships between things, e.g. why the distance from A to B via
C is greater than the distance from A to B via D. A causal
explanation would be required only if the returning twin's clocks
were found not to be retarded by as much as, or to be retarded by
more than, the theory would have predicted.

It is a mistake to suppose that space or space-time have causal
roles in explanations such as these. For the explanations in question are not causal. We cannot say how things would be if there
were no space or space-time, or regard the existence of spatial or
spatio-temporal relationships as effects somehow produced by the
existence of such entities. Hence we cannot consider either space or
space-time to be causes. Things do exist in various spatial and
spatio-temporal relationships; and this is a fact about reality which
we cannot sensibly deny. But it does not follow that these relationships exist because of anything. We may indeed be able to offer a
causal explanation of why a particular thing stands in a particular
spatial or spatio-temporal relationship to another. But any such
explanation must be premissed on the existence of other spatial or
spatio-temporal relationships between things. Hence, any adequate
ontology must have a place for relationships such as these. But I
can see no reason for admitting either space or space-time to
primary ontological status.

It would also be a mistake to suppose that the various abstract
ideals which are apparently referred to in these model-theoretic
explanations have any real existence. Neither Euclidean figures,
nor the abstract ideal entities of which they are composed, can

make any claim to reality. They are precisely on a par with the inertial systems of special relativity, which we have every reason to believe do not exist; and their roles in explanation are similar.

Sets are in much the same boat. They are abstractly considered heaps or collections of things. However, they are not like ordinary heaps or collections. The things grouped together as members of a set need not co-exist in space or time, or be of the same ontological category. They may be infinite in number, or there may be none at all. The membership of a set is eternally fixed, and adding something to a set is not a physical process involving what is added. It is a process of defining a new set – one which has this additional thing as a member. Consequently, sets cannot take part in the causal processes of nature, as any ordinary heap or collection of things might do. They cannot change or be changed. They can only be defined. They are what I have been calling abstract ideals.

For the purposes of number theory, we require sets of any arbitrary cardinality. For we need a model theory which is rich enough in abstract ideals to represent any possible sized grouping of things. Formally, this is like requiring a space for a geometrical model theory which is rich enough in points to represent any possible spatial arrangements. There is no requirement, however, that there should actually be groupings of things of any arbitrary cardinality. For we are concerned here only with possibilities.

I cannot hope to offer anything like a complete account of the nature of mathematical entities. That would take me far beyond the intended scope of this work. Here, I can offer only the bare bones of an account. The account I should give of mathematical entities like sets and numbers is that they have a status which is formally like that of any other abstract ideal in science. They have no causal roles, and they are not any part of the furniture of the world. Their role is to establish ideals or norms against which the actual properties, behaviour or relationships between physical systems are to be compared and causally explained. They are not themselves involved in any such explanations. They merely set the stage for them.

Statements involving abstract ideals, including the mathematical ones, are strictly to be understood counterfactually. They say how things would be, or behave, or be related, if they were ideal. They do not refer to abstract entities, as the Platonist would have it, and say what properties these abstract entities actually have. Nor do they refer to any linguistic entities, numerals or the like, as the nominalist is inclined to think. On the contrary, I am convinced that they are not referential at all. Who, for example, would think of offering a nominalist theory of inertial systems? Nominalism is what you get if you try to combine a dislike for abstract entities with a love for the correspondence theory of truth. Platonism is what you end up with if you stick with the correspondence theory of truth and give up on trying to offer a nominalistic theory of mathematics. In my view it is the correspondence theory of truth which has to be abandoned. But more on this in chapter 4.

1.2 PHYSICALISM AND SENSE EXPERIENCE

Those who would derive their ontology from science cannot accept any form of ontological dualism in the theory of mind. They cannot accept that there are any non-physical mental entities with which there is causal interaction, because the basic forces of nature can operate only between entities which have energy. Anything that did not have energy could not participate in any such causal interactions, because it could not supply the forces needed for them. Therefore, no ontologically dualist theory of mind is acceptable. Yet, surely, the impact of the world upon us *does* cause us to acquire certain beliefs about it, and to have the sensory experience that we do; and conversely, our feelings, beliefs, desires and values surely *do* cause us to act or react in various ways. And if this is so, then we must suppose that these are all physical states, dispositions or mechanisms. All of our thinking and feeling and reasoning – in short, all of those states, processes, events, and so on, which we think of as characteristically mental – must be physical states, processes and events.

Now it would be tedious to rehearse the arguments for and against this view, which have been canvassed over the years. Nevertheless, there is one argument which is so crucial, and has persuaded so many philosophers of the untenability of the physicalist position with regard to mental events, states and processes, that, for fear of losing half my audience, I feel I must say something about it. This is the argument concerning the phenomenological content of sense experience. I do not think that the argument does show that the physicalists are wrong to reject ontological dualism, or to identify mental states, events and processes with physical ones. Nevertheless, I do think it shows *something*.[2]

Many philosophers are willing to allow that mental states and processes are somehow *correlated* with physical ones, but feel, nevertheless, that they cannot be *identified* with them. And for this they appear to have a powerful argument. Why should our experience of thinking or feeling or reasoning have the *quality* that it does? Why should our sense experience appear *phenomenologically* to us as it does, and not, say, systematically otherwise? Why, for that matter, should we be conscious beings at all, if the physicalist view of reality is correct? For surely, if the physicalist world-view gives us a complete picture of reality, there is no role for consciousness, or for the phenomena of consciousness, in either the explanation or the ultimate description of reality. Everything we say or feel or think is, according to the theory, a physical response, a complex neuro-physiological reaction to some stimulus or event occurring in our central nervous systems. And these reactions could, in principle, be described fully and completely in neurophysiological terms, without ever mentioning that we are in any way conscious of them, or that they are experienced in any way. But if that is so, why should these things not occur unconsciously, without awareness, and without associated experience, as they might, for example, in a mechanical replica of the human brain?

This argument is indeed a powerful one. There appears to be no place for the phenomenological content of our experience in a physicalist account of reality. One argument which seeks to demonstrate this is the so-called 'inverted spectrum' argument. We are invited to imagine that one day we wake up and discover that everything is colour-reversed, or at least that it is for us. But we quickly discover that no one else thinks that anything has undergone such a change. To continue to function in society we have to learn to associate the reversed colour impressions with the colour names for the originals. And, after a while, we find ourselves able to do this quite easily. Now we can *imagine*, though none of us would believe, that this could happen without any changes occurring in our neurological responses to colour stimulation. And, if we can imagine it happening to us, then we can imagine it happening to everyone, so that eventually the whole community has done just what we have. Now, when this has happened, we have a strange situation. Everyone is now calling things the same colours they always have. Bananas are still said to be yellow and tomatoes to be red. But phenomenologically, our experiences of colour have been reversed. Moreover, visitors from another community would have no way of knowing that this had occurred (unless we told them), because, by hypothesis, there have been no changes to our neurological responses to colour stimulation.

Next, imagine *we* did not know that this had occurred to us, because, for example, we were born seeing colours differently. Then no one would have any way at all of knowing that the colour experiences of this community were different from those of any other. Moreover, we can go one step further, and imagine that *everyone* was born seeing colours systematically differently from the way that we do in fact see them. Then, the physical description of this world would be exactly the same as ours, and we should say and think and do precisely what we do now. One thing, *and one thing only*, would be different in this imagined world. Our colour experience would be phenomenologically different from the way it is in this world.

If this is a possible world, and I see no conclusive reason to think that it isn't, then an important consequence follows. It follows that the fact that our sense experience is as it is, and not systematically otherwise, is *inexplicable*. It is not just that it is inexplicable on any *physical* theory. It is inexplicable on *any* theory. For in order to explain why our experience is like *this* rather than like *that* we must discover some asymmetry. We must be able to say that our experience is like this rather than like that *because* . . . But if the two imagined worlds are otherwise *identical*, then there is nothing whatever that could fill this gap. And this must be so whatever view of reality we take. Hence, it cannot be a criticism of a physicalist view of reality that it cannot explain it.

Take another case, which has nothing to do with introspective psychology. Think of another world, just like this one except that in it there is left/right reversal. I know that the parity principle does not hold in the world of microphysics. Nevertheless, we can easily imagine it to do so, and it serves as a good illustration. Now this world would be quite different from ours, and if we could somehow be transported to it we should immediately be aware of it, just as Alice was. The books would all be in mirror writing, the type-writers would chug off to the right, the inhabitants would shake with their left hands, and the clocks would run anti-clockwise. But imagine that the inhabitants of this other world speak a language just like English, except that what they call a right-hand thread, or a clockwise motion, or a magnetic south pole is what we should call a left-hand thread, an anti-clockwise motion or a magnetic north pole. Then, if the relevant symmetry principle really did hold, there would be no way of distinguishing the aliens' descriptions of their world from our descriptions of ours. So we have now a situation formally just like the one described in the 'inverted spectrum' argument. And if we ask 'Why is the world *this* way round rather than *that*?', then just because of the supposed symmetry there is no possible answer. That the world is as it is, and not its mirror image would be an *inexplicable* fact about reality, and it could be no criticism of a physicalist, *or any other*, ontology that it could not account for it. It does not matter that the mirror symmetry does not hold in the world of nuclear reactions. There are other symmetries which do. And relative to these, the fact that the world is as it is, and not its systematic reflection in one of these symmetries, is a brute fact about reality.

The point may be generalized. Let us say that two languages are syntactically similar iff they have the same vocabulary, grammar and syntax. That is, every well-constructed sentence of one is a well-constructed sentence of the other. Let L_1 and L_2 be any two such syntactically similar languages. Let W_1 and W_2 be any two worlds describable in these languages. (For the time being you can understand this realistically, if that is your inclination.) Then we may say that the two worlds W_1 and W_2 are structurally similar, relative to L_1 and L_2, iff the L_1 description of W_1 is identical to the L_2 description of W_2. If we imagine L_1 and L_2 to be languages completely adequate to describe these worlds, then we may drop the qualification, and just say that W_1 and W_2 are *structurally similar worlds*. Now what the 'inverted spectrum' and the other symmetry arguments show is that there may well be worlds which are different from, but structurally similar to, our own. But if there are, then the fact that the actual world is as it is, rather than some other structurally similar one, must be totally inexplicable – a fact which cannot be accounted for on *any* theory.

Thus, the argument does show something important. It shows that there may be facts about the world which no theory, physical or otherwise, could possibly account for. It is apparent, upon reflection, that there must be some such facts if the physicalist ontology we have sketched is correct as far as it goes. For, if there are basic entities with intrinsic physical properties, then it must be inexplicable why these entities have these properties. For to explain why they exist, or have these properties, we should have to appeal to some still more basic entities, with some even more basic properties. But if we can do this, then the entities or properties in question are not really primitive. Likewise, if we could explain why the basic forces of nature act as they do, then they would not be basic in the required sense, but forces which exist as modifications of some still more primitive kinds of causal interactions. Every ontology must therefore admit at least some basic facts.

The overall spatio-temporal distribution of things in the universe must be another of these basic facts. For while we may be able to explain why something occurred when it did, or why things are spatially distributed as they are, we can do so only on the assumption that something else occurred when it did, or that things were distributed in such and such a way at some other time. But we cannot explain the *total* distribution of things and events in the universe, because there cannot be any reference point to ground such an explanation. Nevertheless, the spatio-temporal distribution of things in the universe is a fact, or rather, that it is so distributed is a fact about the world which could conceivably have been otherwise; and that it is as it is is something which no theory could possibly explain.[3]

The argument from symmetry principles shows something else. It shows that there may be some basic facts which, ultimately, can only be *ostensively* indicated. For example, until we have established an ostensive link with the world, we cannot tell whether the world we are describing is a world of matter or of antimatter. The universe could be described completely, and in every detail, and it would still be impossible to tell from any internal evidence provided by the description which of two or more possible worlds it describes. But a theory of what exists in reality could never do more than provide a complete description of reality. Therefore, it cannot be any reason to reject an ontology that it cannot explain why the world, or our experience of it, is as it is, and not systematically otherwise. At some point, we just have to say, 'And that is what it is like to see something red', or 'And that is what I call a lump of matter'.

But surely, if I admit that there are such facts as these, I am committed to the existence of another ontological category. Our sensory experience, we might say, has a certain *quality*. But it could conceivably have had a different quality, compatible with our describing, thinking about and responding to the world in the way that we do. Likewise, the physical entities which, for the most part, make up the universe might be said to have a certain *quality* – that of being material rather than antimaterial. Should I not, therefore, admit another category into my ontology – a category of *qualities*?

My inclination is *not* to admit this additional category. I agree that there are ways in which our descriptions of reality, including our descriptions of our sense experience, are realized. And if a quality is anything, then it is a way in which something is realized. But in specifying an ontology, we shall be just naming the categories of things which we must suppose to exist *if we are to give an adequate account of reality*. How our descriptions of reality are realized is relevant to our *understanding* of that ontology, but is not an additional category which belongs to it.

My reasons for taking this stand derive from the *essential incompleteness of descriptions*. Hilary Putnam has made much of this point, drawing upon the Löwenheim–Skolem theorem in mathematics to argue for it. But the point can be made, even without any appeal to model theory. The existence of any general symmetry principle in nature is sufficient to demonstrate the phenomenological incompleteness of any possible description of nature. But, in so far as we are trying to produce an ontology, we are trying to state, in the most general terms, what kinds of things we must suppose to exist, if we are to give an adequate account of reality. But we cannot expect our ontological theory to do what we have reason to believe no theory could possibly do. There is just no way of accounting for the contents of sense experience, or for any other fact about how our descriptions of reality are realized. So we might just as well accept this as a limitation on any ontology, and admit that every ontology must be *phenomenologically incomplete*.

The basic reason for rejecting the additional category of qualities is that it cannot solve the problem of phenomenological incompleteness. For the expanded ontology would *still* be phenomenologically incomplete. There are ways in which it, too, might be realized, and that it *is realized* in the way that it is would have to be a further fact about reality which could not be explained in this ontology. Hence the introduction of first order qualities would only lead to the introduction of second order qualities, and these in turn to third order qualities, and so on. Therefore, there is no way of expanding our ontology to solve the problem of phenomenological incompleteness. Every ontology is *necessarily* incomplete in this way. And if this is the case, then we might as well begin by admitting it, and rest satisfied with aiming for descriptive completeness.

It must be emphasized that this admission does *not* imply that there are any non-physical properties. Whether a particle is of matter or antimatter certainly does make a difference to physical processes. Substitute a positron for an electron in some physical process and the outcomes will be quite different. Likewise, the phenomenological appearance of greenness *is* a physical property. Substitute an apple which presents to us the phenomenological appearance of redness for one which presents greenly, and we will behave quite differently towards it, or say quite different things about it. Hence the quality of our experience *is* causally relevant to some physical processes in which we are involved. What is *not* causally relevant is that *the whole spectrum* of our experiences should be as it is, and not systematically otherwise. But in just the same sense, it is not causally relevant that the world is one of matter rather than antimatter. There are just some brute facts about the world, and these are probably two of them.

1.3 PHYSICAL DUALISM

Many people who would accept a physicalist ontology, and reject any ontological dualism in the philosophy of mind, nevertheless accept a form of *physical dualism*.[4] That is, they speak and think about themselves just as an ontological dualist would, except that they deny its ontological implications. It is, for example, hard to find any epistemologists who do not somehow think of themselves as being detached from the information they receive through sensory stimulation, and using this information to build up a picture of the world. Our knowledge is seen as a kind of building or structure erected by us on a foundation of experience. Man, the agent, freely constructs his view of reality out of the raw data of sense experience, or out of basic beliefs acquired through such experience. And to do this, the agent is supposed to appeal to various canons of inductive or deductive logic which are considered *not* to be laws of thought, but *a priori* building regulations!

Yet it should be clear that this view of the nature of man is still essentially a dualist one. It differs from the position of ontological dualism only in the status it accords to the agent. In ontologically dualist theories of mind, the agent is a non-physical entity which receives and interprets and reasons about the evidence which is presented to it through sense experience, and has *a priori* knowledge of how to do this, although, of course, it is not bound to apply this knowledge. In physically dualist theories of mind it is the same, except that the agent is thought of as a faculty of reason and decision which is separate from the faculty of perception, but which draws upon the evidence which the latter supplies to construct its view of reality. Just what these faculties are is not clear, but presumably they are to be identified with separate compartments or functions of our brains.

However, I should have thought that physical dualism is hardly more tenable than ontological dualism. For it has to deal with most of the problems which make ontological dualism seem so implausible. Physiologically, there is no evidence of a centre, other than the brain itself, where the mind could possibly be located. There are various centres which have more or less distinct functions, e.g. the speech centre, and there are centres for visual, auditory and other kinds of processing, but there is no proper part of the brain whose function it is to do all the sorts of things minds are supposed to be able to do. So the mind cannot be identified with any segment or compartment of the brain which reads, interprets, makes decisions and gives instructions on the basis of what occurs uninterpreted in other parts of the brain. Our faculties of perception are integral parts of ourselves, not just instruments giving us raw uninterpreted data about our bodies or our surroundings.

Nevertheless, some philosophers, e.g. D. M. Armstrong (in Armstrong 1961), who are committed to a physicalist ontology, seem to think of their faculties of perception simply as instruments of this kind, i.e. as being the non-rational means by which we acquire the basic items of belief or knowledge we need to construct our views about the nature of reality. It is supposed that this knowledge must be the foundation of all of our knowledge, and hence that the fundamental questions of epistemology are: 'What sorts of basic items of knowledge can be acquired directly (i.e. without inference), by perception?', 'How can such knowledge be used rationally to build up a picture of reality?', and 'How can the inferences we draw using such data be rationally justified?'.

The ontology is monistic; but the epistemology is still essentially dualistic. From a scientific point of view, neither form of dualism is tenable. The introspective evidence of what knowledge we can acquire directly by perception suggests an evolving programme. We learn by experience to perceive, discriminate and distinguish between things. As a result, we can now, as adults, obtain knowledge directly by perception which we could not have acquired directly as children, e.g. that the telephone is disconnected, that middle C is being sounded, or that the capacity of this glass is greater than that (differently shaped) one. Likewise, as children, we were able to acquire knowledge directly by perception which we could not have acquired as babies or as younger children. There is, therefore, no fixed class of beliefs acquirable directly by perception.

Nor would there appear to be any truly primitive class of beliefs acquirable directly by perception. By the time we are able to acquire beliefs directly (at least, ones we are able to articulate), the sorts of things we can know directly by perception include: (a) what we can see or hear or feel (e.g. that there is a table over there, or a person behind me, or a chair beneath me); (b) what perceivable properties things have (e.g. that this piece of paper is yellow); (c) what is obviously causing what in our surroundings (e.g. that John is lifting a boulder, or that I am eating an apple); (d) what sense impressions we are getting from what (e.g. that this feeling is like the one I had yesterday). No doubt there are also many other kinds of things which are directly knowable. Therefore, if there is a truly primitive class of items of knowledge acquirable directly by perception, it is a very mixed class indeed, and hardly suitable as a basis for a foundationalist epistemology.

My alternative to physical dualism is to suppose that human belief systems develop from amorphous beginnings to fully articulate belief systems by processes of identifying, distinguishing, classifying, generalizing, normalizing, idealizing, explaining, rationalizing, reconceptualizing, theoretically integrating, and so on. The building-construction analogy is all wrong in epistemology: belief systems are not built, they develop out of more primitive attitudinal systems. A better, though still imperfect, analogy would be that of bringing a picture into focus, gradually clarifying and sharpening boundaries, distinguishing colours, making connections, filling in background, and so on, in response to environmental stimuli, and in accordance with an internal value system which has evolved for the purpose. Once formed to the point where our belief systems are articulable, they are refined and further developed by these very same processes. On this view, the main problems of epistemology are to identify the belief-forming processes, including our inductive strategies, and the epistemic value system which monitors them.

The contents of our belief systems are, of course, dependent on what our sensory inputs have been. They also depend on what beliefs we acquired in the processes of learning the language, and being inducted into the culture. So individual belief systems vary enormously, depending on differences in experience, initial programming and social conditioning. Yet, despite the wide variation in content, human belief systems do seem to display some common structures. For the fact is that foreign belief systems are ultimately intelligible to us. They are structured logically more or less as our

belief systems are, and once we understand the cultural backgrounds, and the metaphysical beliefs which are characteristic of
the cultures in which they arise, we can see their rationales. We can
understand why they believe what they do, and why they have the
concepts of evidence they do. Consequently, there is reason to think
that there is more that is innate in human thought processes than
the superficial variety of human belief systems may suggest. I am
convinced, for example, that the laws of logic are laws of thought –
which is something I have argued for at length elsewhere (Ellis
1979). And since these laws are all laws of consistency, which
appeal to us as ideals of rationality, it is plausible to suppose that
our belief systems are structured by a value of consistency. As
human beings we naturally strive to achieve consistent or coherent
systems of beliefs.

However, I would not suppose that consistency is our only innate
epistemic value. There are other intrinsic epistemic values which
determine our concepts of evidence or support, and which lead us
to broaden and secure the experiential basis of our belief systems.

Now is not the time to say what these other values are, or how
they work. That is a question to which I shall return. (See chapter
8.) Here my aim is only to sketch an alternative to physical
dualism. To account for how and what we think, there is no need to
suppose that we have separate faculties of perception, and of reason
and decision. There is no reason to think that our perceptual
judgements are not ultimately monitored by the same forces which
monitor our more considered judgements. All attempts to distinguish what is purely observational from what is theoretical have
ended in failure. There is no such distinction to be made unless it
be between what is perceptually immediate, in the sense that it is a
judgement made without *conscious* inference, and what is not.
Furthermore, we should not think of the laws of logic, or the
principles of reasoning which we employ in making considered
judgements, as *a priori* principles which we are somehow able to
grasp and use for this purpose. Rather we should consider them to
be laws of thought, which exercise control over our thinking processes, and which, therefore, we cannot choose to apply or not as
we wish. We may choose not to think about something, or not to
think about it very much, or not to consider evidence of one kind or

another, or not to carry out investigations of some kind, because we think it unnecessary, unimportant, or dangerous to the social order, or something of the sort. But once we embark on such considerations, their impact on what we believe is not anything over which we can exercise control. So the laws of logic, and in general the principles of reasoning which we use, are not to be thought of as *a priori* principles, but as empirical laws of thought which are to be discovered *a posteriori* by studying and theorizing about how we think.

I do not wish here to defend this view of the nature of thought and of reasoning. I have shown elsewhere (in Ellis 1979) that it gives us a viable conception of the nature of logic, adequate to provide foundations for all of the standard logical systems. And I have argued that the standard objections to psychologism in logic are superficial and unsound. My aim here is just to argue that anyone who accepts a physicalist theory of mind need not accept any form of physical dualism, and that it is contrary to the spirit of a physicalist world-view to do so.

In a paper delivered at a conference in 1968 I wrote:

> On my account there is no one kind of belief acquired by sensory stimulation from which all others are inferred. A landscape is shaped by wind, rain, running water, vegetation, volcanic upheavals, and so on. A particular stretch of land, for example, a field, is thus formed and shaped by its environment. The same with us. Our beliefs are formed, shaped, weakened, strengthened, and undermined by events occurring in our environments and in our heads. To think of a system of beliefs as a construction out of a primitive set of beliefs is to think of the system not as a landscape, but as a building. But since the existence of a building implies the existence of a builder, to think of ourselves in this way is to think dualistically. And this is so, even if we think the foundations of our buildings are insecure, as most neo-empiricists do. (Ellis 1975, pp. 68–9)

I would now add to this that the laws of logic, and the principles of inference which are involved in the processes of learning about the world, and coming to have a better understanding of it, are not to be thought of as *a priori* principles of reasoning of which we are somehow mysteriously aware, but as laws and principles which govern our thought processes, and, as such, can only be discovered *a posteriori*. To think of ourselves as agents freely using these principles to construct a view of reality is to perpetuate the dualist myth; and this is basically incompatible with the view of man which a physicalist world-view requires.

1.4   SCIENTIFIC EPISTEMOLOGY

If the physicalist perspective on human reasoning outlined above is correct, then the role of epistemology must be seen somewhat differently from usual. Traditionally, epistemology has not been seen to be an empirical scientific study, but a *normative* one. Its aims have been to isolate and characterize the foundations of knowledge, to justify accepting foundational beliefs as true, or probable, and to articulate and justify the principles of reasoning, investigation, and so on which we should use in the further pursuit of truth. But if the perspective on human nature which has been outlined here is correct, then epistemology must be viewed as a science of human belief systems, and its aims must be to explain their content, structure and evolution. If we can do this successfully, and separate the rational from the non-rational forces which shape our belief systems, then it should not be too difficult to say how we ought rationally to think. For when we have such an explanation we should have a model of rationality which should appeal to us as a rational ideal.

The kind of explanation we should expect to find is a model-theoretic one; for we cannot hope, at this stage, to offer any account of the microprocesses which are presumably involved in human thinking. Such a theory will provide a model of what is to be explained, and will formulate principles or laws governing the behaviour of the elements of that model. The model, to be useful, must have an intended interpretation. That is, it must be possible to identify at least some features of the physical systems, of which it is the model, with elements in it. There is no requirement that the physical systems should behave exactly as the theory requires. All model-theoretic explanations involve idealizations which we know in advance ignore some of the complexities of nature; and consequently, we should not expect ordinary physical systems to behave as our theories require. We should demand only that the behaviour of the physical systems (or at least those aspects of them in which we are interested) be *explicable* on the models. And for this, it is enough that we should be able to account for the *differences* between the actual, and the theoretically ideal, behaviour.

A difference between an actual state of affairs and a theoretically ideal one is something we think needs causal explanation. Thus, if I ask why the earth is flattened at the poles, I must think of this flattening as an effect, as a state of affairs which would not obtain if it weren't for something. And clearly, the actual shape of the earth is here being contrasted with a theoretically ideal shape. This is the ideal against which the flattening is seen as an effect. And the ideal in question is satisfactory so long as the required causal explanations are forthcoming, and survive critical scrutiny.

Every request for a causal explanation carries with it a certain presupposition. When Aristotle asks what keeps the stone moving after it has left his hand his *causal presupposition* is that it would not do so if it weren't for something. When Newton asks why the stone does not continue to move in a straight line after it has left his hand, his causal presupposition is that it would so do if it weren't for something. When Kepler asks what drives the planets around in their orbits his causal presupposition is that they would not continue to revolve around the sun unless something were driving or pushing them. When the ignorant farmer asks why brown cows don't give brown milk, his causal presupposition is that they would do so if it were not for some causal influence.

Our theoretical ideals determine the structure of our causal presuppositions. They determine the sets of *norms* against which the ordinary behaviour of ordinary physical systems is to be compared and explained. Consequently, the aim of a scientific epistemology must be to construct a model of human thought processes, adequate to explain the content, structure and evolution of our belief systems. We should not expect ordinary human belief systems to evolve, or become structured, in quite the way the model requires.

For ideally rational belief systems will be theoretical ideals which function in the theory of belief systems in much the way that other theoretical ideals do in their respective domains of application. The model must provide a framework adequate for explaining how people think. It must be adequate in the sense that it defines a set of norms of rational thought, against which the ordinary thought processes of people are to be compared, and can be explained. In so far as someone's belief system does not evolve, or fails to become structured as the model requires, we have a problem for causal explanation. The presupposition must be that the system would behave in the required way if certain ideal conditions were to obtain, and the problem for explanation must be to show that there are indeed violations of these conditions in the particular case adequate to explain the differences between the actual case and the theoretical ideal.

The violations of conditions of ideality may be of different kinds. On the one hand, the ideal of rationality may be a kind of limit notion of rational equilibrium – an equilibrium of a kind which may never be reached in any actual belief system. On the other hand, it may involve abstraction from the actual conditions under which belief systems evolve or become structured. I have said enough elsewhere (Ellis 1979) about causes of irrationality of the first kind. Those of the second kind are in some ways more interesting. The physical ideals we use to give model-theoretic explanations of nature are often systems considered in isolation from the forces which act upon them. The law of conservation of energy, for example, applies strictly only to closed and isolated systems, i.e. systems from which there is no outflow or inflow of matter, and which are not subject to the action of external forces. An ideally rational belief system might similarly be one which is not subject to the action of *non-rational* forces.

I shall later have occasion to distinguish between epistemic and non-epistemic values. A value, for me, is just a preference-determining mechanism. An epistemic value is one which, specifically, determines our belief preferences. We do, however, have certain social and personal values which may well influence what we believe, and which, no doubt, in our early years, are largely determinative of what we believe. In trying to specify an ideally rational belief system we should, I think, try to abstract from these forces, since these are the forces which typically, we say, account for our prejudices and blind spots. An ideally rational belief system will be one which is free from the influences of such forces. No doubt, in reality, there cannot be any such belief system. For we do have these other values, and we do interact with other people – and, indeed, must do so to learn the language we need to express our beliefs. So the ideal is certainly unrealizable. But unrealizability has never been considered an objection to any proposed model-theoretic account of reality. We know in advance that there cannot be any inertial systems, perfect fluids, black body radiators, closed and isolated systems, uniform gravitational fields; but no one, to my knowledge, has ever rejected such idealizations on the ground that they are unrealizable. Likewise, it should be no criticism of any ideal of rationality that it cannot in fact, or even in principle, be realized. Science is more concerned to *understand* nature than to describe it, and understanding involves knowing how things would behave in various kinds of more or less idealized circumstances. It does *essentially* involve a knowledge of such counterfactual conditionals.

Given that the aim of a scientific epistemology must be to construct models of rationality adequate to explain the evolution and structure of our belief systems, the traditional aims of epistemology must now be re-evaluated. Firstly, we have no right to assume *a priori* that there is any unique class of theoretically neutral beliefs which is foundational in the traditional sense. Certainly, there are *observationally acquired* beliefs, which are new inputs into our systems of beliefs; and certainly we should expect any model of an ideally rational belief system which was adequate to account for the evolution of our belief systems to allow for such inputs. But we need not suppose that the beliefs which form these new inputs are all of the same kind, or that they have identities which are independent of the systems of beliefs into which they are to be fitted. We need not suppose, for example, that while beliefs ascribing observational properties to objects (e.g. that the wall is white) may be directly acquired, those ascribing causal relationships to things (e.g. that John is lifting a boulder) may not. For we may well, and probably should, allow that any of a wide range of different kinds of beliefs may be fed perceptually into our belief systems. Nor need we suppose that one person's perceptually acquired belief that the wall is white is the same as another's. For they may have quite different conceptions of whiteness (depending on what else they believe) even though they may use the term 'white' coextensively. The problem is not to isolate a unique class of theoretically neutral perceptually acquired beliefs which a rational agent might justifiably use as a foundation for an overall system of beliefs about the world. It is rather to find a model for the acceptance and incorporation of perceptually acquired beliefs on the one hand, or their rejection on the other, which can be used satisfactorily to account for our perceptual performance.

I do not say that a foundationalist theory of knowledge of the traditional kind might not, in the end, prove to be a good theory. Perhaps the assumption of the theory-neutrality of our perceptually acquired beliefs (or of some subset of them) will help us to construct a good theoretical model of rationality. And perhaps it would be better to consider the theory-ladenness of our actual observational judgements to be a complication which it would be better to ignore in our idealization of human thought processes. Moreover, it might be better to assume, for the purposes of theory construction, that perceptually acquired beliefs (or, at least, some of them) have a content and identity which is independent of the systems of beliefs into which they are to be incorporated – even though we may be sure that in fact this is not so. The practical impossibility of a theory-neutral observation language is no barrier to its functioning as a theoretical ideal.

Nevertheless, such a foundationalist theory of knowledge is implicitly dualist, in that it requires us to make a separation, at least in thought, between knowledge which is acquired immediately by perception, and is unaffected by our other beliefs, and knowledge which is not immediate in this sense, but is mediated by various processes of thought in which our other beliefs are involved. It is implicitly dualist because it requires us to think of ourselves on the model of a being which has two distinct and independent faculties – one of perception and one of reason. On the model in question, certain beliefs are given to us in perception, and we, as rational agents, use them to build up our picture of reality. Consequently, it must be doubtful whether a foundationalist theory of knowledge can in the end be satisfactory. It may indeed be very useful for some purposes to assume a kind of epistemological atomism, in which beliefs may be supposed to have an identity which is independent of the belief systems in which they are embedded, but this is unlikely to be a useful assumption if we are concerned with the processes of conceptual evolution, or with how our belief systems evolve. For these purposes it may be better to assume what is nearer to the truth, viz. that the identities of the beliefs we acquire by perception depend on our other beliefs.

However, I cannot say in advance of constructing a scientific epistemology what it would be like in detail. I can only comment on what general features we might expect it to have, given a physicalist ontology. At this point, I would make no stronger claim than this: a foundationalist epistemology is unlikely to be generally satisfactory.

But let us now turn from the question of foundationalism to the questions of justification. On the traditional view, epistemology is not an empirical scientific study of how people think or conceive the world. On the contrary, it is supposed that, as free agents, we are able to think in any way we please. There may be necessary truths or falsehoods, but there are no necessities of thought. Consequently, if we search for laws of thought, we shall search in vain. There are none. There might indeed be interesting sociological or psychological studies related to how people think or form opinions – studies which would be useful, perhaps, to psychotherapists, propagandists or politicians. But these inquiries, it would be said, have nothing to do with epistemology. Epistemology is concerned with how people *ought* to think if their aim is to secure knowledge of the truth, or a better theoretical understanding of nature. Hence, on the traditional view, epistemology is *essentially normative*. And the assumption behind it is that there are no necessities of thought which limit our choice of epistemology. Consequently, the choice of an epistemology has to be justified, and, given the assumptions about human freedom which lie behind the traditional conception of epistemology, the only justification which can be given is that it serves the interests of truth and understanding. Hence any rules, or principles of inference, which we might use to construct our theories about reality must be demonstrably well adapted to these ends. And so arise the problems of justifying the various forms of non-demonstrative reasoning which might feature in any given epistemology.

Karl Popper and his followers do, of course, reject this traditional view of the subject. For them the laws and theories of science cannot be shown to be true, or even probable. They can at most be strongly or weakly corroborated, depending on the severity of the tests to which they have been subjected. But we cannot say of a well corroborated theory that it is true, or even probably true. At most, it has a high degree of verisimilitude. Nevertheless, Popper, like other epistemologists, sees the necessity of justifying his particular choice of epistemology in terms of the goal of truth. An epistemology, to be any good, must lead to the development and acceptance of theories with the highest degrees of verisimilitude, or truthlikeness.[5] The theories, to be acceptable, need not be true, or even probable, but they must possess a higher degree of verisimilitude than any of their rivals.

Popper, like his opponents in epistemology, sees human beings as agents freely constructing their theories about reality out of data provided by sense experience. Like the positivists to whom he is opposed, he makes a sharp distinction between the logic and the psychology of knowledge. But he is more radical than they are because he does not accept any doctrine of 'the given'. The beliefs we acquire directly by sense experience all have the status of hypotheses. The experiences we have, the convictions we feel, the utter certainty that we may have that things are as we perceive them to be – none of these things can show, or even give us any good reason to believe, that any of our perceptual judgements are true. If we accept them, then that is a fact about us, a fact which belongs to the psychology of knowledge, not to its logic. The positivists on the other hand did think that some things were directly knowable, viz. those things that we are directly aware of. They disagreed amongst themselves about what was knowable in this way, i.e. they accepted different doctrines of 'the given'. But at least they thought that there was some basis of known truth on which to build. And the problem for them was how, justifiably, to get from these immediately known facts about particulars to the laws and theories of science. What are the principles of inductive inference, and how can we justify them?

The positivists distinguished between the contexts of discovery and justification. The context of discovery related to what they saw as the psychology of knowledge; the context of justification, including the rational reconstruction of knowledge, related to its logic. Hence, for the positivists, logic had to include some forms of inductive or non-demonstrative reasoning. For clearly the laws and theories of science could not be *deduced* from anything that was directly knowable. Hence the positivists were committed to developing an inductive logic, and demonstrating its rationality.

In a scientific epistemology most of these distinctions would vanish, or be reflected in different ways. Firstly, the distinction between the logic and the psychology of knowledge would have to be rejected. For epistemology, from a scientific point of view, is just the psychology of knowledge. The psychology of knowledge is the study of the principles governing human thought processes. The laws of logic are such principles as these (as I have argued in Ellis 1979). Therefore, the laws of logic belong to the psychology of knowledge: they are laws governing the structure of idealized belief systems in rational equilibrium. Of course, I do not suppose that human beings always think logically, or never contradict themselves. But then, ordinary belief systems are never in rational equilibrium, and are often subjected to non-rational forces. The laws of logic, *qua* laws of thought, are framework principles, which, like other such principles in science, apply only to highly idealized systems, in highly idealized circumstances. But they are psychological laws all the same; and have a role in explaining the structure of human belief systems precisely analogous to that of other framework principles in science in their respective domains. Hence, from a scientific viewpoint, logic is part of psychology, and if any distinction is to be drawn between the logic and the psychology of knowledge, it is a part–whole distinction.

Secondly, there can be no questions of justification of the traditional kind. To justify accepting a scientific law it is necessary and sufficient to show that the theory within which it occurs provides the best available explanation of the accepted data in the domain of the theory's application. Similarly, to justify accepting a law of

thought, it is necessary and sufficient to show that the theory of
rationality within which it is embedded provides the best available
model of our thought processes. Such a justification may or may
not be circular, depending on whether reasoning in accordance
with the principles to be justified is required in giving this justification. If it is, then it is none the worse for that, since our aim is not to
provide an *a priori* justification for thinking or reasoning in one way
rather than another, but an *a posteriori* justification for accepting
some *theory* about how we think or reason. Hence, if what is to be
justified is a theory about how we theorize, the justification must be
circular if the theory is any good. It is beside the point to argue that
if we thought in different ways some other theory of theorizing
might be self-justifying in the same sort of way, since there is no
question of our choosing to think in ways other than we do. Such a
question would only arise if we were able to think in any way we
pleased, and if, consequently, we were faced with the problem of
choosing *a priori* between different ways of theorizing. What is
known as the problem of induction is a problem for traditional
epistemology. But it is not a problem for a scientific epistemology,
which aims to construct a model-theoretic explanation of human
thought processes.

It is possible that a justification for accepting a law of thought
may not be immediately circular. For we may well be able to argue
that the theory of rationality within which a particular law of
thought is embedded is the best available theory, without using any
arguments which can be seen as presupposing that law. The
attempts of Reichenbach and Salmon to justify induction pragmatically were of this kind.[6] For they sought to prove that a certain
principle of inductive reasoning, viz. the straight rule, is the only
principle which satisfies certain *a priori* constraints on rationality.
In particular, they assumed that it is more rational to act on a
principle which must eventually succeed in achieving our agreed
aims, if they are capable of being achieved at all, than any which
need never succeed. However, their attempts at vindicating induction were unsuccessful, because ultimately theories must be involved in making any projection from assumed known facts about
particulars, and these theories are always inductively underdetermined by the evidence for them. Rational projection always de-

pends on what underlying uniformities of nature would best explain the given data, and be most in conformity with our other beliefs about the world. And this question cannot be settled independently of what we consider a good explanation to be, or independently of the background theories against which the question of conformity or non-conformity is to be settled. Consequently, any attempt to justify an abstract principle of induction with which we may be supposed to operate independently of our theoretical understanding of nature, or independently of our criteria of theory evaluation, is doomed to failure.

But quite apart from these objections to the programme of justifying induction pragmatically, there is no avoiding ultimate circularity. First, the theory of probability, which must be presupposed in any pragmatic justification of induction, would have to be shown to be the best available theory of probability; and to do this we should have to show that the theory in question provides the best model-theoretic account of the relationships we suppose to hold between our various probability judgements. Of course, we do not require that the probability judgements of ordinary people should conform to the model on its intended interpretation. But we do require that they be explicable on this model. For if they were not, there would be no reason why we should accept it as a model of rationality, of how our probabilistic belief systems would be structured if we were ideally rational. Hence, if our acceptance of theories ultimately did depend on our acceptance of some inductive principle, we should need this principle to justify our acceptance of the theory of probability which we need to provide the pragmatic justification of this principle. Therefore, any pragmatic justification of induction would ultimately be circular.

It is not for this reason, however, that I reject the Reichenbach–Salmon programme. For, if my other objections could be met satisfactorily, the circularity would not matter. If I am right in thinking that we are innately programmed in certain sorts of ways, then of course we must think in those ways. And it can be no objection to a theory about how we think that this theory is constructed in accordance with the principles which govern our thought processes.

1.5   NORMATIVE EPISTEMOLOGY

The objection that nearly everyone has to a scientific epistemology is that it would not be normative. Epistemology must be concerned not with how people *do* think, or with scientific model-theoretic explanations of their thought processes, but with how people *ought* rationally to think. And this is said to be a question on which a scientific epistemology is necessarily silent. Moreover, it won't do to argue that the question of how we ought rationally to think does not arise because ultimately we have no choice in the matter. The determinist argument for a-rationalism is no better than the determinist argument for a-moralism. There are questions of how we ought rationally to think and of what we ought rationally to believe, and any theory of rationality which did not leave room for such questions, or failed to provide satisfactory answers to them, would be radically unsatisfactory.

Here I wish to argue that a scientific epistemology need not be silent on these issues. On the contrary, it will define a standard, or ideal, of rationality which is not only a theoretical ideal, but also a regulative one. It will provide answers to the questions of how we ought rationally to think and of what we ought rationally to believe. Anyone who aspires to be rational in their search for the truth will strive to meet these standards.

First, any theoretically ideal rational belief system will be one that is isolated from the influence of non-rational forces. Non-rational forces which might influence our belief systems are pressures to believe or disbelieve which result from desires or values which have nothing specifically to do with rational preference. If, for example, I am disposed to believe that *p*, because believing that *p* is socially acceptable, or a condition for parental approval, or necessary to maintain one's self-esteem, or because the rationale for enjoyable or socially respectable practices is underpinned by that belief, then my belief system is influenced by non-rational forces. They are non-rational because they do not refer to specifically epistemic values. The values in question are social or personal ones. Any ideally rational belief system will be one which is supposed to exist in isolation from any such forces. But then, since we are all subject to the action of such forces, we must all have belief systems which fail to satisfy the requirements of the rational ideal. Therefore, if we want to be rational in the search for truth, we should seek to insulate ourselves from the influence of such forces. The theoretical ideal of rationality might thus serve as a regulative ideal.

Secondly, any theoretically ideal rational belief system will be one that is properly integrated. All of us have beliefs which, in one way or another, are not well integrated – their full implications have not yet been realized. We are sometimes slow to recognize the full import of some newly acquired beliefs. Sometimes we just remain in a kind of quasi-stable state of rational disequilibrium. Our beliefs are not questioned or challenged, and the rational adjustments which would occur as a result of such questions or challenges may never in fact occur. Consequently, if a theoretically ideal rational belief system is one that is properly integrated, ordinary belief systems may fail to be rational because they fail to satisfy this condition. Therefore, if we want to be rational in our search for truth, we should seek to expose ourselves to the pressures which would integrate our belief systems. The theoretical ideal of rationality might thus serve as a regulative ideal in this way too.

Thirdly, a theoretically ideal belief system should, perhaps, be one that is well adapted to the world around us. A belief system which was isolated from non-rational forces, and was internally coherent and well integrated, might nevertheless be grossly ill-informed. Recognizing that belief systems can be deficient in this way, we might postulate an ideal of perfect adaptation. The belief systems of ordinary people are always less than perfectly adapted to their environments. New perceptually acquired beliefs may change, reinforce or undermine some beliefs that were previously held. And where this happens we may say that something that we had previously thought to be true or probable is not true or is not probable. In a perfectly adapted belief system we may suppose that this would not occur. New beliefs acquired perceptually would not disturb the existing structure. This ideal too might serve as a regulative ideal; and, in so far as we are influenced by it, we should seek to test our belief systems against experience, and to adapt them as well as possible to the accommodation of new belief inputs.

There are, therefore, various ways in which a theoretically ideal belief system might serve as a regulative ideal. Therefore, it cannot be assumed *a priori* that an empirical theory of human rationality must remain silent on the issue of how we ought rationally to think. Providing a model-theoretic account of rationality may well involve constructing models of ideally rational belief systems, which may serve in a variety of ways as regulative ideals. It is true that from a description of how things *are* we cannot say how they *ought* to be. But it is not obvious that a theoretical model used to define an ideal of rationality is similarly uninformative. To argue from what is the case to what ought to be is certainly a fallacy. But to argue from how things would be in some idealized circumstances to how they ought to be, given that we aim to realize those circumstances, is no fallacy at all. To say that X ought morally to do Y or rationally to believe Z is just to say that X would do Y or believe Z if X were an ideally moral or rational being. Those who would object to a scientific epistemology on the ground that it is necessarily silent on the question of how we ought rationally to think simply do not understand the role of idealizations in scientific theory. They suppose, quite indefensibly, that a scientific epistemology would be simply *descriptive* of how we think. I would say, on the contrary, that a scientific epistemology is *necessarily normative*. It is *essentially* a theory about how we ought rationally to think.

Finally, granting that the theoretical ideal required for a theory of human rationality is capable of serving in various ways as a regulative ideal, the question remains: 'Why should we aspire to be ideally rational in just *this* sense?' The answer is, ultimately, 'Because we are human'. The ideal of rationality required for the model must be an ideal of *human* rationality which refers to fundamental *human* epistemic values, which, being fundamental, cannot be justified with reference to any other values. Our rationality is not, according to the kind of theory envisaged here, an instrumental good to be justified as a means of achieving some non-epistemic objective, such as survival. An ideally rational being, both theoretically and normatively, is simply one who employs optimal strategies for maximizing epistemic value, i.e. one who uses optimal strategies for maximizing their knowledge and understanding.[7] The relevance of this to the problem of induction will be considered in detail in chapter 8.

2

The Ontology of Science

An ontology is a general theory of what there is.[1] It is the attempt to say what sorts of things there are, what basic categories of things we need to postulate to explain their existence, and what kinds of things in each category exist most fundamentally. Given the scientific world-view, we naturally turn to science, particularly to fundamental physics, to answer these questions. However, it is not clear what science can tell us about what there is, or what exists most fundamentally. For philosophers and scientists themselves disagree about what the ontological commitments of science are. Naive scientific realists are inclined to take what scientists say in presenting their theories fairly literally and uncritically in deriving their ontologies. Empiricists, on the other hand, would mostly deny that theories are to be taken literally in this way, and insist upon an instrumentalist reading of them.

To derive an ontology from science, scientific realists rely heavily on an argument from the best explanation: if the world behaves *as if* entities of the kinds postulated by science exist, then the best explanation of this fact is that they really do exist. This is the main argument for realism about theoretical entities. Properly understood, it is a powerful argument, although its scope and application are matters for debate. Anyone who argues in this way is called 'a scientific realist'. Scientific realists have generally presented the argument crudely as an argument for the existence of 'things like atoms and electrons' – as though this were all that needed to be said. However, the argument is not a good argument for the existence of some kinds of theoretical entities (such as space-time points), and it is a good argument for the existence of certain kinds of properties and relationships which many scientific realists do not believe in.

The chief difficulty with the main argument for realism about theoretical entities is that it is not always clear when we should say that the world behaves *as if* things of such and such a kind exist. If you believe in things of this kind, it is likely to be because you think the world behaves as if they exist, and if you do not think they exist, you are not likely to agree that the world behaves as if they do. The main argument for realism must therefore be used with some caution if it is to do more than just reinforce one's ontological preferences. It does not provide us with an easy way of constructing an ontology. To do this we need to do quite a lot of work.

2.1 ONTOLOGICAL REDUCTION

We say that things of a kind A can be reduced ontologically to elements of the kinds B iff it can be shown: (1) that As could not exist, even if they were miraculously to come into being, unless elements of the kinds B existed; and (2) that As consist of elements of just these kinds. That is, the existence of elements of the kinds B must be severally necessary and jointly sufficient for the existence of As. If As can be so reduced, then we may say that the existence of As *depends on* the existence of elements of the kinds B. If elements of these kinds cannot themselves be ontologically reduced, then we may say that they *exist fundamentally*.

It is possible, given these definitions, that the elements to which a thing may be reduced should turn out to be ontologically *interdependent*. For example, it is consistent to hold that the universe consists of fundamental particles *and* their basic properties, although neither could exist without the other. Some philosophers will take a different view on this, and insist that things in each of the basic categories should be capable of existing independently of things in any of the other categories. However, I can see no good reason to insist on the independence assumption – at least across categories. A good deal of ontological reduction is possible without it, and, as we shall see, it would prevent the construction of some very neat and satisfying ontologies to demand it.

For reasons to be given shortly, we should expect an ontology to be highly reductive in each of the basic categories of existents it assumes. I stress, however, that the economy required concerns *kinds* of things rather than their individual instances. This is because the reductiveness of an ontology is unaffected by how many individual things we may have to suppose there are of any given kind.

The basic items in any given category must be simple, i.e. not constituted of, or divisible into, other things in this category. For if they were not simple, they would be reducible to these other things, and so would not exist fundamentally. For example, if quarks are postulated as basic items in the category of physical entities, then it must be supposed that they are not reducible to any more fundamental things in this category. Nor can it be that the basic items of a given category are reducible to things in other categories. For example, if we have an ontology which includes fundamental particles as basic items, we cannot consider the particles to be just co-instantiations of particle properties at points in space. For this would be to make points in space and particle properties the more fundamental categories.

2.2 COMPREHENSIVENESS, REDUCTIVENESS AND EXPLANATORY POWER

An ontology seeks to establish a system of categories of the sorts of things which exist fundamentally, and to explain how other things either fit into these categories, or depend ontologically on the sorts of things that do. To be acceptable, it should be a good theory by the usual criteria for theory evaluation. However, because an ontology must be a supremely general theory to be any good, comprehensiveness must be a very important consideration in evaluating an ontology. Other kinds of theories can afford to be more restricted in scope. On the other hand, we should not expect an ontology to be predictive, as we would a scientific theory, because such a general theory, as an ontology must be, is bound to be programmatic. It would be an extraordinary ontology if it were able to predict the existence of some new kind of entity, although I do not say that this is impossible. However, a good ontology should be able to influence our beliefs about what there is in the sort of way that a good moral theory should be able to influence our beliefs about what is right. That is, by systematizing, and seeking to explain and justify our beliefs, it should ultimately correct them.

An ontology should also be highly reductive, not only because we want it to be as simple as possible, but also because differences between supposedly fundamental existents must be held to be inexplicable. For example, when there were just a few fundamental particles known to exist, they could all be accepted as basic items in an ontology. But when the number grew to a hundred or more, we should have had to suppose that all this diversity could exist without any underlying structure which would explain it, if we still wished to accept all of these particles as ultimate constituents of matter. Some diversity, somewhere in the fundamental categories, is needed to explain the diversity we know exists. But too much diversity leaves too many differences at the fundamental level unexplained; and to accept the ontology is to suppose that these differences are finally inexplicable. Consequently, it is a considerable virtue of an ontology, if the number of basic items posited for each category is small.

As with any theory, the most important virtue of an ontology is its *explanatory power*. Consequently, there is not much point in eliminating a category of things from an ontology, if to do so does not increase our understanding. The Humean reduction of causes to regularities, for example, made an ontology without a category of causal relationships possible. But it did so at the expense of our understanding of reality. Hume's own psychological account of the genesis of our causal concepts is certainly unsatisfactory, and epistemological theories about the nature of causal laws do not explain their apparent necessity to everyone's satisfaction. An ontology which included a category of causes, and explained more, might be better than one which was more highly reductive, but explained less. Reductiveness is not an autonomous virtue, but is derivative from considerations of simplicity, and the concern of ontologists not to leave too much diversity unexplained at the fundamental level.

According to the mechanistic ontology which was commonly accepted after Newton as sufficient for the material world, all physical changes are fundamentally changes of position. Even for

Descartes, the world consisted just of matter in motion. Consequently, the regularity theory of causation would allow all causal relationships to be understood as being fundamentally spatio-temporal. This mechanistic ontology had the advantage of being highly reductive. However, since the advent of quantum theory, mechanism is no longer tenable, and there is now no prospect of reducing all changes to changes of position. Therefore, other kinds of changes must be envisaged as being at least as primitive. In particular, the sorts of interactions between fundamental particles which cannot be analysed simply as changes of position may be in a category of their own, and not reducible to anything else. If so, then perhaps we can reduce all causal processes to these primitive causal interactions between the fundamental particles. We shall consider this possibility in detail later.

2.3 REALISM ABOUT THEORETICAL ENTITIES – THE MAIN ARGUMENT

The main argument for realism about theoretical entities applies most obviously to what I call 'causal process theories', i.e. to theories which are, or are intended to be, descriptive of underlying causal processes. It applies, for example, to the atomic and molecular theories of nineteenth-century chemistry, and to the Bohr theory of the atom. For these theories were clearly intended to be taken literally as descriptions of unobservable physical structures. The entities postulated in these theories were assumed to have certain properties, similar in some ways, but different in others, from things we already know about, and to participate in various causal processes to give rise to the phenomena to be explained.

For these theories the usual arguments for realism concerning the entities postulated are mostly sound. If A is agreed to be the best causal account that can be given of the occurrence of some event E, and A is otherwise a satisfactory theory, then the entities postulated in A as the *causes* of E must also be thought to exist. To say that it is just *as if* they existed would always be to weaken the explanation, for it would immediately raise the further question why this should be so; and the realist answer, 'Because they *do* exist', would appear to be the only satisfactory one. We should, therefore, always be realists about the theoretical entities postulated to exist in the causal process theories we accept.

The main argument for realism applies to the theoretical entities of *causal process* theories because of the roles these entities are supposed to have in bringing about what is to be explained. In these cases, it can truly be said that the world behaves *as if* these things existed, because the explanation we are offering shows how the events to be explained appear to be causally dependent on the entities we have postulated. This is why the argument is a good argument for the existence of things like atoms and electrons, as its proponents claim it is.

However, to argue as though all, or nearly all, scientific theories are causal process theories, as some scientific realists seem to do, is to show no awareness of the variety of aims of theory construction, of the diversity of kinds of theoretical entities in science, or of the different sorts of roles that scientific theories may have. There are many important, indeed fundamental, theories which plainly are not intended to describe hidden structures or processes, and realism about the theoretical entities postulated in these theories is often quite unwarranted.

Physical geometries, for example, are constructed to systematize the range of *possible* spatial or spatio-temporal relationships. In doing so, they postulate an infinite set of *possible* locations, or points in space or space-time, and construe the actual world as consisting of things or events occupying some or other of these points. However, such theories should not be interpreted realistically. First, physical things and events are not so precisely located. Therefore, real spatial and spatio-temporal relationships between objects and events are not like those postulated to hold between geometrical points. Secondly, physical geometries are not, and are not intended to be, causal explanatory theories. Therefore, we do not need an ontology which includes infinitely many space or space-time points *in addition* to the physical entities which we suppose may occupy them. If points in space or space-time have no causal explanatory roles, how we can argue that the world behaves *as if* they existed? What difference could they possibly make?

Other theories appear to describe how certain *ideal* systems would behave in various specified circumstances, e.g. in the absence of certain forces (which may never in fact be absent). Thus, the laws of conservation of energy and momentum apply strictly only to closed and isolated systems, although there are no macroscopic systems other than the universe as a whole which are like this (and whether these laws apply to the universe is at least problematic); the principles of special relativity tell us how things would behave in inertial systems (although general relativity implies that no such systems can exist); certain of the laws of thermodynamics apply only to perfectly reversible heat engines (which other principles of thermodynamics clearly prohibit). Theories of this kind are not unusual, and the laws they contain are among the most fundamental in science. Therefore, they cannot simply be dismissed as anomalies. On the other hand, they cannot be taken literally as true generalized descriptions of reality either, for then they would all be vacuous.

To determine the scope of the main argument for realism, we need to be able to distinguish clearly between those entities which are supposed to be involved in causal processes and those that are not. I do not know precisely how to do this, but one distinguishing mark appears to be that they should have effects other than those they are defined as having. The point derives from James Clerk Maxwell who held that a quantity must be related to other quantities, independently of how it is defined, if it is to count as a genuine physical magnitude. Otherwise, he said, it is a 'mere scientific concept'.

Maxwell made this distinction when discussing Lord Kelvin's analogy between the laws of electrostatics and heat conduction (Maxwell 1881, paras. 65 and 66). Kelvin observed that, in certain circumstances, the two sets of laws are formally the same; so that concepts used in the one field have formal analogues in the other. Maxwell argued, however, that these formally analogous concepts do not have the same *ontological* status. In particular, he claimed that the electrical potential at a point in a field, which is the formal analogue of the temperature at a point in a conductor, is not, as temperature is, a genuine physical magnitude. Physically, he said, it is only potential *difference* which has effects, whereas temperature has effects independently of temperature differences.

Whether Maxwell was right about this particular case does not matter. What is important is his insight that causal connectivity is what characterizes real things. That is, real things should have a range of different properties, and so be capable of participating in various causal processes. Therefore, we should not expect the properties of a real thing to be given wholly by definition, or to be just those it is postulated as having in some particular theory. Rather, we should expect it to have properties, and hence effects, others than these, and so to manifest itself in different ways. Consider place, time and direction, for example. If mere position in space and time has no effects, and space is isotropic, then place, time and direction are all 'mere scientific concepts' by Maxwell's criterion. The physically real quantities here (assuming a Newtonian world) are just distance, time-interval and angle; for these are the properties which make a difference in physical causal processes.

While the main argument for realism about theoretical entities is limited in its applicability to certain of the entities postulated in our causal process theories, it is important to appreciate the full strength of the argument. It is not, as I see it, just an argument for the existence of material particles, and things that are constituted of them. It is also, *prima facie*, an argument for the existence of certain properties, e.g. the properties that these particles are supposed to have. For, we may ask, 'Why do the fundamental particles behave *as if* they had these properties?' The only satisfactory answer seems to be : 'Because they *really do* have these properties'. To try to reduce them (the properties) to sets of material particles, as Smart is inclined to do,[2] is to make a mystery of the similarity of behaviour of these particles. For this fact could hardly be explained by their common set membership, if it is being denied that there is anything which unites the members of this set, save that they have the same general name. The set theoretic reduction of particle properties to sets of particles is more in the spirit of logical atomism than scientific realism, because it seeks to cut our ontology to fit our logic rather than our science.

The main argument for realism about theoretical entities is also, apparently, an argument for the existence of forces, fields, numbers, sets, spatio-temporal relationships, possible worlds, and many other kinds of things. The question is, what other sorts of things must we believe in if we accept the main argument? There is no simple way of answering this question. I think we should believe in some of these things, but not in others; it is a question of which ontology is most elegant, comprehensive, explanatory and plausible.

2.4 THE ONTOLOGICAL REDUCTION OF PHYSICAL ENTITIES

In the category of physical entities I include everything that is thought to possess energy.[3] The category includes all material objects, all of the fundamental particles, and all of the force fields of the kinds recognized in Quantum Field Theory. It does not include numbers, sets, propositions, sentences, or other abstract particulars. It does not include properties or relationships. And it does not include forces. If we believe that any of these other sorts of things exist, and are not reducible to things in the category of physical entities, we must say to what other category or categories of things they belong.

Until quite recently, some philosophers of science argued against the existence of fields. P. W. Bridgman did so, for example, in Bridgman (1954), p. 59. Bridgman sought to eliminate fields and to construe statements about them as being strictly about the dispositions of charged particles, or whatever they are supposed to act upon, to behave in certain characteristic ways, depending on where they are in relationship to other particles.

There are, however, good reasons to be realists about fields. One such reason derives from the main argument for scientific realism. The best theory we have of the causal interactions which take place between particles is Quantum Field Theory. This theory is a causal explanatory theory; for the fields are required as mediators in interactions between particles, and they are quite essential to the explanation, because they are the carriers of the energy which is transferred in these interactions. Without them energy would not be conserved in these processes. Therefore, by the main argument for scientific realism, we should be realists about fields.

Realism about fields [margin annotation]

Next, an ontology of fundamental particles, interacting without the mediation of fields, is untenable, given that some of the most fundamental laws of quantum mechanics are expressed as wave equations, and that the energy transfer processes involved in particle interactions are best described by these equations. Indeed, an ontology of fields, in which particles are understood to be more or less stable wave packets, is now generally accepted. Moreover, the distinction between particles and resonances is hard to make, and particles are coming to be seen more and more as field phenomena, which are incapable of existing, except in the fields in which they are embedded. Therefore, the direction of ontological reduction which now seems most plausible is from particles to fields.

Even classically, there is good reason to believe in fields, since they have always been required as the bearers of potential energy. When opposite charges are separated, it is conventional to say that they each acquire a certain amount of potential energy. But in a classical ontology of particles, moving under the influence of mutually attractive or repulsive forces, potential energy can only be understood dispositionally, if fields are not considered to be real. For the particles are not changed in any way as a result of being separated. Therefore, if we do not have fields in our ontology, we must say that, in acquiring potential energy, the particles simply acquire a disposition to accelerate towards each other. To explain such a disposition, however, we need a categorical basis other than mere separation. A field which is created in the process of separating the particles, and which bears the potential energy, is the best explanation we have.

If fields are the more basic kinds of physical entities, this raises important questions about their nature. What sorts of things are they? The evidence seems to be that they are entities which are propagated as waves, but act as particles; the probability of a field acting at a point being a function of the wave amplitude at that point. The difficult question is how this is possible. If the energy is localized somewhere in the field, then there is the problem of explaining the interference phenomena that are observed (e.g. in the 'two slit' experiment). If the energy is dispersed throughout the field in the process of propagation, then there is the problem of explaining how the field can collapse, apparently instantaneously, in the process of particle interaction. For this would seem to imply that energy localization may occur instantaneously, or at least at superluminal velocities. I favour the second view, despite its apparent conflict with relativity theory, because a probability field seems more like a mathematical fiction than a physical entity. What is physical has energy, and if fields are physical entities, then the energy must be dispersed throughout them. In any case, the empirical evidence is only that there is an upper limit to the speed of energy *transmission*, not that there is an upper limit to the speed of energy *localization*. These two kinds of processes must be just fundamentally different.

2.5 THE ONTOLOGICAL REDUCTION OF PHYSICAL SUBSTANCES

Ordinary physical substances are ontologically reducible to their pure chemical constituents, and these, in turn, are reducible to various combinations of the chemical elements. The pure chemical substances, and the elements to which they may be reduced, are all natural kinds. That is, the distinctions between them are distinctions which exist in nature. They are not distinctions imposed by us for our own classificatory purposes, like those between the various kinds of chocolate. To explain the existence of these natural kinds, we need more than just an ontology of physical entities. We need an ontology of *kinds* of physical entities. For it is not enough that there should just be things which possess energy. There have to be certain specific kinds of things possessing energy – kinds which are distinguishable from each other by their naturally distinctive properties.

The properties of, and differences between, these natural kinds are to be explained by the more fundamental differences which exist at the atomic and molecular levels. For these properties and differences can in principle be accounted for in terms of the properties of the kinds of atoms and atomic bonds which exist. The properties of the atoms and bonds may, in turn, be accounted for by the subatomic nuclear and shell structures of the atoms, and by the fundamental forces which operate at this level. The kinds of entities we need for these explanations are, therefore, physical entities and forces. These kinds of entities would all appear to be natural kinds, including the forces. For their properties are distinctive, and the distinctions between these various kinds of entities are not ones we have had to impose: they exist in nature.

2.6   THE ONTOLOGY OF EVENTS

Scientific realists must suppose that all events are physical events, where physical events are changes in physical systems. Such events always involve changes in form or distribution of energy. So, without loss of generality, we may define a physical event as any change of distribution of energy in any of its forms. Of course, many events, so understood, will be phenomenologically indistinct parts of larger events, and so not thought of as separate events. Nevertheless, this definition of 'physical event' fits well with our conception of a physical entity, and it does not include any changes which are clearly not physical. It does not include mental events, for example, if these are not changes in the distribution of energy in the universe.

Not all physical events have the same ontological status. Changes of shape, for example, are ontologically reducible to systematic changes in the relative positions of parts of things; and changes which occur in them are ontologically reducible to changes in their parts, and so on. But not 'and so on' indefinitely. For we now know that there are many physical changes which are not reducible to changes of position. The question for ontology, then, is what sorts of physical events must we consider to be most fundamental.

Changes of position within physical systems are certainly physical events by the definition we have given; and there is no reason to suppose that they are reducible to any more fundamental physical changes. All attempts to develop causal theories of space-time, which would permit the reduction of spatio-temporal relationships to causal ones, have so far been unsuccessful, and the prospects for their success in future are not good (Heathcote 1984). The temporal order is perhaps identical to the causal order, and hence reducible to it, as Hans Reichenbach once argued (Reichenbach 1927, para. 21). But the complete reduction of spatio-temporal relationships to causal ones does not seem to be possible. Therefore, we should, at least provisionally, recognize changes of position occurring within physical systems as a primitive category of events.

In addition to changes of position, I think we also need to recognize that there are some essentially different kinds of changes occuring in the interactions between fundamental particles. On current theory, as I understand it, these interactions can be reduced to four basic kinds – the strong, the weak, the electromagnetic and the gravitational – although there is reason to think that some reduction in the number of kinds of basic interactions may be possible (Freedman and van Nieuwenhuizen 1978). These basic kinds of interactions are thought to be governed by characteristic conservation and symmetry principles, and the general theory of particle interactions based on these principles is elegant, comprehensive and highly reductive. Therefore, it is reasonable to speculate that all physical events are ultimately reducible to interactions of these kinds, and the characteristic wave/particle emissions they produce.

2.7 THE ONTOLOGY OF CAUSATION

This ontology of events immediately suggests an ontology for causal relationships. For it is plausible to suppose that all causal interactions are reducible to basic interactions between fundamental particles. Thus, if the billiard ball A collides with the billiard ball B, then this event is presumably just the sum of the interactions between their particles; and the subsequent motions of A and B are the continuing consequences of these interactions (compounded by those of any further interactions there may be between the balls and the table or other things in their surroundings).

I postulate that no causes are required to sustain a continuing consequence of a causal interaction – such as an inertial motion, or the propagation of an electromagnetic wave. These chains of events will continue indefinitely, or until they become involved in some new basic interactions. The only causes involved in these processes, I wish to say, are the interactions which would initiate, change or destroy such motions or waves. The case for regarding inertial motion as a kind of 'natural' motion, not requiring any cause to sustain it, has been argued at length in the literature (see Ellis 1965a). The case for taking a similar view of electromagnetic radiation is also compelling, although I have never seen it argued. It is that there is no good reason to distinguish radically between electromagnetic (e.g. gamma) radiation, on the one hand, and alpha, beta, and other forms of radiation resulting from particle interactions, on the other. If the motions of the latter are considered to be inertial, then those of the former should be too. Let us call any motions like these, which require no causes to sustain them, *energy transfer processes*.

A basic problem for the theory of causation is to say how causes are related to their effects. Plausibly, the answer is that they are related either directly by the action of forces, or indirectly by energy transfer processes. Certainly, many causes produce their effects in these ways. However, there are also some negatively acting causes which produce their effects by blocking or modifying energy transfers which would otherwise have occurred. For example, I may darken my room by pulling the blinds. The issue is further complicated by the fact that an effect may be produced by a combination of positively and negatively acting causes, which may be acting either in series or in parallel. However, it would seem to be at least a necessary condition for an event A being causally related to an event B that it be serially related to B by some such combination of processes.

This ontological account of causation is comprehensive, highly reductive, and offers a satisfying explanation of the nature and variety of causal relationships. It identifies their direction as that of the forces or energy transfer processes involved; it explains why there is an upper limit to the speed with which causal influences may be transmitted (because there is an upper limit to the speed of energy transfer); it explains how there can be unique, never to be repeated, cause-and-effect relationships (such as the Big Bang causing the expansion of the universe), which regularity theories cannot satisfactorily account for; and it explains how causes may operate in an indeterministic world, which no regularity, or natural necessitation, theory of causation can do. According to our ontological theory, *all* causal influences are transmitted by processes which are fundamentally *indeterministic*.

These energy transfer processes are also said to transmit the *forces* which are involved in particle interactions. Thus, the electromagnetic force is supposed to be transmitted by photons or electromagnetic waves, the strong force is thought to be transmitted by gluons, gravitation by gravitons, and so on. All of the changes which occur in particle interactions are said to be produced by the actions of these forces. Now, this way of speaking suggests that forces are just kinds of causal influences. And, so conceived, there is good enough reason to believe in them. If there are four basic kinds of causal interactions between particles, there are four basic kinds of direct causal influences.

There is another way of speaking about forces, however, which suggests that they are things necessarily present when the effects they are said to produce occur, and are necessarily productive of these effects. This is the conception of force as an entity which *intervenes* between a material cause and its effect, but is not itself a material cause. For reasons I have given elsewhere (Ellis 1976), I see no reason to believe in forces of this kind. In principle, they are eliminable from physics, and if we have an ontology which includes primitive causal influences, we are not left having to believe in a Hume world. When we know how fields and particles interact, and how the effects of their interactions are transmitted, we know what there is to know about primitive causes, and how they are related to their effects.

2.8 FORCES

According to J. R. Mayer (Mayer 1842, p. 233), the essential characteristics of all causes are that they are *quantitatively indestructible* (since a cause must equal its effect), but *qualitatively convertible* (since causes and effects need not be similar). He went on to say:

> Two classes of causes occur in nature, which, so far as experience goes, never pass into one another. The first class consists

of such causes as possess the properties of weight and impen-
etrability; these are kinds of Matter: the other class is made up
of causes which are wanting in the properties just mentioned,
namely Forces, called also Imponderables, from the negative
property that has been indicated. Forces are therefore *indestructible, convertible, imponderable objects.*

In classical physics, forces were generally conceived of as immediate causes – as entities which are produced in some way by
material circumstances and are necessarily, and immediately, productive of their effects. Mayer's conception of force is clearly very
different from this; it is much more like our present-day concept of
energy. Indeed, Mayer is often given credit for being the first to
have stated the law of conservation of energy in its most general
form.

Mayer rejected the conception of force as an immediate cause
because he believed it confused the concept of a property with that
of a cause. For example, he thought it was a mistake to think of the
weight of a body as the cause of its acceleration downwards when
falling. This is a mistake, he said, because: '. . . precisely that which
is the essential attribute of every force – the *union* of indestructibil-
ity with convertibility – is wanting in every property', and 'If
gravity be called a force, a cause is supposed which produces effects
without itself diminishing, and incorrect conceptions of the causal
connexions of things are thereby fostered' (p. 199).

I agree with Mayer that the conception of force as a property is
unsatisfactory. Heavy bodies do not fall just because they have
weight. As Mayer himself observed, they have also to be raised;
and the raising of a body is no less part of the cause of its falling
than its weight. What is lost in the process of falling is its height
above ground; what is gained is a velocity proportional to the
square root of the distance fallen. If, therefore, the measure of the
cause of falling is proportional to the height from which a body
falls, then, by the principle that a cause is equal to its effect, the
measure of the effect of its falling must be proportional to the
square of the velocity it acquires.

But Mayer's conception of force as energy will not do as a
substitute for the classical conception of forces as directed magni-

tudes, which are subject to laws of vector addition, and are productive of accelerations. Something like the classical conception of forces seems to be needed in addition to the energy conception. It is true that forces of this sort can always be eliminated from physics. For every kind of force there are *laws of distribution* which enable us to calculate the strength and direction of the forces acting in the given circumstances; there are *laws of combination* which we can use to calculate the resultant forces acting on various things; and there are *laws of action* which enable us to calculate their effects on these things. And these three kinds of laws can always, in principle, be combined to produce laws of distribution of effects, i.e. laws which would enable us to calculate directly the effects which should occur in the circumstances.

But the elimination of forces cannot be effected without loss. Forces link together and explain disparate phenomena in ways in which laws of distribution of effects cannot. To eliminate gravity from a Newtonian world, we must suppose that every body is naturally disposed to accelerate towards every other body in the universe (why, we may not ask) with an acceleration directly proportional to the mass of the other body and inversely proportional to the square of its distance away. Hence we must suppose that gravitational accelerations which are not caused by forces are essentially different from other sorts of accelerations which are. There is thus a loss of uniformity in the account we must give of nature if we make this move. Similar effects must be assigned very different kinds of causes.

If all forces were eliminated in the same sort of way as gravity might be in a Newtonian world, then the result would be even less satisfactory. Accelerations and other changes would just occur, or have some finite probability of occurring, in various circumstances. (And again, we may not ask why.) There would be laws which should enable us to predict what changes would or might (with some probability) occur in given circumstances. But these events would be seen to occur as if by magic, for the world would be viewed as a world without causal connectivity. Events of one kind would be followed more or less regularly by events of another, but there would be no causal connection between them. It would be a Hume world.

But is a world with forces any more connected than a world without them? The answer depends on what sorts of things forces are conceived to be. If forces are conceived to be entities which mediate between causes and effects, as further links in a causal chain, then connectivity cannot be increased by them, for they too will need to be connected to their causes, and so on. Moreover, if forces are causes, like the events or circumstances which give rise to them, then they are curiously disembodied causes. They are defined as having certain effects, but they do not appear to have any properties or effects other than those they are defined as having, and so do not behave as we should expect real things to do. They are what Maxwell would call 'mere scientific concepts'.

But suppose we took a different view of the nature of forces, and thought of them, not as causes on a par with the events which give rise to them or the effects which they produce, but as *primitive instances of the relation of cause to effect*. Then forces would not themselves be regarded as the causes of anything, and the usual argument from their eliminability, that they are redundant in causal explanation, would lose much of its force. For if forces were instances of the causal relation, they would belong to a different ontological category from the things they related. The length of an object is not an entity of the same ontological type as the object itself; if it were, we could ask how long it is, and so generate an infinite regress. But it does not follow that lengths do not exist. Likewise, the force which is needed to bring about a certain effect is not itself a cause or effect; if it were, it would be appropriate to ask what force is needed to bring it (the force) about. But it does not follow that forces do not exist. To argue for this conclusion, we should have to show that we do not need a category of causal relations in our ontology, or, at least, that we do not need to include forces in this category.[4] I take it that the reductiveness, comprehensiveness and explanatory power of the ontology of causal relations I have developed here is sufficient to justify the inclusion of forces as instances of causal relations (and kinds of forces as species of causal relations).

2.9 PROPERTIES AND RELATIONSHIPS

The main argument for realism about theoretical entities requires us to be realists, not only about forces, but about other kinds of physical properties and relationships as well. For there are many different effects which forces may have, depending on the physical properties and relationships of their sources and objects. These physical properties and relationships must therefore be part of the causal story of why things behave as they do. Thus, we must say that the world behaves *as if* things had these physical properties, and were related physically to each other in these ways; and the best explanation of this fact must be that they really do have these properties, and are in fact so related.

It is not easy to say what sorts of things physical properties and relationships are. Consider properties. Some would simply identify them with sets of individuals (every set being a property); others would say that they are universals which individuals may or may not instantiate; and some would say that there are no property-universals, only property-instances or tropes. However, I am not satisfied with any of these accounts of the nature of properties. For reasons to be given presently, I am sure that properties are not just sets of individuals; and the other two theories cannot easily account for the structure we find in the system of the most fundamental properties we know about. For example, how does one explain the relationship between *different* properties of the *same* kind, like spin ½ and spin ³⁄₂, on a theory of universals or tropes? What seems to be needed for science is an ontology which recognizes the funda-mentally *quantitative* nature of the most basic properties of particles and fields; and such an ontology must somehow include such multi-valued properties or their values as primitive.

I do not know precisely how to construct such an ontology, because I have no adequate theory of what quantities, or more generally, what multi-valued properties, are. They are not property universals, as they are usually understood, because property uni-versals are not multi-valued. They may be multiply *instantiated*. But different instances of a property-universal must be *the same* in respect of this property, i.e. they must be single-valued. In *Basic*

Concepts of Measurement (Ellis 1966), I argued that quantities are the objective linear orders into which things possessing them may be arranged, and that the measurement of quantities consists in assigning 'numerals' to things according to their positions in these linear orders. By doing so, I sought to avoid the extremes of operationism, which would pointlessly have divided our quantitative concepts according to how they are measured, and naive realism, which would have located quantities and their magnitudes wholly in the objects possessing them – independently of their relationships with other things. However, I no longer think my earlier account will do. To give a satisfactory account of quantities, we must assume that there are quantitative universals.

The need to postulate the existence of quantitative universals is clear, I think, where the same linear order may be generated in any of a number of different ways. For on any other assumption, the existence of different ways of ordering things in respect of the same quantity seems entirely fortuitous. Conversely, the hallmark of any genuine quantity is that things may be ordered in respect of it in more than one way. Real things, as Maxwell observed, have properties other than those they have by definition.

If we think of a quantity as just any objective linear order, then at least we must distinguish between *real quantities*, *phenomenal quantities*, and *quantitative constructs*. For any real quantity q, there is a relation $>_q$ defining the order of q which is a universal. To be more precise, the real quantity q exists iff there is an asymmetrical and transitive relation $>_q$ of being greater in respect of q which imposes at least a partial ordering on things of a certain kind K. The things of kind K are then said to *possess* q. The ordering is complete iff, for any two distinct things A and B of kind K, either $A >_q B$ or $B >_q A$. It is partial iff there are things A and B of kind K which are equipollent in all q-relationships, so that neither 'A $>_q$ B' nor its converse, 'A $>_q$ B', holds. Such things are said to be equal in q ($=_q$). For real quantities, the relations $>_q$ and $=_q$ must be universals, and so hold independently of the results of measuring operations and the responses of measuring instruments (including people). That is, if A and B are any two things of the kind K, then one or other of $>_q$, $<_q$ and $=_q$ must hold between A and B, even if we cannot say which.

For *phenomenal quantities*, such as subjective brightness, and *quantitative constructs*, such as the product of a person's height and age (hage), there are no such ontologically objective relations. In the case of phenomenal quantities, the linear orders are determined by the results of measuring operations, or by the responses of complex systems or organisms, but not by any single relational universal; and quantitative constructs, like hage, are just more or less arbitrary functions of the measures of other quantities.

But not all quantitative constructs are as uninteresting as hage. Consider, for example, the space-time co-ordinates of the hypothetical events referred to in the Lorentz transformation equations. Since there are no inertial systems, and the events referred to are suppose to be occurring in such systems, they cannot be the measures of real quantities. They are what Maxwell would have called 'mere scientific concepts'. Moreover, even if the events represented were real events, their positions, times and directions from each other would not be physically real quantities; for the things which have effects would be only the *differences* in position, direction and time, i.e. the angles, distances and time-intervals between these events. Real quantities have effects, depending on their magnitudes; they belong to the causal net.

Such quantities as time-interval, distance and angle are fundamentally relational, and do not depend on the properties of the things they relate. For the time and place of an event are not properties that the event would have independently of other events; and the direction of a line is not a property of the line itself, but depends on how it is related to other lines. The ordering relations for these quantities must therefore be first order universals. However, the quantitative ordering relations for other quantities often seem to depend on the properties of the things they relate. Charge and mass, for example, seem to do so. My earlier view was that all quantities are fundamentally relational; and I claimed that it made no sense to speak of the charge or mass of an object except in relation to other objects. Thus, I held that to say that an object has a certain charge or mass is just to say that it bears certain relationships to other charges or masses.

However, I no longer think that this theory will do. For it does not explain how there can be things belonging to natural kinds which all have the same mass or charge, or why there should be fixed relationships between the charges or masses of things of different natural kinds. By contrast, there are no natural kinds which all exist at the same place, or all occur at the same time, or all point in the same direction; and there are no fixed relationships between the places, times or directions of any natural kinds. To explain these differences, I now want to say, as Swoyer does (Swoyer 1987), that the ordering relations for mass and charge are relations between certain quantitative properties of the things they are said to relate. If these quantitative properties are first order universals, then the quantitative relations which depend on them must be relations between first order universals, i.e. they must be second order universals. On this point I agree with Swoyer.[5]

Like Swoyer, I accept that the results of measuring operations cannot be adequately explained unless it is assumed that there is an underlying structure of quantitative properties and relations. The world certainly behaves as if this structure existed. Therefore, by the main argument for scientific realism, we should believe it does exist.

I am tempted by an ontology which identifies quantities with second order universals embracing particular quantitative values. Mass, for example, could be construed as a second order universal, the instances of which are the various particular masses which things may have. Likewise, temperature might be regarded as the property which all particular temperatures have in common. On this account, the particular masses and temperatures are fundamental, because they are the real first order properties which things may possess independently of anything else, and mass and temperature ordering relationships must be just more or less accurate ways of comparing things in respect of these quantities. However, such an account will not do generally for quantities; for some quantities, like date and longitude, are essentially relational, and their values do not exist independently of the systems of relations which define them.

I am also doubtful whether an ontology of quantities, as second order universals, will suffice. For there are many fairly basic relationships in nature besides the quantitative ordering relationships which define scalar quantities, like length and temperature.

Vectors, for example, have both magnitude and direction, and are additive in certain sorts of ways. But it is hard to see how directed quantities, like vectors, can be reduced to scalars, without the introduction of co-ordinate systems. The ontological reduction of tensors is even more problematic.

It is easier to say what physical properties and relationships are not than what they are. In formal logic, it is usual to represent a property as a set of individuals, and an n-place relationship as a set of ordered n-tuples of things – thus leaving the question of what sort of thing a property or relationship is wide open. This is fine for the purposes of logic, but it would be a mistake to make too much of the usefulness of this particular representation, and suppose that properties are nothing more than the sets of individuals which possess them, or that relationships are nothing more than the sets of ordered n-tuples which instantiate them. For what has to be explained is what the various members of these sets have in common. And it is not at all helpful to say that they all satisfy the same predicates, for this leaves the point of having these predicates wholly unexplained.

Moreover, to regard properties just as sets of individuals, and n-place relationships as sets of ordered n-tuples of individuals, is to make nonsense of the idea of *discovering* a new property or relationship. Sets are defined or constructed, not discovered; and there is nothing easier than defining a new set. Yet scientists surely *do* discover new properties and relationships, and what they do is by no means trivial. Murray Gell-Mann, for example, was awarded the Nobel Prize for Physics for his discovery of the set of relationships among certain properties of the fundamental particles known as the 'Eightfold Way'. A consistent scientific realist must hold that this symmetry existed before it was described.

Whatever general account of properties we may eventually give, we may define a *physical* property as one whose value is relevant, in some circumstances, to how a physical system is likely to act. It is a property which thus makes a physical difference. The most fundamental physical properties we know about are the multi-valued properties of fields and fundamental particles. They include such quantities as mass, charge, spin, interaction potential, hypercharge, strangeness, colour, charm, flavour, and many others. But perhaps the most important of all multi-valued properties is energy itself. I think a scientific realist must believe that energy exists, and is conserved in all fundamental interactions.

The account we give of physical properties should give us the lead for an account of physical relationships. For the most important physical relationships are also quantitative. In many cases, the quantitative relationships we speak about are ontologically dependent on the physical properties of the things related. This is normally the case, for example, when we speak of two things being equal or unequal in respect of some quantity. Therefore, we do not need to have an independent theory of relationships like this, if we have an ontology of quantitative universals. However, there appears to be at least one class of relationships which cannot be so reduced, viz. spatio-temporal relationships. For position in space-time does not appear to be a physical property in the sense in which we are here using this term. The laws of nature are supposed to be invariant with respect to position in space-time; therefore, mere position in space-time cannot make a difference to the propensity of a physical system to act in any way. Therefore, we must recognize that there is at least one ontologically irreducible class of physical relationships, viz. the spatio-temporal ones.

The theory of multi-valued universals I have proposed as a possible solution to the problem of ontologically reducing the category of properties and relationships to its most basic elements, is so far not much more than a suggestion. But if it can be made to work, it promises to yield a theory which is no less reductive or comprehensive in its own realm than the reduction of all physical entities to particles and fields is in its domain.

2.10 NUMERICAL RELATIONSHIPS

There is one more category of things we certainly need, viz. a category of numerical relationships. For there is no reason to suppose that these relationships can be reduced to those of any of the other categories. However, realism about numerical relationships does not imply realism about numbers. For numbers, abstractly considered, belong to the theory of *possible* numerical relationships, and so are not supposed to be causally effective. They are like geometrical points in this respect, and a scientific realist need not believe in them.

The simplest kind of numerical relationship is the *actual number*, or *degree of instantiation* N(P), of a physical property P. It is what we should ordinarily call 'the number of Ps'. This relationship is an objective, quantitative relationship between P and the world. In the terms of our earlier discussion (see section 2.9 above), it is a real quantitative property of P. The actual number of things with the property P is a real property of P, because it makes a physical difference how many things there are with this property. And it is what I have called a quantitative property, because N(P) has a magnitude which is both objective (i.e. independent of our knowledge and sensory apparatus) and not definable simply by its place in an objective linear order. Degree of instantiation is thus a real quantitative property in the sense that, say, charge is real. It is, indeed, a rather special quantity, since it is fundamental to all measurement, and its magnitude may sometimes be determined just by counting. But it is a fundamental quantity, nevertheless, and it surely deserves a place in our ontology.

Numerical relationships of this kind are the physical basis for the abstract concept of natural number. For the natural numbers are the idealized counterparts of actual numbers in the theory of all possible numerical relationships. They are not the actual numbers of any particular properties; for the abstract theory speaks of numbers as though they were independently existing entities. Nor do we need to suppose that for every natural number there is a property which has the corresponding degree of instantiation. For we can easily imagine a heap or collection which consists of just one thing. And if we can imagine a heap or collection of n things, we can always imagine adding one more thing to it. Therefore, by mathematical induction, every natural number is possibly the actual number of things in some heap or collection. Therefore, the natural numbers are just the set of all possible degrees of instantiation, and there is no need to be realistic about them.

There is also no good reason for a scientific realist to be realistic about sets. For sets are idealized heaps or collections. They have determinate membership; heaps do not. The membership of a set may not vary; but a thing may at one time be, and at another time not be, something that belongs to a given heap. The things that belong to a given collection must belong to the same ontological category; sets are not so restricted. But sets are not supposed to have any causal roles. Like numbers, they are incapable of changing or being changed. Therefore, a scientific realist is not required to believe in them. It may be useful to postulate them for certain purposes, just as it is useful to speak of other sorts of idealized systems. However, a sophisticated scientific realist should not be realistic about every sort of thing it is useful to postulate, but only those things they have to believe in to accept the causal process theories they do.

Smart disagrees with me about whether a scientific realist should believe in sets (Pettit, Sylvan and Norman (eds) 1987, p. 183). He argues that scientific realists have to believe in sets because they have to believe in numbers. The laws of nature cannot be expressed, except with reference to numbers. Moreover, he argues, if we have sets in our ontology, we do not need properties or relations, since properties and relations are reducible to the sets or ordered n-tuples of the things which have or bear them. However, Smart's argument for scientific realism does not require him to be a realist about either numbers or sets. He has to believe that there are numerical relationships between kinds of things, if he is to believe, for example, that there are more planets than suns, and he has to believe in properties if he is to believe in kinds of things. But he does not have to believe in the abstract theoretical entities of number or set theory, since these are the inventions of theoreticians who are not, *qua* logicians or mathematicians, concerned at all with the causal structure of the world.

To revert to the main argument for scientific realism, the world does not behave *as if* sets existed, because sets *must* exist iff all their members exist, and they are, therefore, ontologically reducible to them. But it *does* behave as if there were certain properties, like that of being negatively charged, and this is reason enough to believe in such properties, as well as in the things which possess them. The world does not behave as if the natural numbers existed, for the general theory of numerical relationships would not be affected by any conceivable changes in the real world. But different physical properties have different degrees of instantiation, and any increases or decreases of these degrees would have physical effects. Therefore, the world does behave as if these numerical relationships existed, and this is good enough reason to believe in them.

The ontology to which a scientific realist is committed does not, therefore, include all of the categories of things Smart would wish to include, and it does include some kinds of things which Smart may not wish to have in his ontology. Nevertheless, Smart's original argument for scientific realism (developed in Smart 1963) is a powerful one, and properly deployed it can be used to develop a comprehensive and highly reductive ontology for science.

2.11 ABSTRACT PARTICULARS

Things like numbers, points, propositions and sets are usually conceived to be *abstract particulars*. Abstract particulars are ghostly sorts of entities which are to be distinguished from both *concrete particulars*, like physical objects and events, and *universals*, like properties and relations. They are different from concrete particulars in that they are not physical, and do not have physical properties, causes or effects, and so cannot participate in physical causal processes; and they differ from universals in that they are not properties of, or relationships between, physical things. They are Platonic entities, in the sense that they are eternal and unchanging. If they exist at all, they do so timelessly; and they cannot change without changing identity.

The question is whether a scientific realist can have any good reason to believe in such things as these. I think not. A scientific realist can (and indeed should) believe in their physical counterparts, in the actual numbers of things in various heaps or collections, in the spatio-temporal relations between real physical things existing in space and time, in the sounds or inscriptions we make when we assert things by speaking or writing, and in the groups of things we may sometimes describe as sets. But a consistent realist should not believe in their abstractions or idealizations as things existing in their own right.

The basic reason for resisting abstract particulars is that the world we can know about would be the same whether or not they existed. There would be the same spatio-temporal relationships between real things, the same degrees of instantiation of physical properties, the same utterances (assuming our beliefs are the same), and the same heaps or collections of things. Moreover, we could have the same geometrical, mathematical and logical theories as we have now; we should just not take them, as mathematical realists do, as referring to real things.

It is not that the world behaves as if abstract particulars existed. For it is characteristic of abstract particulars that they do not have causal roles. They do not affect, and cannot be affected by, anything else. Only the physical entities of which they are abstractions have causes and effects. Therefore, the world behaves in ways independently of whether they exist, and hence the main argument for scientific realism fails as an argument for their existence. However, in the absence of a good argument for the existence of abstract particulars, our assumption must be that they do not exist.

I have no objection to saying that numerical relations of the kinds John Bigelow talks about (in Bigelow 1988) exist, because these relations are genuine universals which are physically instantiated. According to Bigelow, the natural numbers (which, he says, start with 2) are relations of mutual distinctness; so that the number n, for example, is the relation of n-fold mutual distinctness – a relation which is instantiated by any group of n mutually distinct things. The negative numbers, the rationals, the reals, and the complex numbers are also genuine universals, according to him. But they are more or less complex relations of proportion, which are second order universals. I am not sure that Bigelow's theory of number, which is clearly compatible with a physicalist ontology, will prove to be adequate for the whole of number theory. This may or may not be so. But it does not really matter if mathematicians want to talk about more numbers than Bigelow can identify as physically instantiated universals. For number theory is not the theory of what actual numerical relations there may be, but the theory of all possible numerical relations.

2.12   THE UNIVERSE AND LAWS OF NATURE

An ontology which is adequate for science must find a place for laws of nature. If they are descriptive, then what do they describe?

If they are not descriptive, then what is their role in science? It has frequently been observed that laws of nature often seem to be concerned not just with the way the world is, but with all the ways it might be (or have been). For the laws of nature define what is *physically possible*. It is tempting, therefore, to suppose that laws of nature describe, not just the actual world, but the set of all possible worlds. Realism about possible worlds is not, however, an option for scientific realists (as will be argued in chapter 4). Therefore, we need another account of the nature of scientific laws which explains adequately their role in defining what is physically possible.

The simplest account of the nature of laws which is compatible with scientific realism is the theory that they, or at least any which may reasonably be called laws of nature, are just universal generalizations which are distinguished from other (accidental) generalizations by their complete generality; so that they may be supposed to apply at all times and places to all members of the classes over which these generalizations are made. There are, of course, many variations on this theme, the details of which need not concern us; they can be found in almost any textbook on the philosophy of science. However, neither this theory, nor any of its variants, is able to account satisfactorily for the *necessity* of laws. For, if laws are just generalizations, the necessity of a law has to be supposed to be either a *psychological* necessity, or an *epistemological* one. That is, it has to be supposed that the necessity of laws has no *ontological* foundation, but is grounded in the psychological necessity of thinking in certain ways, or in the need to preserve certain generalizations in order to retain a viable theoretical system. However, the supposition that laws of nature hold at all times and places cannot be explained adequately by any psychological or epistemological theory of our disposition or need to believe that they do. There would actually have to *be* complete regularities in nature for them to do so. What is needed, therefore, is an explanation of why these complete regularities exist at all, not an explanation of why it is satisfying or useful to believe they do.

It is true that hypotheses postulating complete regularities can be defended in various ways. Exceptions can be barred, and monsters adjusted, as Imre Lakatos has shown (in Lakatos 1963). As a result, generalizations may sometimes take on the character of conceptual truths – just by being treated as such. The necessity of laws is thus sometimes considered to be a kind of quasi-logical necessity. This is how conventionalists explain the necessity of laws. But not every generalization can be defended in these sorts of ways without doing great violence elsewhere to the system of knowledge to which it belongs. Indeed, the only complete, non-trivial generalizations which seem to be defensible in methodologically acceptable ways are ones which we think really do tell us something about the structure of the world. At least, we should have to suppose that there is an underlying structure of the world reflected by what we take to be laws of nature, if we are to explain why the generalizations we accept as laws of nature are defensible in the sorts of ways they are.

The most recent, and currently the most popular, realist account of the nature of laws which explains their necessity is the theory that they are actually *relations between universals*.[6] Thus, the law that all Fs are Gs is said to be true in virtue of the existence of a relation of causal or nomic necessitation between F-ness and G-ness, which relationship is supposed to explain why laws have the kind of necessity they do, and hence why some things are physically necessary or physically impossible. The theory seems to be able to do what is required of a theory of laws, viz. to explain their necessity ontologically. Moreover, it also gives a good account of the rationality of believing that something is a law of nature. The inference from the sample of Fs which have been observed and found invariably to be Gs to the statement that all Fs are Gs, is not just a statistical inference. For such an inference could never justify much confidence in the complete generality of the law. The inference is rather an inference to the best explanation. The observed results are to be explained, not by the extremely high proportion of Fs which are Gs (which is all one can ever derive from uniform statistical evidence in favour of a generalization), but by the supposed nomic connection between F-ness and G-ness (which guarantees that there are no exceptions to the generalization).

However, laws of nature do not normally have the form of universal generalizations like 'all Fs are Gs', where F-ness and G-ness are plausibly universals. For, in most cases, what we call laws of nature apply strictly only to idealized systems and circumstances which we have every reason to believe do not exist. In the days of Newton, one could believe that the laws of nature applied directly to physical entities existing in the world. The atoms which constituted the physical world could be supposed to be constrained to move in accordance with a definite set of completely general principles, such as the law of gravity, and the laws of mechanics. But nowadays, we have to recognize that many of the propositions we call laws of nature are really just simplified solutions to the field equations which ultimately determine the dynamical properties of things, and the probabilities of various events. The Schrodinger equations, and the laws of special relativity, are like this. They are solutions to the most general field equations obtained by making some more or less gross simplifying assumptions about the systems to which they are to be applied, and the circumstances in which they are to be found. Therefore, they do not describe how real things actually behave, or determine what the real probabilities of the events they predict are.[7]

The most fundamental laws of nature are not, however, just simplified solutions to field equations. They are the conservation laws which the field equations are designed to preserve. So if anything is a genuine law of nature, it is a conservation law of fundamental physics. The best known of these, and one of the few to survive the quantum-mechanical revolution in physics, is the law of conservation of energy. Others are the laws of conservation of momentum, charge, spin, etc. These laws are supposed to govern interactions between particles. But interactions between particles are really interactions between fields. Hence, the conservation laws are basically laws determining what kinds of interactions between fields are possible.

The law of conservation of energy strictly applies only to closed and isolated systems, i.e. to systems which are not subject to the action of external forces, which do not receive energy from external sources, and from which no energy escapes. But given the unlimited range of certain forces, the only system which could possibly be closed and isolated is the universe itself. Other conservation laws, like those of momentum and charge, also apply only to closed and isolated systems, not to the kinds of open systems which we should ordinarily encounter. These laws may nevertheless be applied successfully to predict the results of particle interactions, because systems of interacting particles may always be regarded as closed systems if all of the exchange particles involved in these inter-actions are included. For then, the external forces acting on the particles may be adequately represented by the exchange particles we suppose to be absorbed or emitted.

The question then is whether our conservation laws may be regarded as relations between universals. I think the answer to this is 'No'. What is conserved is a real property of a field, or of the universe. To regard the conservation laws as relations between universals, we should have to suppose that energy, charge, momen-tum, etc. *at any one time* are different properties from energy, charge, momentum, etc. *at any other time*, and that these properties-at-times are related by relations of sameness. It would be better, surely, to regard the fields, and the universe itself, as instances of natural kinds, which are to be distinguished from other fields, and other possible universes, by their total energy, charge, momentum, etc. For then we could explain the necessity of the fundamental laws of nature as being the kind of natural necessity which attaches to the essential properties of things.

Accordingly, I postulate that the universe is an instance of a natural kind, and that the laws of nature describe the essential properties of things of this kind. The conservation laws describe those properties which must be conserved through all physical causal changes. Other laws describe the structural principles which must be satisfied by any universe of the same kind as ours. Thus, I would explain the necessity of all laws ontologically, as other realist theories of laws have sought to do, but avoid the naivety about laws which these theories often seem to display. I think the theory that the laws of nature are of the essence of the universe is a better theory than any of its rivals (a) because it gives a uniform expla-nation of the source of natural necessity, and (b) because it is compatible with the holism of modern physical science.

The postulate that the universe is an instance of a natural kind characterized by its laws of nature does not imply that there are any other possible universes, and it is certainly not to be equated with modal realism. It is of course compatible with there being other universes of the same kind as ours, and it would be perfectly legitimate to call any such things other physically possible worlds.

Hence we can capture the intuition which many people have that the business of science is to define what is physically possible without having to embrace the kind of realism about possible worlds which requires us to believe that every logically possible world exists necessarily. There may be other physically possible worlds like ours, or there may not be: science can go about its business independently of whether there are or not.

3

Scientific Realism and Empiricism

Not everyone who takes the scientific point of view would accept the kind of ontology I have described.[1] For there is a long tradition in philosophy of science of people who are very sceptical of the ontological claims of scientists. The tradition is that of empiricism. The earlier writers in this tradition were the positivists, Ernst Mach, Henri Poincare, Moritz Schlick and Hans Reichenbach, who argued for the conventionality of many of our laws and theories, which they said were neither true nor false. As philosophers of science, these writers saw their main task as being to distinguish clearly between what is true as a matter of fact in scientific theories, and what is only a matter of definition or convention. These philosophers were accordingly known as conventionalists. The conventionalist programme was actively pursued by philosophers of science, particularly by those working in the philosophy of the physical sciences, until the late 1960s or early 1970s, when scientific realism became the dominant philosophy in the area. Most recently, the empiricist tradition has been revived by Bas van Fraassen, who elaborates and defends a position he calls 'constructive empiricism' (van Fraassen 1980 and 1985).

The challenge to scientific realism presented by this tradition is important because it threatens the main argument for realism about theoretical entities on which all scientific realists rely. The main argument used by empiricists against scientific realism is from the empirical underdetermination of theories by evidence. The argument depends on the claim that no theory is uniquely satisfactory empirically, because all theories have empirically equivalent variants. That is, for any theory we care to construct, it is always possible to construct another theory which is empirically indistinguishable from it. To choose between two such theories, we can only rely on pragmatic considerations, such as those of simplicity, elegance, etc. – at any rate, only on considerations which are usually supposed to have nothing to do with truth. However, if the empiricists are right about this, then the main argument for realism about theoretical entities can never get off the ground. For, if it can be said that the world behaves as if entities of such and such a kind exist, then it can equally be said that it behaves as if entities of some other kind, postulated in some equivalent theory, exist.

In this chapter, I will consider several empiricist arguments against scientific realism. In particular, I will consider some conventionalist arguments against what I call 'the objectivity thesis' of scientific realism. I will also examine some important arguments for the underdetermination of theory by evidence which have been used recently to undermine what I call 'the central thesis' of scientific realism. I will argue that these arguments are not at all compelling. In fact, because of what I call 'the openness of the field of evidence' for a theory, the strong empirical underdetermination thesis, required for the main argument against scientific realism to go through, cannot be demonstrated without relying on arguments for global scepticism; and these are arguments which only metaphysical realists have to take seriously. Therefore, a scientific realist, who is not also a metaphysical realist, has nothing to fear from the argument from empirical underdetermination.

3.1 FOUR STRANDS OF SCIENTIFIC REALISM

The position of scientific realism is not well defined. We can say that scientific realists would all accept the main argument for realism about theoretical entities. For this, at least, is characteristic of their position. Consequently, scientific realists must have an ontology they think is adequate for science. But, as we have seen, the main argument cannot, by itself, resolve all ontological questions about theoretical entities. As a result, there are disagreements between scientific realists about what a realist ontology should include. I suppose it would be almost universally agreed that it should include the fundamental particles in a category of physical entities. But this is about as far as agreement would reach. It would be disputed whether there should also be categories of physical properties, spatio-temporal relations, forces, sets, numbers, space-time points or qualia in the ontology. But enough has already been said in chapter 2 about these issues.

A second strand of scientific realism concerns the status of scientific laws and theories. All would say that these are to be understood realistically rather than instrumentally. Scientific realism thus stands opposed to *instrumentalism* in the philosophy of science. Realists believe that the laws and theories of science are genuine claims about reality, not mere instruments for prediction which are more or less useful for this purpose. This is what I call *the central thesis* of scientific realism, and every scientific realist subscribes to some version of it.

It is not at all clear what the central thesis of scientific realism entails. Basically, the idea is that there are things in the world to which our laws and theories refer, and of which they are true or false. They are, that is, to be understood as referring to real existents and ascribing genuine properties to them. But what does this mean? On a naive interpretation, we must suppose that there are Hilbert spaces, perfect gases, inertial systems, and ideal incompressible fluids in steady flow in uniform gravitational fields. For it is to things like these that many of our laws seem to refer. But my impression is that most scientific realists do not really want to take the ontological commitments of laws or theories, which are apparently about such entities, at face value. Their commitment is not to understanding all of the laws and theories of science in such a *naively* realistic way, but only to those which can be so understood compatibly with their ontology. The rest would have to be suitably reduced, and the apparent references to theoretical ideals parsed away, to avoid any unwanted commitments.

A third strand of scientific realism is the *objectivity thesis*: that the laws and theories of science are objectively true or false, not merely conventional. Every scientific realist is committed to some version of this thesis. The objectivity thesis is rarely distinguished from the central thesis of scientific realism, and is often confused with it. But, as I understand them, they are really quite distinct. The central thesis of scientific realism stands opposed to instrumentalist readings of scientific theories; the objectivity thesis stands opposed to *conventionalism* in the philosophy of science.

The main difficulty with the objectivity thesis derives from conventionalist arguments which seem to show that at least some of the most fundamental theories in science are empirically under-determined – not just in the weak sense of being inductively underdetermined, but in the strong sense that even if *all* the empirical consequences of the theory could be checked, and it could be *known* that they have all been checked, it would still be possible to construct another theory compatible with the evidence.

A fourth tenet of scientific realism is the correspondence theory of truth. Most scientific realists believe that we must have such a theory if we are to be realists about scientific entities – or, for that matter, about anything else non-mental. In defending the correspondence theory of truth, realists see themselves as being opposed to *idealism* in the philosophy of science – to the view that reality is a construct out of experience, rather than something existing independently of it. I believe that scientific realists who make this connection are profoundly mistaken. We need not have a correspondence theory of truth to accept a physicalist ontology, or believe in an independently existing reality. On the contrary, I think that anyone who has a physicalist ontology should not also hold a correspondence theory of truth – as I shall argue in the next two chapters.

3.2 CONVENTIONALIST ARGUMENTS AGAINST THE OBJECTIVITY THESIS

Conventionalists argue that there are many questions in science which call, not for further empirical investigation, but for decision. Is the one-way velocity of light equal to its round-trip velocity? Is the geometry of space Euclidean? Does a body which is not acted upon by forces continue in its state of rest or uniform motion in a straight line? These questions, and many others, have been said by conventionalists not to be questions about what is true of reality, but ones which can only be resolved by stipulation or definition.

Concerning these questions there is said to be no truth of the matter.

Conventionalists do not argue that all theoretical questions are like this. On the contrary, they see it as their task to distinguish those questions which are empirical or factual from those which are a matter for stipulation. A conventionalist might maintain that it is a matter of convention whether we should say that light travels in straight lines, but few conventionalists would claim that it is conventional whether we should say that photons exist. Indeed, most conventionalists have a fairly orthodox scientific ontology. Their quarrel is with the objectivity thesis of scientific realism, not the central one. They reject the thesis that the laws and theories of science are objectively true or false. Some are; some are not. The laws, they would say, are mostly conventional, reflecting decisions on how we choose to measure things; but the existential hypotheses which occur in our causal process theories are mostly factual claims, and whether they are true or false is a matter for empirical investigation, not for stipulation.

There are three main arguments used by conventionalists for considering the statement of a law or theory to be conventional. First, there is *the circularity argument*, which was frequently used by Reichenbach. For example, in arguing for the conventionality of the principle that the one-way velocity of light is the same in all directions, he tries to show that we should have to presuppose the principle in order to prove it. He argues that to measure the one-way velocity of light we should need clocks in synchrony at different places, i.e. reading the same at the same time. Consequently, we must know what it is for two events (readings), occurring at different places, to be simultaneous. But ultimately, he claims, we cannot determine whether two such events are simultaneous, unless we make some prior assumptions about the one-way velocity of light. And he then goes on to say that: 'The occurrence of this circularity proves that simultaneity is not a matter of knowledge, but of a coordinative definition, since the logical circle shows that a knowledge of simultaneity is impossible in principle' (Reichenbach 1927, p. 127). He concludes that the law in question is conventional.

It has now, I think, been conclusively established that Reichenbach was wrong in thinking that one has to make some assumption about the one-way velocity of light in order to determine the simultaneity of distant events. There are in fact several procedures which could be used to establish clocks in a relationship of distant synchrony which, logically, do not depend on this assumption.[2] Consequently, there are several logically independent criteria for distant simultaneity, and the 'standard signal synchrony' criterion is just one of them.

However, conventionalists have a second argument to fall back on – *the argument from the need for definition*. It may be conceded that distant simultaneity is a multicriterial concept, so that any of a number of different criteria for distant simultaneity might be chosen to define this relationship. Still, a choice has to be made. And the law or principle which underlies the choice will have to be considered to be true by definition. This principle might be the one-way light principle (that the one-way velocity of light is the same in all directions) or the principle of slow clock transport (that locally synchronized identical clocks transported sufficiently slowly remain in synchrony), or it might be some other principle. But surely at least one of these laws or principles must be regarded as conventional if the concept of distant simultaneity is to be well-defined. If the one-way light principle is the chosen one, then it is conventional, and all the others are empirical.

It is, however, arbitrary to pick *one* law out of a law-cluster like this, and say that it is conventional while the rest are empirical, if no good reason can be given for choosing it. And if the choice is arbitrary, then we might as well have chosen another one. Consequently, any given law in such a law-cluster might arbitrarily be regarded as empirical or conventional, depending on how we choose to axiomatize our system. Assuming that the 'simultaneity' law-cluster is like this, and that the one-way velocity of light has been set equal to the round trip velocity by definition, then the principle of slow clock transport is empirical. It is, however, a matter of convention that the one-way light principle is conventional, and it is also conventional that the principle of slow clock transport is empirical. For we could equally well have reversed the roles of these two principles. Assuming that the special theory of relativity is correct, we know that the 'simultaneity' law-cluster exists. In all of the vast literature on distant simultaneity there is no argument for preferring the standard light signal to the slow clock transport definition of distant simultaneity, or conversely; and we may reasonably assume that there is none. Therefore, it is arbitrary which principle we choose to call conventional and which empirical.

This being the case, why should we choose at all? What difference would it make, either to our practice, or our beliefs, if we thought of all the laws in the cluster as empirical laws? Suppose that, contrary to the predictions of the special theory of relativity, we found that clocks synchronized by slow transport were not in standard signal synchrony? Would it make any difference to how we should proceed which of the two principles we had chosen to call true by definition or convention? It is my belief that it would make no difference at all. A radically new space-time theory would be needed, and I do not believe that, in constructing it, we should feel in any way constrained to accept what we had earlier said was true by definition, or to reject what we had said was empirical.

In general, the empirical/conventional distinction is of no practical importance in science. Scientific practice is not affected by what we might choose to say is conventional, or what we might think of as empirical. So we can just as well regard all of the laws and theories of science as empirical – at least in the sense that they are open to revision in the light of experience. The argument from the need for definition is, therefore, no good argument for conventionalism. For, in general, there *is* no need for definition. It may be useful or even necessary to offer a definition of a term when introducing it to the profession, or to students, for the first time. But the statement of that definition enjoys no privileged immunity to revision, or even rejection, in the light of further experience.

The third, and perhaps most important, argument for conventionalism is that from *empirical underdetermination*. We can discover empirically, perhaps, that the 'simultaneity' law-cluster exists. But this does not bind us to accepting any, or even the conjunction of all, of the laws in the cluster as defining the relationship of distant simultaneity. For we are free to adopt some non-standard signal or transport definition of distant simultaneity, say one which makes the one-way velocity of light a function of direction, or relative clock-rates a function of their relative positions, and use this to determine what all of the other laws in the cluster are. Given such a definition, there will still be a 'simultaneity' law-cluster, but it will be a different one. No doubt, such a co-ordination would seriously complicate our physics, but, so the conventionalist maintains, it cannot be ruled out on any *a priori* or empirical grounds. Consequently, there can be no truth of the matter concerning *any* of the laws in the cluster. They are *all* conventional.

This move is the most serious one for scientific realists who wish to retain the objectivity thesis along with the correspondence theory of truth. For it makes the truth unknowable in principle. It is the main reason why those positivists who accepted the correspondence theory, rejected the objectivity thesis for some form of conventionalism; and it is one of the main reasons why some, who wish to retain the objectivity thesis, have rejected the correspondence theory of truth in favour of some form of coherence theory. The point is that the coherence theorist can argue that what is true is what occurs in the best (ultimately best) theory, and is not embarrassed by this conventionalist argument. For no one would pretend that a non-standard definition of distant simultaneity would produce a theory which was anything like *as good* as the special theory of relativity. It might be empirically equivalent, but we should have to allow that there are some strange spatial asymmetries in many of our laws of nature – asymmetries for which we have no adequate explanation.

These conventionalist arguments against the objectivity thesis of scientific realism do not refute the claim that the laws and theories of science are objectively true or false. Nevertheless, they pose difficulties for those who think that where two or more theories are empirically equivalent, the true theory is not necessarily the one we should consider to be the best theory. If the sorts of considerations (e.g. of symmetry, isotropy, simplicity, etc.) which would lead us to prefer one of a cluster of empirically equivalent theories are not enough to single that theory out as the true one, then we cannot reasonably hope to discover which laws or theories occurring in such clusters are true.

3.3 CONSTRUCTIVE EMPIRICISM

The most recent challenge to scientific realism, and hence to the ontology discussed in chapter 2, is from Bas van Fraassen's 'constructive empiricism'. In *The Scientific Image* (1980) van Fraassen locates the basic difference between empiricism and realism as a difference of view about the *aim* of science. Empiricists, he says, see the aim as being to 'save the phenomena', and hence to produce theories which are *empirically adequate*. Scientific realists, on the other hand, generally see it as being to *describe* the fundamental processes by which things occur in nature. My position is different from both empiricism and realism. I would defend the ontology of chapter 2, using the scientific realists' main argument for realism about theoretical entities. But I would not accept that the aim of science is just to describe reality. Nor would I accept that the aim is just to save the phenomena. In my view, the aim of science is to *explain* what happens in nature, to give the best possible theoretical account of it.

The different views about the aim of science lead naturally to different views concerning its theoretical achievements. For scientific realists, van Fraassen says, well-established and accepted theories must be considered to be literally true – not just useful models for predicting what will occur. For empiricists, such theories are just models of reality which are, and which we believe will continue to be, empirically adequate. Whether they are true or not, van Fraassen maintains, is of no importance – although he does not deny that they have truth values.

According to van Fraassen, the scientific realist's position is this:

(1) Science aims to give us, in its theories, a literally true story of what the world is like; and acceptance of a scientific theory involves the belief that it is true. (1980, p. 8)

Van Fraassen's concept of literal truth is a correspondence concept; a statement is literally true if, literally interpreted, it accurately describes or corresponds to reality. The rules for literal interpretation are not clearly specified, but he has in mind at least this: any apparent reference to a theoretical entity is to be construed as a genuine attempt to refer, unless there are good, and specific, reasons for not doing so.

Against the scientific realists' conception of the aim of science, van Fraassen argues that it is not required either to motivate science or to explain its practice. It is enough for these purposes to see the aim as being the provision of empirically adequate theories. Moreover, on the basis of a general thesis of empirical underdetermination of theories, he argues that we cannot rationally demand more of any theory than that it be empirically adequate. For once we get down to those theories which are acceptable by his criterion of empirical adequacy, the choice between them cannot be made on grounds which have any bearing on whether or not they are true. The choice has now to be a pragmatic one. So if we required belief in the *truth* of a theory as a condition for its acceptance, we could not rationally accept any theories at all, even though we had good empirical *and* pragmatic reasons for doing so. Conversely, if we did accept any theories as being literally true, we should have to allow that the pragmatic reasons (simplicity, elegance, and the like) which we have for preferring them to other empirically equivalent theories are actually grounds for believing them to be true.

Van Fraassen thus arrives at the following position:

(2) Science aims to give us theories which are empirically adequate; and acceptance of a theory involves as belief only that it is empirically adequate. (ibid., p. 12)

I assume that van Fraassen intends this statement to be understood normatively, and that the same applies to the statement of position he attributes to scientific realists. Presumably, it is a question of what we ought to consider the aims of science to be, and of what beliefs ought to be involved in accepting a scientific theory. Nevertheless, since the principal theses are not presented as normative judgements, and there is a lot of discussion of modern physical theories, I cannot help seeing van Fraassen's position as being, at least in part, a reflection of what he thinks are the attitudes of scientists to the dominant physical theories of today.

At the time when the dominant theories in science were mechanistic, it was easy to see the aim of science as being to discover and describe the underlying mechanisms of nature. Think of nine-teenth-century chemistry. Of course, the atomic-molecular theories of the time were usually seen as describing basic chemical pro-cesses; and to accept them was to believe that they truly described these processes. But the image of science has changed a great deal since then, and the dominant theories are no longer mechanistic. Think now of quantum mechanics and geometrodynamics. Is scientific realism any longer the philosophy of science which we feel naturally compelled to accept? I should think that many space-time and quantum physicists would be quite puzzled by the suggestion that the theories they accept, and work with, might literally be true, since they have no clear conception at all of the reality with which these theories might correspond. And I can well see many of them agreeing with van Fraassen that the aim of science is only to give us theories which are empirically adequate. I think that van Fraassen, rightly or wrongly, draw some comfort from this, and sees scientific realism as a philosophy of science more appropriate to another age.

I am convinced that anyone who accepts, as van Fraassen does, that the only considerations relevant to the truth or falsity of a claim are empirical or logical, and that such considerations alone can never determine what theories are true (because of empirical underdetermination), is in trouble defending scientific realism. For given these premises, it follows that we can never have any good reason to believe that a theory is true. Therefore, anyone who believes in the literal truth of the theories they accept must do so irrationally. To counter this argument, it is necessary either to challenge the empirical underdetermination thesis, or deny that the only considerations relevant to the truth or falsity of a theory are empirical or logical. One might, for example, try to argue, as pragmatists do, that the true theory is just the one that is ultimately the best, all things considered.

However, most scientific realists are in a serious bind. For they see acceptance of a correspondence, rather than a pragmatic, theory of truth as being essential to their position. Pragmatic theories, they think, go together, not with realism, but with ideal-ism. So most scientific realists are likely to focus either on the empirical underdetermination thesis, or else on the claim that pragmatic considerations, such as those of simplicity, symmetry and explanatory power, are not relevant to questions of truth or falsity, as the weak point of the argument. However, the empirical underdetermination thesis is very widely accepted, and seldom challenged; and most scientific realists would be reluctant to give up the empirical/pragmatic distinction, which gives the argument from underdetermination such force, since doing so would seem to undermine the correspondence theory of truth which most scientific realists believe to be essential to their position.

Nevertheless, I think that they *must* do one of these things if they wish to defend scientific realism. The correspondence theory of truth is *not* essential to their position; nor is the empirical/pragmatic distinction. For scientific realism can be combined with a pragmatic theory of truth; and, given such a theory of truth, all of the criteria we use for the evaluation of theories, including the so-called pragmatic ones, can be seen as being relevant to their truth or falsity.

In opposition to van Fraassen's constructive empiricism, I would propose the pragmatist thesis:

(3) Science aims to provide the best possible explanatory account of natural phenomena; and acceptance of a scientific theory involves the belief that it belongs to such an account.

Scientific realists who accept a pragmatic theory of truth can accept this thesis. For they can agree that the best possible account, if it exists, is *necessarily* the true one. But I suppose not many scientific realists would accept this pragmatist defence of their position. For most of them would insist that truth is a correspondence relationship. However, I do not think they have much choice. They have either to reject the correspondence theory of truth, or follow van Fraassen down the road to constructive empiricism.

3.4 THE AIM OF SCIENCE

It is dangerous to generalize too quickly about scientific theories and explanations. The danger is that what seems to be true of

theories and explanations in one field, may not be true in others. I
think that both empiricists and realists are guilty of drawing broad
unwarranted conclusions from a few selected examples. Scientific
realists are inclined to take nice homely examples of causal explanations, e.g. from nineteenth-century physics or chemistry, as
typifying scientific explanations generally. These simple mechanistic theories were obviously intended by their authors to be understood realistically. Their philosophical position is thus given a
strong flavour of initial plausibility. Van Fraassen's position, on the
other hand, probably derives more from his earlier work on space-
time theories, where it is not at all obvious that the theories were
intended to be anything more than models of some kind which
could be used with greater or less facility to 'save the phenomena'.

In fact, there are different sorts of theories and explanations
which arise as answers to different sorts of questions. I follow van
Fraassen in thinking that any request for explanation is a request
for information. A *causal explanation* is information about the causal
history of something, or about the causal processes which result in
something. A *functional explanation* is information about the role of
something in some ongoing system – about the contribution it
makes to sustaining it. A *model-theoretic explanation* is information
about how (if at all) the actual behaviour of some system differs
from what it would be ideally, if it were not for some extraneous
influences. A *systemic explanation* is information about how the fact to
be explained is systematically related to other facts.

Theories, on the other hand, provide us with the general sche-
mata for giving such explanations. *Causal process theories* attempt to
describe the basic causal processes of nature. *Functionalist theories* are
concerned with ongoing systems of various kinds, and with the
kinds of mechanisms, described in terms of their functional roles,
necessary for their maintenance. *Model theories* define norms of
behaviour against which actual behaviour may be compared and
(causally) explained. *Systemic theories* set forth some general organizational principles adequate to determine the basic structure of
some system of relationships between things. Euclidean geometry,
for example, is such a theory for the system of spatial relationships.

The main argument for scientific realism is persuasive concerning the theoretical entities of causal process theories. For to accept

that A is the cause of B is to accept that both A and B are real existents (or events). But no such argument applies to the theoretical entities of model theories. For the hypothetical entities of model theories are not the postulated *causes* of anything. Consequently, there is no parallel argument that to accept a model theory involves the belief that the entities to which it apparently refers really exist.

Van Fraassen's view, on the other hand, seems to come from taking model and systemic theories as typical. For the value of such theories derives, not from any insights they may provide about the workings of nature, but from their capacity to systematize our knowledge of it. Consequently, it does not matter whether these theories are literally true or false. What matters is whether they are adequate to the task for which they were devised. Plausibly, therefore, to accept such a theory involves no more than the belief that it is so adequate – that it is, in van Fraassen's sense, an empirically adequate theory.

Scientific realists run into trouble when they try to generalize about scientific theories. To cope with laws which hold only for ideal systems, and which would strictly be false for actual systems, many scientific realists think of them as being only good *approximations* to the truth. So, instead of van Fraassen's characterization of their position, they would accept something like this:

(1a) Science aims to give us, in its theories, a literally true story of what the world is like; and acceptance of a scientific theory involves the belief that it is at least approximately true.

Thus they would consider such laws as conservation of energy and conservation of momentum, which strictly apply only to closed and isolated systems, as being only good approximations to the truth about actual systems. What is strictly true, they would say, is that the energy and momentum of any more or less closed and isolated system are more or less conserved. And, as science progresses, these essentially 'inaccurate' laws should be replaced by more accurate ones involving less idealization and hence greater faithfulness to the actual relationships among things. Think, for example, of the replacement of the ideal gas laws by van de Waal's equation. Many scientific realists thus envisage the eventual replacement of model theories by systemic ones in which all of the laws and principles are just true generalization about how actual things behave.

However, if science is aiming to achieve such a result, it seems often to be pointing in the wrong direction. For a great deal of theoretical scientific research goes into devising increasingly abstract model theories; and relatively little into reducing the degree of idealization involved in our theories in order to make them more realistic. It is true that in economic forecasting, weather forecasting, and in the applied sciences generally, researchers labour to develop increasingly elaborate computer simulations of real systems, taking into account as many as possible of the relevant variables, so as to maximize the accuracy of their predictions. And I do not deny the importance of such research. But basic theoretical development in science tends, if anything, to proceed in the opposite direction – to greater abstraction and generality.

Take the development of Newtonian mechanics from 1700 to about 1900. In this period no major scientist working in the field of mechanics developed theories which they thought were closer to the truth than Newton's. Most of them would have said that Newton's theory was true already. Nor, for that matter, did they think they were developing theories which were empirically more adequate than Newton's. So it seems wrong to suppose that they were aiming to increase either the realism or the empirical adequacy of the basic theory they were working with. Yet the great works of classical mechanics of Euler, the Bernoulli's, d'Alembert, Fermat, Lazare Carnot, Lagrange, Laplace, Gauss, Coriolis, Hamilton and Jacobi surely contributed *something* to fulfilling the aims of science. For they improved greatly our knowledge and understanding of mechanical processes. They solved many previously unsolved problems; they applied Newtonian theory in new ways; they discovered new principles and unsuspected symmetries; and they invented powerful new mathematical techniques for handling complex mechanical problems. I think we may conclude that scientists, *qua* pure scientists, are not always greatly concerned to make their model theories more realistic or more adequate empirically. They have other much more interesting things to do.

Van Fraassen adds to his troubles by construing all theories as model theories. For this commits him to saying that the postulated entities of causal process theories are just like other theoretical constructs. Atoms, creatures of the Jurassic Period, inertial systems and possible worlds are all on a par, according to him, and to accept theories which apparently make reference to such entities, involves only the belief that the theories are empirically adequate. Now, if the theories we are talking about are special relativity and 'possible worlds' semantics, van Fraassen's position is at least plausible. But it loses all plausibility if the theories in question are historical theories or theories of chemical combination. And the reason, I think, why this is so is that the postulated causes of the phenomena must be supposed to exist if the theory is to be accepted as doing what it purports to do; and normally we should expect to be able to find independent confirmation of their existence from various sources.

The situation is quite different with the theoretical entities of abstract model theories. Since they are not postulated as causes, they are not supposed to have any effects. So we should not expect them to leave any traces, or to manifest themselves in other ways, or indeed, in any way at all. And that is why, apparently, we can play with them as we like, and assign any properties to them we wish, to produce a better theory. We know that no astronomers are going to discover inertial frames which don't have the properties we assign to them, and that travellers are not going to stumble across other possible worlds where they shouldn't be, and so spike our theories about conditionals.

The status of the theoretical entities of causal process theories is not like this, however. When the theory is accepted, we think we know only *some* of their properties. We know we might be wrong about them in some ways; and we might expect our picture of them to change somewhat. But typically, we expect to discover more about them – to add to, and refine, our knowledge of them, and explain why they have the properties they do. That is, we expect them to be like other physical things, and to participate in various ways in causal processes, depending on what their properties are, and what the surrounding circumstances are like. In short, we think of them, and expect them to behave, as real things do. Moreover, our reasons for believing in them are not basically different from our reasons for believing in more ordinary things. If the existence of atoms, or of the moons of Jupiter, were a legal issue, I think almost any jury would find the case proven by the ordinary rules of evidence.

I think van Fraassen is aware of all this. I don't think he embraces constructive empiricism out of naivety, or any failure to distinguish between causal process theories and model theories. His philosophical position probably arose out of a less ambitious theory about the status of the laws of special relativity, and other abstract model theories. Originally, he argued that many of the principles involved in these theories were conventional. For example, he argued that it is ultimately a matter of convention whether we say that the one-way speed of light is the same in all directions. About this, he would have said, following Reichenbach and the other positivists, there is no truth of the matter. However, he has now come to believe that his arguments for the conventionality of such principles apply *right across the board*. So, consistently with his earlier position, he ought to conclude that *in general* there is no truth of the matter concerning the fundamental laws and theories of science. But, as I understand him, van Fraassen does *not* accept this general conclusion. There *is* a truth of the matter, he now wants to say, *but we cannot really know what it is*. For the best that we can ever hope to do is construct a system of empirically adequate theories. Anything beyond this is necessarily beyond our grasp.

3.5   THE EMPIRICAL UNDERDETERMINATION THESIS

The implications of the conventionalist argument from empirical underdetermination are serious for the scientific realist. For empirical underdetermination would appear to be a feature of *all* of our theories. Consequently, it threatens to make even the realists' belief in a physicalist ontology unjustifiable. If it is always possible to construct another theory which is incompatible with a given theory, but is empirically equivalent to it, then all theories are empirically underdetermined. Therefore, if one believes that the sorts of pragmatic considerations which could decide between empirically equivalent theories are never justificatory, one may be forced to consider belief in the truth of any theory to be unjustifiable – a conclusion which would be unavoidable if the general principle of empirical underdetermination were accepted.

This thesis of empirical underdetermination is not, of course, the obvious point that our theories are *inductively* underdetermined by the evidence we have for them. Things might turn out to be grue or bleen rather than green or blue. The point is that there are incompatible theories which are empirically equivalent in the sense that *no* empirical evidence could ever distinguish between them; and the claim is that our theoretical understanding of the world would be underdetermined even by the supposed totality of empirical evidence. This thesis, if it is true, is the real threat to scientific realism. For what reason could we have to believe in the existence of any theoretical entity, if we could be assured that there is another theory, empirically equivalent to the one in which it is postulated, which may assume the existence of other quite different kinds of entities?

Although the general thesis of empirical underdetermination is commonly asserted, the arguments for it are not as compelling as they are usually thought to be. First, there is the failure of Carnap's programme of reductive analysis.[3] All attempts to define the theoretical terms of science in an observational language have been unsuccessful. Even the simplest theoretical predicates have stoutly resisted such an analysis. Consequently, the conviction has grown that theories say more than anything that can be said in an observational language. It is not just that they go beyond the evidence. All inductive generalizations do that. They go beyond anything for which there could be inductive support. For they cannot even be *expressed* in a language the terms of which are purely observational. Consequently, it is held that all theories must be strongly underdetermined by evidence. Even if all possible observations had been made, and were known to have been made, and our theories were compatible with this supposed totality of evidence, our theories would still say more than this, and so be underdetermined by it.

This argument is plausible, and I think many philosophers are persuaded by it. But it is really not a good argument for the underdetermination thesis. For it relies on a rather naive view of the nature of explanation and of inductive support. The crucial premiss of the argument is that if A cannot be expressed in an observation language L, then no amount of evidence expressible in L can give us good reason to believe that A is true. But this premiss is untenable. For the best explanation of the facts stated, or statable, in L that are to be explained may well be in terms of a theory which is not statable in L. Explanation is not just a matter of subsuming what is to be explained under a general law, as the argument seems to presuppose.

A second argument, which was very influential with the early positivists, is that all causal process theories have a-causal phenomenological equivalents which do not refer to any unobservable things or processes. N. R. Campbell showed us, years ago (in Campbell 1957, chapter 6), how to construct a formal theory, empirically equivalent to the kinetic theory of gases, which does not postulate the existence of any atoms or molecules. Such a theory may be said to be the *phenomenological equivalent* of the kinetic theory. Presumably, the same technique will yield the phenomenological equivalent of any other causal process theory. But the phenomenological equivalent of a causal process theory does not have the same ontological implications as the theory itself; it does not postulate the existence of any specific causal processes by which the events to be explained come about. However, the phenomenological equivalent of a given causal process theory T is empirically equivalent to T; and hence, there cannot be any reasons, other than pragmatic reasons, for preferring T.

This argument will be discussed at some length, because it is probably the main reason why the empirical underdetermination thesis is so widely accepted. It will be shown that the plausibility of the argument depends on an untenably narrow view of the field of evidence for a theory, and that when it is recognized that the field of evidence for a theory is an open one, it becomes clear that the empirical equivalence claim on which the argument depends is hollow.

A third argument derives from the existence of empirically equivalent theories of space and space-time. It has long been argued that there are distinct, but empirically equivalent, theories of space and space-time, depending on what congruence definitions are chosen to determine the space and space-time metrics. The congruence definitions required are said to be conventional. If these arguments are sound, then our theories of space and space-time must be empirically underdetermined because of the need for these congruence definitions. But all measurement depends on congruence definitions of one kind or another. Therefore, all quantitative theories must be empirically underdetermined in the same sort of way as our theories of space and space-time.

This argument is never explicitly stated, although it seems to be the argument which empiricists are implicitly using when they generalize from the empirical underdetermination of theories of space and space-time, which they claim to be able to demonstrate, to the empirical underdetermination of all theories. For one cannot establish that all theories are empirically underdetermined by showing that some are. So presumably, the claim must be that the reason why our theories of space and space-time are empirically underdetermined, viz. because of the need for more or less arbitrary congruence definitions (to define relations of quantitative equality at different times or places), applies to quantitative theories generally. The argument is an interesting one. If indeed our theories of space and space-time are conventional for this reason, and non-trivial congruence definitions are required for the metrization of mass, or temperature, or any other quantity, then all of our quantitative theories will be conventional in the same way, and for the same reason.

I do not wish to discuss this argument here. Peter Bowman and I have argued at length in 'Conventionality in Distant Simultaneity' (Ellis and Bowman 1967), that the choice of congruence definition for distant simultaneity is not just an arbitrary convention, and in two recent papers, 'Conventionalism in Measurement Theory' (1990), and 'Comments on Forge and Swoyer' (1987b), I have argued that while there are always conventions involved in defining scales of measurement, the radical conventionalist thesis suggested in the previous paragraph is untenable. There are objective relationships of quantitative equality and inequality in nature, and at least some of these relationships are based on objective properties of the things related. But even if the conventionality thesis were established, the argument would not show that it is just a matter of convention what physical entities exist; it would only show that it is conventional how we should measure them.

Finally, there are well-known arguments for the conventionality of the laws of dynamics which seem to have ontological implications. These arguments make no claim to demonstrate the conventionality of *all* theories, but they do suggest that it is at least not a question of fact whether forces exist, but a question of what kind of dynamical theory we prefer. For reasons my colleagues, John Bigelow and Robert Pargetter and I, have given in detail elsewhere (Bigelow, Ellis and Pargetter 1988), I no longer wish to defend the conventionality claim that I once made (in Ellis 1965a) concerning the existence of forces. But even if the case for the conventionality of our theories of dynamics were established, the general thesis of the empirical underdetermination of theories by evidence would still need to be demonstrated. For it might be possible to isolate our dynamical theories, and admit that some of the entities, such as forces, which they postulate are not real, and, at the same time, maintain a realist position concerning the entities postulated in our causal process theories. This is the strategy I had in mind when I spoke of 'scientific entity' realism (Ellis 1979, p. 45).

It is worth emphasizing that the main arguments for the conventionality of space-time and dynamical theories do not carry over as arguments for the conventionality of causal process theories. For, if the entities postulated in process theories exist, we should expect them to manifest themselves in various ways, and to participate in causal processes *other* than those described in the theories we have so far developed. Consequently, we should expect confirmation of causal process theories to come from various unexpected sources as these theories are developed. Hence, theories which cannot be distinguished empirically in one theoretical context may be distinguished in another. New theoretical developments may show some empirical considerations to be differentially relevant to the truth of the two theories, which previously would have been considered to be empirically equivalent.

It is possible, for example, to construct two theories of chemical combination to explain why one volume of hydrogen combines with one of chlorine to form two volumes of hydrogen chloride. One is the classical causal process theory of Avogadro; the other is a phenomenological theory which postulates the existence of certain 'gas numbers' characteristic of elemental and compound gases, and certain laws relating these gas numbers to combining volumes.[4] In terms of empirically testable consequences, the two theories are equivalent. Nevertheless, they are very different theories. One postulates the existence of atoms and molecules and paramechanical processes of chemical combination. The other does not offer any account of how elements combine to form compounds, and just, to make sure that the two theories are incompatible, we may add that the gas-number theory denies the existence of atoms and molecules.

Despite the fact that these two theories have the same empirically testable consequences, they are not, and never were, empirically equivalent. For they offered quite different prospects for development, and, as a matter of fact, as new theories (in related areas) were developed, new facts became relevant to the acceptance of one of the two theories (viz. Avogadro's theory) in preference to the other. The facts of electrolysis, for example, are not empirical consequences of either Avogadro's theory or the gas-number theory. But they certainly supported Avogadro's theory rather than the gas-number theory, because they could readily be explained on Avogadro's atomic-molecular model.

Many philosophers think of theories as being equivalent to sets of observational conditionals, i.e. sentences of the form:

$$C_1 \ \& \ C_2 \ \& \ \ldots C_n \supset O$$

where C_1, C_2, ... C_n are empirically determinable boundary conditions and O is an observation statement, such as that an event of kind K is occurring in the space-time region S. This model of a theory is so widely accepted and used that it may reasonably be called 'the standard model'. On this model, it is natural enough to say that two theories are empirically equivalent iff they imply the same set of observational conditionals. For, only if this is so will they have the same empirical consequences. Yet, according to this criterion, my 'gas-number' theory is empirically equivalent to Avogadro's – which in my view is absurd. It is absurd because the evidence in favour of Avogadro's theory, and against the gas-number theory, is now overwhelming. For, the original theory of Avogadro has become embedded in a very general, and powerful, theory of chemical combination, which has well-established links with (in the sense that it has hypotheses in common with) a wide range of other physical and chemical theories. Avogadro's theory has gained support from these other theories because it has become

an integral part of them. Therefore, the evidence in favour of
Avogadro's theory cannot be identified with the confirmation that
its observational consequences has received – at least, not if
'observational consequences' is understood as narrowly as the
standard model would suggest.

The point is a Duhemian one. Theories do not normally occur in
isolation; and evidence for or against a theory can come from
unexpected quarters. This evidence may be unexpected, not because we have failed to carry out the relevant deductions from the
axioms, but *because it is not a consequence of these axioms at all*, at any
rate, not these axioms *alone*. It may be evidence which can be seen
to be relevant to the theory in question *only* because some new
linked theoretical development has occurred. Therefore, unless we
can know in advance what theoretical developments might occur,
we cannot say in advance what evidence, if any, might distinguish
between theories which, on present indications, are empirically
equivalent. Therefore, assuming that we cannot know what theoretical developments will occur, we cannot ever be fully justified in
claiming that two incompatible theories are empirically equivalent
in the sense that no evidence could ever distinguish between them.
That they cannot be distinguished, given our present theoretical
understanding of the world, does not imply that they cannot ever
be distinguished. Scientific realists may therefore be able to defend
their position against the case study arguments for the empirical
underdetermination of theories. For, they can argue, no genuine
case of empirical equivalence, in which the equivalence is not
determined by fiat, can be demonstrated.

The reason for this perhaps needs stressing. It derives from the
openness of the field of evidence. By the field of evidence of a theory I
mean the set of possible empirical discoveries relevant to its truth
or falsity. This set is to be clearly distinguished from the set of
empirical consequences of the theory. The empirical consequences of a
theory are the observational conditionals entailed by it; hence the
set of such consequences is a subset of the set of logical consequences of a theory. But not so the field of evidence. There can be
evidence for a theory which is in no way entailed by it, and
evidence against a theory which does not contradict it. Faraday's
laws of electrolysis, for example, certainly supported the atomic-

molecular theory of Avogadro, since the atomic-molecular model, which was proposed by Avogadro to explain certain facts about chemical combinations, could readily be adapted to explain the facts of electrolysis. But Avogadro could not, without making additional assumptions, have deduced Faraday's laws from his original theory. The failure of the Michelson–Morley experiment, on the other hand, surely proved to be evidence against Newtonian mechanics, even though this null result was compatible both with Newton's laws of motion, and with his law of gravity. Newton's laws of mechanics simply had *nothing to say* about the behaviour of electromagnetic radiation.

This point is of considerable importance in the present context. For it implies that claims of empirical equivalence should be treated with caution, and, in any case, be relativized to a given stage of theoretical development. From the fact that two logically distinct theories have the same empirical consequences (in the sense that they imply the same set of observational conditionals) it does not follow that there is no evidence which could distinguish between them. Nor does this follow from our inability to think of any way in which they might be so distinguished. For, so long as the theories we are concerned with are logically distinct, it is always logically possible that unforeseen theoretical developments will occur which will enable us to devise tests which would decide between them. To justify accepting any empirical equivalence claim, therefore, we should at least need a good theoretical argument that no such developments could occur.

Defenders of the thesis of the conventionality of distant simultaneity claim to have just such an argument. They claim that the facts relating to signal speeds and slow clock transport make it impossible for us ever to distinguish empirically between standard relativity theory, and non-standard theories which make the one-way speed of light in an inertial system some kind of function of direction.[5] I am not convinced by these arguments. However, even if it were established that there is some significant conventionality in our theories of space and time, this would not establish the *general* thesis of empirical underdetermination which empiricists need.

As far as I know, the only way of demonstrating the empirical underdetermination thesis for causal process theories is to build empirical equivalence into the specifications of the theoretical alternatives. For example, instead of the theory T, we might have the theory T', where

T' = Although the world is not as theory T says it is, the world behaves, so far as we can ever tell, as if T were true.

Of course, there are all sorts of variants of this, like

T'' = Actually, we are all brains in a vat, but . . .

or

T''' = Actually, the world began five minutes ago (local time?), but . . .

But the variations just illustrate the general strategy. So the fundamental issue which needs to be considered is whether the metaphysical realism presupposed by such specifications of alternative theories is acceptable to a scientific realist.

I think not. The position of scientific realism depends fundamentally on accepting the relevance of arguments to the best explanation to questions of ontology. For, roughly speaking, what scientific realists believe is that the world is more or less as our best theories say it is. At least, they have to believe that, for the most part, the things postulated in our causal process theories really do exist. Therefore, they cannot consistently adopt a position of global scepticism with regard to scientific knowledge, by saying such things as 'For all we know, we might all be brains in a vat'; and if their theory of truth or reality requires them to say such things, then to maintain their position, they will have to revise their theory of truth or reality.

Part II

Truth

4

The Programme of Analysis

An adequate theory of truth must preserve or explain those intuitions which make the correspondence theory of truth seem so
obviously right to so many people. There is no point in denying
that in many standard cases, at least, truth does seem to be just a
kind of correspondence relationship. Some word or phrase is used
to refer to something, and something is said about it. And what is
said is true iff what is referred to is the way it is said to be. This all
seems so obvious that one would have to be mad to deny it. So
whatever theory of truth we may eventually arrive at, this intuitive
account must somehow be preserved for these cases, or if not
preserved, then at least fully explained within the framework of
some other theory. A theory of truth which did nothing to explain
this intuition could reasonably be accused of ignoring the facts.

It is also a fact, which no one who wants to construct a theory of
truth can reasonably ignore, that many different kinds of statements are held to be true or false. These include not only those
statements whose truth or falsity seems so obviously to depend on
whether the required correspondence relationship holds, but also
many whose relationship to reality is not at all perspicuous. If it is
true that A caused B, then what is the fact which corresponds to
this claim? What are the facts which correspond to true statements
of laws or theories or conditionals? In virtue of what is it true that A
believes B, or that A explains B, or that A is probable, given B?
What makes it true that $2 + 2 = 4$, or that the one-way speed of
light is constant with respect to all inertial systems, or that the
earth is bigger than the moon? What are the facts which correspond
to true necessity and possibility claims? What makes it true that
there is no elephant in this room? Any adequate theory of truth
must be able to account for the *variety* of the truth claims we make.

If there are any truth claims which we should all confidently accept, the truth of which cannot be explained on our theory, then we should require some explanation for our misplaced confidence.

Defenders of the correspondence theory of truth have worked hard, and with great ingenuity, to solve these problems. They have tried to account for the truth or falsity of these various kinds of claims by analysing them as truth functional compounds of certain primitive statements whose truth or falsity can readily be understood in correspondence terms. This is what the programme of analysis has been all about. Yet despite the effort that has been put into it, many of the problems of analysis seem to be no nearer solution. Perhaps it is time to reconsider the truth theory which gives rise to this programme.

In this and the next chapter I shall be arguing against the correspondence theory of truth. I shall begin by considering the research programme of analysis which it generates, ignoring for the time being any difficulties there may be with the primitive correspondence relationships in virtue of which various kinds of claims may be supposed to be true or false. The question of whether, even in the most favoured cases, truth can be identified with any such relationship will be discussed in the next chapter. I want first to consider the research programme, because my own doubts about the correspondence theory arose from its apparent failure.

I think we can distinguish four main phases in the development of the programme of analysis. The first was *the early positivist phase*, which had its origins in Hume's empiricism. It was the attempt to identify the concepts we use to describe the world with the empirically ascertainable conditions necessary and sufficient for their application. To say that one thing is the cause of another, for example, is just to say that a certain kind of regularity exists; and if we think that there is any kind of necessary connection between cause and effect, or power resident in the cause which is productive of the effect, then we are mistaken, for the impression which corresponds to this idea is not one of external sense, but of internal sentiment. The attribution of causal powers to objects is, therefore, according to Hume, strictly meaningless, since we are incapable of forming any such idea.

The second phase was that of *logical atomism*. With the near success of the logicist programme of reducing mathematics to logic, logic was seen as an immensely powerful tool in the programme of analysis. For the first time, it seemed, we could give an account of the nature of mathematics which promised to explain its necessity, objectivity and a priority, compatibly with an empiricist epistemology, and a none too lavish ontology. To believe that $2 + 2 = 4$, for example, one did not have to believe in the existence of any abstract particulars, such as numbers, which were so related.

Encouraged by this result, Russell sought to use logical techniques more widely to attack philosophical problems, in the belief that if we really understood the logical structure of the claims we made about reality, we should not be led into paradox, or into drawing false or absurd conclusions about what exists. His programme was to identify the logically simplest statements that we could make about the world, the atomic propositions, and to analyse all other statements as truth functional compounds of these atomic constituents – the atomic propositions being those which could be most immediately understood in correspondence terms as expressions of atomic facts.

The third phase was the logical positivist movement which grew out of the discussions of the philosophers of the Vienna Circle in the 1920s. The movement was characterized by a wholesale rejection of metaphysics, and of metaphysical questions, as meaningless. Metaphysical statements were described as those which were neither logically nor analytically true or false nor empirically decidable. Clearly they had in mind the kinds of statements over which philosophers could argue apparently endlessly and fruitlessly. For example, the questions supposedly at issue between realists and idealists were regarded as meaningless on these grounds. Realist and idealist ontologies, while formally incompatible, are both, apparently, consistent with any possible experience. So, according to the logical positivists, these questions are meaningless.

While many logical positivists accepted the view that truth is correspondence with the facts, this view was not central to their philosophical position – as it had been to the logical atomists. Indeed, some logical positivists rejected it as metaphysical, and so meaningless. For it was clear that the relationship of correspondence could not be a logical one. Logical relationships can hold only between statements, not between statements and any other kind of thing. On the other hand, it did not appear to be a relationship which we could investigate empirically. We do not reject any belief because it fails to correspond to the facts which we somehow, independently, know about, but because it conflicts with something else that we believe, and which we are not prepared to, or cannot, abandon. So, by the logical positivists' own criterion, it seems that the correspondence theory of truth should be counted as one of those metaphysical, and therefore meaningless, doctrines which philosophers can argue endlessly and fruitlessly about. However, most logical positivists were, understandably, reluctant to draw this conclusion. If our perceptual judgements could not be said, in some sense, to correspond to the facts, or to reality, or to be in some other way objectively true, then why should we accept them, or the scientific systems which are founded upon them? So they lived in the hope that someone would come up with a correspondence theory of truth which they *could* reasonably accept.

The fourth and current phase of the programme is that of *semantic analysis*, which derives from Tarski's semantic theory of truth (Tarski 1936). Many of the logical positivists had been uneasy about the correspondence theory because the postulated correspondence relationship could not be investigated or even clearly articulated. Tarski succeeded in constructing a theory of truth which many felt they could accept without qualms. He did so by defining truth for certain kinds of formal languages, using just the primitive semantic notions of denotation and satisfaction. For languages of the appropriate kinds, truth could be defined recursively in a metalanguage, so that the truth of any sentence of the language is determined by what its primitive terms denote, and what things, or sequences of things, satisfy its primitive predicates.

The primitive semantic relationships are semantic in the sense (and only in the sense) that they relate words to things. So, any true sentence of a language for which there exists a Tarskian truth theory (i.e. Tarskian language) must correspond to reality in some more or less complex way, viz. in the manner specified by this truth theory. Consequently, Tarski's theory of truth is really a sophisticated correspondence theory. Ealier versions, e.g. Russell's in

Russell (1918), of the correspondence theory of truth required us to believe in an ontology of facts. For the only primitive semantic relationship (i.e. word–thing relationship) countenanced in Russell's theory was the unanalysed relationship of correspondence. Elementary sentences were the semantic units. In Tarski's theory, however, the relationship of correspondence is a complex one, and whether it holds or not in a particular case depends on what denotation and satisfaction relationships hold. Now the relata of these relationships are names and predicates, on the one hand, and things or sequences of things on the other. Consequently, one does not have to believe in an ontology of facts to accept Tarski's theory. It is compatible with almost any ontology.

The programme of semantic analysis derives immediately from Tarski's theory. It is a programme pursued in the belief that whatever is true is so, ultimately, in virtue of what things exist, and what descriptions they satisfy. However, a Tarskian truth theory does not exist for any natural language, and there is reason to think that no such theory could be provided for such a language. Nevertheless, any truth that we can express in a natural language *may* be expressible in *some* language for which a Tarskian truth theory can be given. So, the problem of semantic analysis is seen as being to construct Tarskian languages rich enough to express whatever we may believe to be true. Now, if this can be done compatibly with an ontology we are willing to accept, then the correspondence theory of truth is at least extensionally adequate. For, quite generally, we can say that a belief is true iff it has an expression S in a Tarskian language whose primitive terms denote only real objects, and whose primitive predicates are satisfied, if at all, only by such objects, or sequences of them, and S corresponds to reality in the manner specified by the Tarskian truth theory for this language.

The programmes of logical atomism and semantic analysis are formally quite similar. Both seek to explain meaning atomistically by specifying truth conditions. In Russell's case, the atoms of meaning are the direct relationships of correspondence which exist or not between atomic propositions and facts. In Tarski's case, the atoms of meaning are primitive semantic relationships which the elementary terms and predicates of a language may bear to things in the world. Nevertheless, there are analyses which are acceptable to many followers of the programme of semantic analysis which would not have been acceptable to Russell or his followers. The 'possible worlds' analyses of modal and conditional statements, for example, would not, I think, have been acceptable to Russell. They would have offended his 'robust sense of reality'. For Russell, analysis was subordinate to ontology. True, it required an ontology of facts; but it was silent on the question of what the facts were. An analysis acceptable to Russell would not existentially quantify over entities he did not believe to exist. For many followers of the programme of semantic analysis, however, the opposite is the case. If we *must* existentially quantify over sets or possible worlds or possibilia to provide formally satisfactory analyses of the statements we believe to be true, then these things must exist. For them, Tarski's version of the correspondence theory of truth is to be preserved, even if we must adjust our ontology to fit the semantics.

In this chapter, I shall argue for the failure of the programme of analysis by first presenting a brief account of its history, and of the reasons why the various shifts in the programme have occurred. It is important to do this, because I want to argue that this programme really is at the end of its tether. The successive modifications and refinements of the programme have each led to insuperable difficulties, and the problems which confront the present semantic phase are at least as great as any which led to the overthrow of any of its predecessors. I cannot, of course, prove that the programme of analysis cannot be revived in some new form. But the difficulties that now confront it are so great, and have been with us for so long, that it is surely reasonable to doubt that it can be revived at all. When *rigor mortis* has set in, death can reasonably be pronounced. But if it is pronounced dead, then the correspondence theory of truth which gives rise to it cannot be adequate.

4.1 THE LEGACY OF EMPIRICISM

The correspondence theory of truth has strong links with empiricism. It is the kind of theory one is likely to arrive at by taking perceptual judgements as paradigms of truth – as most present-day empiricists do. For the truth of a perceptual judgement does seem to depend just on whether what is observed has the properties attributed to it. It is not, perhaps, the kind of theory one would naturally develop if one thought of truth as the aim of rational inquiry – as some scientific realists do. A Peircean concept of truth might then seem to be more appropriate. Nor is it the kind of theory which would naturally appeal to those seeking self-knowledge. For such people, what is important is what is true for them – and that, they would say, is all we can ever know. Nor, again, is it the kind of theory that is readily suggested by the mathematical paradigm. If one's paradigm of truth is the mathematical theorem, then one is likely to think that truth has little or nothing to do with the reality we can observe, just as Plato did.

I am not saying that an empiricist *must* hold a correspondence theory of truth. Nor am I saying that *only* an empiricist can hold such a theory. The point is just that there is a kind of natural association between modern empiricist epistemology and the correspondence theory.

Empiricists believe that all knowledge which is not purely conceptual derives from experience. They suppose that some things are known directly by experience, while others have to be inferred. Accordingly, the epistemic problems of empiricism are to say what can be known directly, and to explain, and if possible justify, the inferences we make. Experience, they say, gives rise to certain immediate perceptual judgements, which are the sole foundation of all of our legitimate or justified beliefs about the world. With perhaps some rare exceptions, they are true, and known to be true, if anything is. And in this sense, they are paradigms of both knowledge and truth. So naturally, when empiricists ask what truth is, they focus on judgements of this kind. Truth must be basically whatever it is that makes such judgements as these true. And what is that? Obviously, that the things referred to have the properties ascribed to them. For this reason, the correspondence theory of truth often appears to be almost a corollary of empiricism; and it would be hard to find many empiricists today who did not subscribe to some version of it.

In accepting the correspondence theory of truth for immediate perceptual judgements, empiricists are committed to explaining what would make other kinds of judgements true. Obviously, they do not want the sense in which they are true to be essentially different, or they would be forced to say that truth is an ambiguous concept. So the problem must be to say what facts about the world, of the kind which make immediate perceptual judgements true, are the truth makers for statements which are not of this kind. Any empiricist who accepts the correspondence theory of truth must be committed to some such programme.

To meet this commitment, empiricists have generally tried to develop theories of meaning which would enable them to analyse complex judgements, or judgements which seem to have unacceptable ontological implications, so that the corresponding relationships upon which their truth or falsity depend may be clearly displayed. To develop such theories of meaning, empiricists have naturally turned once again to their paradigm of empirical knowledge, but now adopted it as a paradigm of *understanding*. For surely, if anything is paradigmatically known, it must be clearly understood. For an empiricist, therefore, immediate perceptual judgements serve, not only as paradigms of knowledge and truth, but also of understanding.

The problem of meaning for an empiricist is thus seen as being to specify the meanings of sentences, which, though they purport to describe the world, cannot be used to report anything which might be directly observed. Sentences which can be so used are assumed to be sufficiently well understood, and so not in need of explication. There is a problem of meaning for an empiricist only where the sentence in question cannot be used to express an immediate perceptual judgement.

In the case of direct observation reports, there does not seem to be any distinction to be drawn between knowing what they mean, and knowing what would make them true. So that, in the paradigmatic cases, it seems that to know the meaning of a sentence is to know its observational truth conditions. Empiricism thus gives rise to positivism. It leads directly to the view that two sentences mean the same iff they have the same observational truth conditions, and by a short further step to the equation of meaningfulness with verifiability by observation.

Hume comes close to this line of reasoning when he writes in 'The Abstract' (referring to himself in the third person):

... wherever any idea is ambiguous, he (Hume) has always recourse to the impression, which must render it clear and precise. And when he suspects that any philosophical term has no idea annexed to it (as is too common) he always asks *from what impression that idea is derived?* And if no impression can be produced, he concludes that the term is altogether insignificant. It is after this manner he examines our idea of *substance* and *essence*; and it were to be wished that this rigorous method were more practised in all philosophical debates. (Hume 1740, p. 340)

Immediate perceptual judgements are always clear and precise, according to Hume, because there are always impressions of outward sense corresponding to the terms that are used. So, Hume certainly accepts such judgements as models of clarity and precision. In the case of claims which are not immediate, the question is from what impressions the ideas contained in them are derived. If these can be specified, then the significance of the ideas is clear. If not, then they are not significant.

In the context, Hume is talking about claims purporting to state 'matters of fact'. There is no evidence that he would apply this criterion to judgements concerning 'relations of ideas'. Moreover, we should be cautious in interpreting the phrase 'altogether insignificant'. When Hume says that ideas which are not derived from impressions are altogether insignificant, he may mean only that they lack signification, or, as we should say today, denotation or reference. I leave that to Hume scholars to decide. I do not wish to pin positivism on Hume on the strength of just this passage.

Hume's 'rigorous method' is well illustrated by his discussion of causation. There he argues persuasively, and many think conclusively, that judgements of cause and effect are not immediate perceptual judgements; for, there is no impression in the single instance which corresponds to the idea of causation. He also argues that such judgements do not merely express relations of ideas. So if 'cause' signifies any real power or property in an object which is designated a cause, there must be some impression produced by the repetition of instances which is not present in the single case. There is, however, no such impression, or at least none of outward sense.

So, he concludes that the term 'cause' does not signify any such power or property of the object. The impression which does correspond to the idea of causal power or necessary connection is an internal one. The repetition of instances of event sequences of certain kinds, of which we are perceptually aware, produces in us a certain habit, or disposition of mind, of which we are reflectively aware, to expect an event of the kind we call the effect to follow one of the kind we call its cause. So, the idea of causal power corresponds to nothing external, nothing which belongs to an object which is a cause.

Hume notes that we may judge one thing to be the immediate cause of another when, and only when, we observe, or otherwise have reason to believe, that the cause is contiguous in space and time with its effect, precedes its effect, and that things similar to the cause are always conjoined in this way with things similar to the effect. So that, if there are any relationships between the external events which we suppose to be causally related, they are just these. There is no further relationship of necessary connection between the events, and there are no causal powers which are productive of the effect.

Hume's analysis of causation has been an inspiration to empiricists ever since. The 'rigorous method' that he used has been followed, although perhaps not so rigorously, by empiricist philosophers in almost every field of philosophical inquiry. Think of Hertz on forces, or Mach on the concepts of absolute space and time, and on other concepts of physics such as mass and temperature, or of Reichenbach on simultaneity and length congruence. The attempt to understand statements about the world in terms of their observational truth conditions, or where this has proved to be impossible, to replace them by less metaphysical ones which could be so understood, or where even this has proved to be impossible, to banish them altogether as metaphysical or meaningless, has characterized empiricist philosophy more or less since the time of Hume. There have, of course, been many variations and refinements of the programme, some of which we shall look at shortly. But it is not too misleading to say that this is what empiricist philosophers have been doing, or trying to do, ever since Hume.

But while Hume's analysis of causation has been an inspiration, it has also been something of an embarrassment. For most empiricists are uneasy about accepting the conclusion that there are no dynamical forces or causal powers or nomological necessities in nature, only *de facto* regularities. Yet Hume's analysis has proved to be extraordinarily difficult to improve upon, given the requirements of Hume's 'rigorous method'. There seems to be no way of avoiding Hume's startling conclusion that, while there are regularities in nature, there are no forces productive of these regularities. Some regularities, it is true, may be produced by others, so that they may be explained by subsumption under them. But fundamentally, there must be some basic regularities which cannot be explained in this way. That these basic regularities exist must be just the way things are.

There is worse to come. If the argument that there are no dynamical forces or causal powers in nature is sound, then, by a parallel argument, there are no static forces either. For Hume's argument will go through against these sorts of forces as well. Consider the following very well known passage from Hume's *Inquiries* – modified as an argument against static forces:

> . . . upon the whole, there appears not throughout all nature, any one instance of connexion which is conceivably by us. All [parts of objects] seem entirely loose and separate. They seem *conjoined*, but never *connected*. And as we can have no idea of any thing which never appeared to our outward sense or inward sentiment, the necessary conclusion *seems* to be that we have no idea of connexion or [binding force] at all, and that these words are absolutely without any meaning, when employed either in philosophical reasonings or common life. (Hume 1777, p. 74)

(The words in the original passage, of course, are 'events' instead of 'parts of objects' and 'power' instead of 'binding force'.) Now Hume's arguments in the *Inquiries* can be systematically transformed in this way as arguments against the existence of any kind of bonding between the parts of objects. So the Hume world is a very strange world indeed. Not only are all events loose and separate in this world, so are (or should be, by parallel reasoning) all the parts of objects. Moreover, if we have no good reason to believe that the future will resemble the past, or even that it will exist, then by parallel reasoning, we have no good reason to believe that those parts of objects which are not immediately perceived are as we believe them to be, or even that they exist. So Hume's 'rigorous method' sometimes appears to empiricists to be just a bit *too* rigorous.

Yet the programme of analysis, in one form or another, has survived. The immediate perceptual judgement remains the paradigm of knowledge, truth and meaning; and it is still maintained that to know the meaning of a statement is to know its truth conditions. What has occurred since Hume, and since the demise of positivism, is that epistemic questions have been distinguished more clearly from questions of truth and meaning. In the positivist tradition, there is no distinction to be made between what a statement means and what would show it empirically to be true. But such a distinction is now fairly generally drawn. What remains of the doctrine is the view that what a statement means is to be identified with the set of necessary and sufficient conditions for its truth – these conditions being specifiable in a language whose primitive terms denote only real objects and whose primitive predicates are satisfied only by such objects. It is allowed, for example, that there may be nothing which would *show* an unrestricted universal generalization to be true, or an open existential statement to be false. But such statements may, nevertheless, be true or false, and what they mean is determined by the sets of conditions which would make them so.

The correspondence theory of truth is still retained, since the perceptual judgement remains the paradigm of truth. Therefore, the analytic programme, which seeks to specify truth conditions for statements in such a way that their truth or falsity can be seen to depend on what primitive correspondence relationships hold, remains intact. The theory of meaning, however, has undergone some change, since sentences are now allowed to be meaningful, though there may be nothing which would show them empirically to be true or false. To explicate the meaning of a statement it is thought to be enough if we can specify truth conditions for it which are intelligible in terms of primitive correspondence relationships.

Moreover, it is often allowed that there may be structural or pragmatic aspects to meaning which would distinguish between statements which have the same empirical truth conditions. Though what they state to be the case may be the same, the statements may have different logical structures or occupy different positions in our theories, or suggest different models or analogies, and so have different pragmatic roles in theory development.

The theorems of logic and mathematics, for example, are supposed all to have the same empirical truth conditions, since what they state to be the case (viz. nothing) is the same. But they may have different logical forms, or different roles in the logical and mathematical systems of which they are part. So, in the fuller sense, which allows for such differences, they may have different meanings. Similarly, theories which have the same truth conditions may, nevertheless, be distinguished pragmatically, and so, in the stronger sense, be distinct in meaning. If Reichenbach was right in thinking that there is no truth of the matter whether space is Euclidean, equivalent Euclidean and non-Euclidean cosmologies might not, nevertheless, be equivalent *as theories*, since the two may offer quite different prospects for development, or one might leave unexplained something which the other is easily able to account for.

The correspondence theory of truth has always been in some difficulty with the theorems of mathematics. If they are true, then what are the facts to which they correspond? The truth of these theorems, surely, does not depend on what the world is like. So their truth cannot depend on what actually exists? If their truth is independent of what actually exists, however, then they cannot be true because of it. So, either they are not true, or their truth depends on something other than what is actual, or, like logical truths, they are vacuous. Frege and Russell concluded that they were like logical truths; and so they tried to reduce mathematics to logic. Others, e.g. Wittgenstein, argued that they were neither true nor false, because they were just rules which were more or less useful for calculating and measuring, but which, in themselves, made no claims about reality. I think the fault lies with the theory of truth which makes the truth and meaning of mathematical theorems so problematic.

4.2   RUSSELL'S PROGRAMME OF ANALYSIS

Russell's programme of analysis, which he called logical atomism, was to display the logical structure of the facts which make propositions true or false. He distinguished two kinds of propositions, atomic and molecular. Atomic propositions, he held, are elementary propositions of a logically perfect language with the structure of the predicate calculus, whose primitive terms are logically proper names of simple particulars knowable by acquaintance, and whose primitive predicates ascribe unanalysable properties and relations to these particulars. 'This is red' is an example of the kind of proposition he had in mind. Molecular propositions are propositions constructed from atomic ones by the operations of negation, disjunction (or just by the single operation of conjunction–negation, i.e. 'not both . . . and . . .') and universal generalization.

Russell seems not to have required, as Wittgenstein did, that all atomic propositions should be logically independent of each other. For he was evidently prepared to countenance 'This is red' as an atomic proposition, even though it is incompatible with 'This is green', which is, presumably, also an atomic proposition. He thought it was enough that all *true* atomic propositions should be logically independent. Thus, Russell held that if two or more true propositions are not logically independent, then they cannot all be atomic propositions.

Russell thought that atomic propositions assert the existence of atomic facts, and hence are true if these atomic facts exist. But molecular propositions, if they are true, must correspond to the facts in a more complex way. Roughly, a molecular proposition will be true if the atomic facts which exist are such as to make it so (by making the atomic propositions of which it is compounded true or false in an appropriate combination).

Russell's programme of logical atomism, then, was to display the structure of the facts which make true propositions true by expressing these propositions in a language with the structure of the predicate calculus using only terms which refer to objects of actual (or possible) acquaintance, and simple, unanalysable, observational predicates. The programme was thus an empiricist one agreeable to the philosophical climate of the time. But it was not, in any way, an idealist philosophy. If any of our beliefs are true, Russell held, then they are true because they correspond in some way, which may or may not require philosophical analysis to reveal, with the facts.

Russell's programme failed for a number of reasons. Firstly, Russell needed negative facts as well as positive ones, and general facts as well as singular ones. A negative fact seems to be needed to correspond to the true statement that there is no elephant in this room, and a general fact seems to be needed to correspond to any true universal generalization (which is not merely tautological). It is not what is in the room which makes it true that there is no elephant here, because it would still be true even if these things were not in the room. So the presence of these things is not necessary for the truth of the statement. Moreover, the true positive singular existential claims concerning the contents of this room do not together entail that there is no elephant here. So the presence of these things is not even sufficient for the truth of the claim. So there are no positive singular facts which correspond to the true statement that there is no elephant in this room. It is possible that if we had general facts, as well as singular ones, we should not need negative ones. For it might be the fact that all elephants are outside the room which makes it true that none are inside. But the totality of the singular facts about the locations of elephants does not entail that none are in the room, because we also need the general premiss that there are no other elephants.

The main trouble with negative facts is that they look so artificial and insubstantial. The fact that there is no elephant in this room does not seem to be a *thing* in the sort of way that the fact that there *is* an elephant in this room might be; and it does not, in itself, seem to differ from the fact that there is no walrus in this room. It is easy enough to believe that the things that exist in this room somehow make the claims that they exist true, but it is not so easy to believe that the truth of a negative claim about what exists in this room is to be explained in the same sort of way. Negative facts thus have the hallmarks of being entities postulated *ad hoc* to save Russell's theory, and hence his programme of analysis, from refutation.

Secondly, after some early successes of the programme in

mathematics, and in the theory of descriptions, there were few
successful analyses. It became increasingly implausible to claim
that anything which could be said about the world could in
principle be said in a language with the structure of the predicate
calculus, if the elementary sentences of this language had to be
atomic propositions. Statements of laws, theories and conditionals
defied analysis, and many were persuaded that even so-called
'indicative conditionals' are not truth functional. Statements attributing beliefs and other propositional attitudes to people could
not be analysed satisfactorily. Judgements of causal connection also
resisted analysis. Hume's efforts in this direction had never been
entirely successful. And no one had any satisfactory account to give
of necessity or possibility claims, at least where the necessities or
possibilities involved were not logical ones. So, all in all, the
programme did not live up to its early promise.

With the revival of positivism in the 1920s, the programme of
analysis moved into a new phase. The new positivists, who called
themselves 'logical positivists', or 'logical empiricists', accepted the
importance of logical analysis, but many of them rejected the
doctrine of logical atomism, which had been its foundation, as
metaphysical or meaningless. The claim that the world consisted of
atomic facts was neither empirically verifiable nor analytic. So it
had to be rejected. Nevertheless, a programme of analysis similar to
the one which Russell had begun was continued, but now with the
aim of determining the empirical significance, if any, of the claims
we make. Those which are, in principle, neither verifiable nor
falsifiable empirically, and are not analytically true or false, were to
be rejected as meaningless, and empirically equivalent claims were
to be regarded as different ways of saying the same thing.

4.3   LOGICAL POSITIVISM

The philosophers of the Vienna Circle, the so-called 'logical positivists', agreed with Russell that logical analysis is the key to
understanding the cognitive significance of what we say about the
world. Like Russell, they sought to analyse statements as truth
functions of elementary statements whose meaning and truth con-

ditions could be supposed to be known, and whose truth or falsity could be determined directly by experience. They took the view that if a statement could not be analysed in this way, then it was not an empirical or factual claim. If, nevertheless, it was accepted, then it could only be so as a matter of definition or convention. There could be no truth of the matter whether p, if no empirically satisfactory analysis of 'p' could be offered.

Reichenbach's discussion of length congruence (in Reichenbach 1927, pp. 14–19) is a good example of positivist analysis. If two straight rods (which are not too long) are lying side by side, and there is no overlap, then we can judge immediately that they are equal in length. This is the only *direct* experience we can have of length equality. There is no such experience, however, where the rods are not side by side. Rods at different places, or the same rod at different times, cannot be directly compared. So, if we judge them to be equal in length, when they are not so disposed, this cannot be an immediate perceptual judgement. Some analysis of what we mean by saying that two things, when apart, are equal in length, or that something remains the same in length, is therefore required. For, these concepts cannot be assumed to be meaningful in the absence of any such analysis. To be acceptable, the analysis must specify some tests for length equality – a method verifying it which we could, in principle, carry out. What we mean by saying that two things are equal in length then depends entirely on this specification. In the absence of such a specification, it would just be *meaningless* to say that two rods which are not in a position to be compared directly for length are equal in this regard. The meaning of this claim depends on the method of its verification.

Reichenbach argues that the only restriction which we *must* put on any operational (i.e. co-ordinative) definition of length equality is that it should be compatible with the 'no overlap' criterion. He does not even insist that the relationship of length equality, however it might be defined, must be symmetrical and transitive. He then points out that this restriction is not enough to determine how length congruence is to be defined. It is not even enough if we insist that, however it might be defined, the relationship should be both symmetrical and transitive (and so formally an equivalence relation). There are infinitely many formally admissible operational definitions of length equality compatible with the 'no overlap' criterion, and with the transitivity and symmetry requirements on length congruence. So Reichenbach concludes that there is no fact of the matter whether two things which are not in a position to be compared directly for length are congruent. The question can become a factual one only *after* we have fixed upon some operational definition of length equality.

It is typical of positivist analyses that they try to distinguish like this between what is factual and what is conventional. This distinction is usually considered to be different from that between analytic and synthetic. That analytic statements are true can be discovered just by attending to the meanings of words; they are *trivially* conventional. But the kinds of conventions which the logical positivists looked for were conventions adopted, wittingly or otherwise, for purposes of theory construction. And these, typically, were propositions which could not be seen to be true just by attending to the meanings of words. If Reichenbach is right, for example, about the conventionality of the one-way light principle, then this must be because it is neither analytically nor empirically demonstrable that the one-way velocity of light is equal to its round-trip velocity. He argued that *a new determination of sense* is required if all talk of one-way light velocities, and ultimately of all one-way velocities, is not to be meaningless; and this can be achieved only by some more or less arbitrary stipulation. If *now* we say that the one-way velocity of light is the same in all directions, then this reflects a decision we have made. We have chosen to *set* the one-way light velocity of light equal to the round-trip velocity *by definition*, and so, by this decision, *make it analytically true*.

Until quite recently, many philosophers who rejected the analytic–synthetic distinction nevertheless continued to operate with an empirical–conventional distinction. Quine, for example, who led the attack on the analytic–synthetic distinction in the 1940s and 1950s, held that there is no fact of the matter whether a translation from one language to another is correct. A translation can only be correct, he said, *in relation to a given translation manual*.[1] Now a translation manual is a system of rules for co-ordinating the sentences of one language with those of another. It is good if it would enable the speakers of one language to communicate with those of another without apparent misunderstanding, and it is as simple as any viable alternative. But there can be no question of its being correct, or incorrect, according to Quine, because there is no empirical test of whether a sentence of one language means the same as that of another. That two sentences have the same *stimulus meanings* does not imply that they mean the same. But ultimately there is no way of comparing what people mean, except by reference to stimulus meanings. Therefore, it cannot be a factual question whether a sentence of one language is correctly translated by a sentence of another: it must be conventional. If, nevertheless, we speak of correct or incorrect translations, then this must hold implicit reference to some system of co-ordinative definitions, i.e. to a translation manual.

However, if one rejects the analytic–synthetic distinction, I do not see how the empirical–conventional distinction can be maintained. For suppose the argument for the conventionality of the one-way light principle is sound. Then we must have established that at least this principle is not empirical. So, if now we choose to set the one-way velocity of light equal to the round trip velocity by definition, it cannot be an empirical question whether the one-way velocity of light is equal in both directions. Therefore, there must be at least one thing which is true by definition or convention, and hence analytic. Similarly, if Quine's arguments for the conventionality of translation manuals are sound, then all statements of translation rules in all currently accepted translation manuals must be analytic. For, if they were otherwise, it would be an empirical question whether a given sentence of one language is correctly translated by a sentence of another language. There would have to be a fact of the matter.

In my view, Quine was right to reject the analytic–synthetic distinction, but wrong to defend inter-linguistic conventionalism. He ought to have held that it is an *empirical* question whether 'Gavagai' is correctly translated as 'Lo, a rabbit'. He should not have been looking for hidden conventions in the manner of Reichenbach. He should have been arguing that the empirical–conventional distinction is as bogus as the analytic–synthetic. He should have taken the view that even *explicit definitions* are not purely conventional, or true just because they have been offered as definitions.

Historically, there is considerable support for this position. Definitions in science have been rejected for precisely the same sorts of reasons as other law-like statements. At one time, for example, a chemical compound was defined as a pure substance made up of elements combined in definite proportions by weight. Now that we know about isotopes this is no longer considered to be true. At another time, temperature would have been defined as the pressure of the caloric fluid. But when the caloric theory was overthrown, no one, *absolutely no one*, concluded that temperature did not exist.

Where explicit definitions have never been offered, or if offered, then never widely adopted, it is impossible to distinguish clearly between what is conventionally true and what is not. Is it true by definition that a whale is a mammal, or is this just a fact about whales? Is it true by definition that the molecular formula of water is H_2O, or is this a fact about water? Does oxygen have the atomic number 8 by definition, or is this a fact about oxygen? How, in general, can we distinguish between defining and other characteristics when there are no universally agreed definitions to which we can refer? 'Definitional' itself is not an observational predicate. We cannot, just by inspection, decide which characteristics are definitional and which are not. For, to do Hume's trick, what is the impression of outward sense or inward sentiment which corresponds to it?

The test that has most plausibility is a kind of thought experiment. In general, a claim may be considered to be true by definition or convention iff it can rationally be accepted, but cannot rationally be denied by any member of the language community who correctly understands the terms involved. So, if we have a statement which is generally accepted, and presumably rationally so, and we wish to determine whether it is conventionally true, we must decide whether there are any circumstances in which it could rationally be denied by anyone who understands it properly. In particular, if it is generally agreed that an A is a B, and we want to know whether it is true by definition or convention that this is so, then the test would be to ask whether any member of the language community can think of circumstances which would make it rational to believe that some A was not a B. If no one can think of such a case, then B-ness may, at least for the time being, be considered to be a defining characteristic of A-hood. If someone can produce a convincing case, however, then it may be concluded that B-ness is not a defining characteristic of A-hood.

The test is, nevertheless, unsatisfactory by empiricist standards. Firstly, it may not always be clear what it would be rational to believe. If the circumstances are extreme, for example, we may simply have no idea what to think. Secondly, while it might be rational for someone to deny that p if their understanding of 'p' is somehow deviant, the test requires that their understanding of 'p' should not be deviant. Therefore, to use this test to show that a statement is not true by definition or convention, it would have to be shown that it could rationally be denied, even though it was correctly understood. But that someone understands something correctly is no more a datum of direct experience than the judgement that some statement is true by definition or convention. If we could say what it is to understand something correctly, then no doubt we could make the distinction. But unfortunately we can't do this without begging the question.

The test for analyticity (i.e. truth by definition or convention) is as elastic in practice as it is in theory. Is it true by definition that a whale is a mammal? Well, one can easily imagine circumstances in which it would be reasonable to believe that it was a mythical beast, or a creature which was brought to earth from another planet, and which, therefore, did not belong to the Animal Kingdom. So, apparently, even the claim that a whale is an animal is not true by definition or convention. On the other hand, it could be said that anyone who had either of these beliefs about whales would have a different concept of whalehood, and would not understand the term 'whale' as we do. Both answers are plausible. It is plausibly a factual question whether whales are mammals, since it is not difficult to imagine circumstances which would lead one to deny it. And it is surely a factual question whether these circumstances obtain. However, it is also plausible that anyone who thinks that a whale is not a mammal has a deviant concept of whalehood. Yet, without some way of deciding between these alternatives the test for truth by definition or convention is useless. The distinction between what is conventionally true and what isn't, is, by empiricist standards, a meaningless one.

My own view is that the alternatives are *not* mutually exclusive. My concept of whalehood depends on the *totality* of my general beliefs about whales, and so *partly* on my belief that a whale is a mammal. Therefore, anyone who disagreed with me about this must have a different concept of whalehood. But this is not to say that I hold *any*, much less all, of these beliefs about whales to be true by definition or convention. My concept of a whale is of a large aquatic mammal, fishlike in appearance, and with a flat tail. But I am willing to allow that I could be wrong on any of these points. Certainly, I can imagine circumstances in which I would be convinced otherwise about them. So I want to say that the beliefs which determine my concept of whalehood are not things which I just accept as being true by definition or convention. I accept them because the evidence in their favour seems, currently, to be over-whelming. No doubt others have more or less sophisticated concepts of whalehood. They know more or less about whales. But there is *no* set of statements true by definition or convention about whales which anyone *must* accept to have a concept of whalehood. There is no such thing as *the* concept of a whale. My concept of a whale is of a thing of the kind I believe a whale to be. You may have a different concept.

The case for distinguishing between what is true by definition or convention and what isn't is clearer where explicit definitions have been offered, and widely accepted. For, if anything which is not tautological can be said to be true by definition or convention, then surely explicit definitions can be. But we should not too hastily conclude that explicit definitions do not make significant empirical claims about the world. They can be, and frequently are, rejected for precisely the same sorts of reasons as claims which everyone agrees to be empirical are rejected, viz. that they prove to be incompatible with too many other beliefs we hold, and which we cannot, or are not willing to, jettison. At one time, for example, the units of time-interval were defined astronomically, so that the rate of rotation of the earth relative to the 'fixed stars' was fixed as being uniform by definition. But we now have good reason to believe that the rate of rotation of the earth is *not* constant. In geological time, the energy of rotation of the earth has been dissipated by tidal forces, and there is good reason to think that its size, and hence its moment of inertia, has changed significantly since its formation several billion years ago. So it would now be quite generally agreed that what was once accepted as being true by definition or convention is false. The astronomical definition of equality of time-interval had to be rejected because it proved to be incompatible with the laws of conservation of energy and angular momentum, and with certain well-justified assumptions about the earth's history.

The sorts of reasons we have for rejecting the astronomical definition of equality of time-interval are theoretical immediately, but ultimately empirical. They are like the reasons Newton had for considering Galileo's law of free fall to be only a first approximation to the truth. It is not that the length of the siderial day has been measured by some other standard and found to change slowly. It is just a *theoretical* prediction that if it were measured by standards which were theoretically invariable over a sufficiently long period of time, the variations in the length of the day would become apparent. Likewise, Newton had *theoretical* reasons for rejecting Galileo's law of free fall. He did not have, or at any rate did not need, experimental evidence that the gravitational acceleration of a body in free fall is a function of its distance from the centre. It was just a prediction of his theory that this was so. In relation to theories, therefore, there are definitions which enjoy no privileged epistemic status. In the context of the theory, they are treated as ordinary empirical hypotheses, to be accepted or rejected on the same basis as any other hypothesis. They are rejected if they come into conflict with any laws or theories which we are not willing to reject in their favour. They are retained if no such conflict arises, and no better (e.g. theoretically more fundamental) definitions are offered in their place.

Therefore, if there are any definitions which are immune from empirical refutation, they can only be ones which cannot come into conflict with any laws or theories which we should be unwilling to abandon on the ground that they do so conflict. The mere fact that some concept has been explicitly defined in a certain way does not confer upon the statement of this definition any immunity from refutation. That we *call* it a definition indicates, perhaps, something about how we have chosen to axiomatize our system. But it tells us nothing whatever about the epistemic status of the statement of this definition.

Now I do not wish to deny that there are definitions which are immune from empirical refutation. The legal definition of murder, for example, could hardly be refuted empirically. For 'murder' is not a term which occurs in any empirical laws or theories. So there can be no question of this definition being in conflict with any laws or theories which we should be unwilling to abandon. The possibility of such a conflict arising depends on whether the defined term occurs anywhere in the statement of laws or theories independently of the definition provided. If it does, then the possibility of a conflict of the kind which would lead us to reject the definition exists. If it doesn't, or at least so long as it doesn't, there is no possibility of such a conflict. It may be useful, therefore, to distinguish between empirical and non-empirical definitions. *Empirical definitions* are definitions of terms occurring in empirical laws or theories. *Non-empirical definitions* are definitions of terms which have no such empirical role. To illustrate: this definition is itself non-empirical.

Definitions in science are typically empirical. For, in science, there is little point in defining any term which is not needed to express any of our laws or theories. But if a term so defined is needed for this purpose, then there is always the possibility of a conflict of the kind we have described. There is always the possibility that, where such a conflict arises, we should prefer to accept the laws or theories rather than the definitions. So I want to say that empirical definitions are empirical claims. We can have good empirical reasons for accepting, modifying or rejecting them. I do not say that all definitions in science are like this. Sometimes a definition is no more than a convenient abbreviation – and such a definition is certainly non-empirical. But many definitions in science are more than this. They are offered as definitions of terms which already have wide currency in scientific literature in the belief that by defining them their meaning can be fixed. But in my view there is no such process as that of 'fixing meaning by explicit definition', at least where scientific concepts are involved. My understanding of what an *A* is *changes* as I learn more and more about *A*s. My concept of *A*-hood is *enriched* as a result of this learning, and what I mean by saying that something is an *A* depends on what I know or believe about *A*s. Therefore, so long as we continue to investigate, and to learn new things, *meaning cannot be fixed*. New information about the properties of *A*s *must* change my concept of *A*-hood.

We are thus left with the conclusion that if there is anything that is true just by definition or convention then it is either the statement of a non-empirical definition, or a logical consequence of such statements as these. The truth of anything else, whether or not it has been called a definition, is not just a matter of convention. But even this distinction depends on that between empirical and non-empirical definitions, which is itself fairly obscure. So, I think we might as well forget about it. It is unlikely to be of much value in analysing the truth claims that we make. The hope of the early positivists that we could distinguish clearly between the empirical and the conventional, and provide adequate analyses of the truth conditions of significant empirical claims, has now largely faded. The critique of the analytic–synthetic distinction has thus undermined the empirical–conventional distinction which the logical positivists needed for their analyses. The logical positivist programme has, therefore, collapsed.

4.4 SEMANTIC ANALYSIS

The programme of semantic analysis derives from Tarski's theory of truth (Tarski 1936), which is a sophisticated form of the correspondence theory. In the earlier Russellian theory, truth was supposed to be a relationship of correspondence between propositions and facts, and the elementary correspondence relationships were those which held between atomic propositions and atomic facts – these being the ultimate, mutually independent, constituents of reality. On Tarski's theory, truth is a relationship between words and things, i.e. a semantic relationship, but it is one which is to be analysed in terms of the two more primitive relationships of denotation and satisfaction. *Denotation* is that relationship which holds between names and the things they name. *Satisfaction* is the relationship between predicates and the things, or sequences of things, which satisfy them. They are *semantic* relationships in, *and only in*, the sense that they relate words to things. It is not a semantic question, in the sense that it can be answered just by considering what the terms involved mean whether a given thing, or sequence of things, satisfies a given predicate. In all standard cases this must be discovered empirically.

In the simplest kind of case, a sentence contains a name, or a sequence of names, and a predicate. Evidently, such a sentence is true iff the thing, or things, named exist and satisfy this predicate. Thus, 'Fa' must be true iff what 'a' denotes exists and satisfies 'F', i.e. iff Fa. In such a simple case, this is probably an adequate analysis of the correspondence relationship. But clearly it will not do as a general analysis. A theory of truth which applied only to the most elementary sentences of a language would not be acceptable as a general theory of truth. What is needed is a definition of 'truth' applicable to *all* of the sentences of the language which are true or false.

Tarski showed us how to provide such a definition for a language like first order predicate calculus, using only the primitive semantic concepts of denotation and satisfaction. Assuming that the primitive terms of this language denote only real objects, and that its predicates are satisfied, if at all, only by such objects, the truth or falsity of any sentence of the language can now be shown to depend on what real things, or sequences of such things, satisfy its primitive predicates. Consequently, if we had a language like this, we should have no difficulty in saying what would make its sentences true or false.

Tarski's theory of truth leads us naturally to ask this important question: can every truth be expressed in some language whose primitive terms denote only real entities, and whose primitive predicates are satisfied, if at all, only by such entities, or sequences of them? That is, *can every truth be expressed in a realistically interpretable extensional language?* The question is important, because if all truths can be expressed in such a language then truth is at least *extensionally* equivalent to a complex correspondence relationship. A sentence of such a language will be true iff it corresponds to reality in the manner specified by the Tarskian truth theory for this language. If, on the other hand, there are truths which cannot be expressed in such a language, then either the correspondence theory of truth must be wrong, or there are primitive word–thing relationships besides denotation and satisfaction which we can use to construct truth theories for more elaborate kinds of languages which are adequate for the purpose.

There are various ways in which formal languages can be defined, which have greater expressive power than the predicate calculus, and for which, nevertheless, a Tarskian truth theory can be provided. For example, we can define truth for a language with predicate modifiers by requiring that the extension of a modified predicate be included in that of the predicate unmodified. But this language is still one, the truth theory for which is Tarskian, in the sense that the primitive word–thing relationships required for the definition of truth in this language are just denotation and satisfaction. The question is whether there are any other primitive word–thing relationships which might be used to define a different kind of correspondence theory. If not, then the fate of the correspondence theory must depend on whether every truth can be expressed in a language for which a Tarskian truth theory can be provided, and whose terms and predicates can be interpreted realistically, i.e. as denoting or being satisfied only by real entities.

There are, to my knowledge, no other kinds of primitive word–thing relationships which might be used to define a satisfactory concept of correspondence. We can easily define languages which have terms that can be used to refer to properties and relationships in addition to those which designate individuals. Indeed, given the ontology I would defend, I should certainly want to have such a language to express formally what I believe to be true. When I say that something is red, I am attributing the property of redness to it; I am saying that it *possesses* this property. When I say that *a* is taller than *b*, I am saying that *a* stands in a certain relationship to *b*; I am asserting that this relationship holds between them. I see no reason to deny that properties and relationships exist. I would deny that they exist uninstantiated, but then I should also deny that objects exist unqualified. Neither objects nor properties, it seems to me, can exist without each other. Therefore, I see no future in trying to construe properties as sets of objects, or n-place relationships as sets of ordered n-tuples of objects. This seems to me as futile as trying to construe objects as bundles of properties and relationships. These categories of things are just not reducible to each other. Therefore, I have no metaphysical objection to quantifying over properties and relationships. They have as much claim to primary ontological status as the entities which possess them.

To construct a formal language which includes names of properties and relationships, as well as of individuals, we must introduce some primitive predicates which are not themselves to be construed as property or relationship names; for if they were, we should be led into an infinite regress. In particular, we must have predicates that we can use to ascribe properties and relationships to individuals. For we must be able to say what *has* what property, or what *bears* a given relationship *to* something. In the truth theory for *this* language, these predicates could only be extensionally defined, i.e. defined in terms of the primitive relationship of satisfaction. So the truth theory for this language would still be essentially Tarskian. The primitive relationships in terms of which truth is defined would still be just denotation and satisfaction.

I am persuaded that Tarskian languages can be defined to accommodate any ontology, i.e. that anything which we may believe to exist can be named and spoken about in some language for which a Tarskian truth theory can be given. If, for example, we believe in second order properties or relationships, such as those of bearing or being instantiated, it should not be too hard to construct a Tarskian language in which we could talk about them too. The requirements on Tarskian languages would appear to place no limits on ontology.

So the crucial question remains: can every truth be expressed in a realistically interpretable extensional language? If so, then the correspondence theory of truth is extensionally adequate. If not, then the correspondence theory had better be abandoned. For I see no prospect of defining a semantic concept of correspondence in any substantially different way, and if it has to remain undefined, or only partially defined, then the theory is either vacuous or inadequate.

The programme of semantic analysis is to show how any statement which we believe to be true or false can be expressed in a language for which an adequate (Tarskian) truth theory can be provided, i.e. *an extensional language*. It is, or should be, a requirement on the adequacy of any semantic analysis, not only that the language in which it is given be an extensional one, but also that the terms and predicates occurring in the analysis should be capable of being understood realistically, i.e. of denoting or being satisfied by real objects. Let us call this the *requirement of realism*. If the requirement of realism has not been met by some proposed analysis, then the truth or falsity of the statement being analysed cannot yet be understood in correspondence terms. An analysis of the analysandum would be needed.

4.5 MODAL REALISM

The programme of semantic analysis has often been pursued without much regard for the requirement of realism. Think of the 'possible worlds' analyses of modal and conditional propositions. Of course, there are some philosophers who think that these analyses *do* satisfy the requirement of realism. They believe in possible worlds. But there are many who do not think this, and who, accordingly, have sought to analyse propositions about possible worlds so that they can be realistically understood. There are also some who consider the question of the reality of possible worlds to be relatively unimportant. What interests them is what can be done with this kind of analysis by ringing the changes on accessibility and similarity relationships between possible worlds.

For our purposes, though, the requirement of realism cannot be ignored. For unless we can provide adequate semantic analyses, for example, of modal and conditional claims, compatibly with this requirement, Tarski's theory of truth cannot be philosophically satisfactory – however useful it might be for logic. It would not do as a general theory of truth because it could not be used to account for the truth of at least some of the claims we make.

The main trouble with possible worlds (other than the actual one) is that we can have no good reason to believe in them. First, there cannot be any evidence for the existence of other possible worlds of the kind that there is for things in the past. For the past leaves traces in the present, but other possible worlds can leave no traces in the actual world. Second, there can be no evidence for the existence of other possible worlds which is at all like that for the occurrence of future events. Present events can cause future ones, but what occurs in the actual world is supposed never to influence anything that happens in other possible worlds. Third, there can be no evidence for other possible worlds like that for the existence of what is topologically elsewhere; for these objects and events are causally related both to our past and to our future. The light cones surrounding them intersect with ours. But the light cones of events occurring in other possible worlds do not intersect with ours. Consequently, the hypothesis that there are other possible worlds is not a physical, causal hypothesis, which is needed to explain, or which can be inferred from, anything which actually happens. Therefore, there can be no good physical reason to believe in them. Yet possible worlds are supposed to be not mere abstract entities, like complex numbers or Hilbert spaces, but (usually, at least) physical realms which beings like us can occupy. So, from the point of view of a physical scientist, the hypothesis that there are other possible worlds is gratuitous.

There might indeed be other physical worlds which are inaccessible to us. And there could even be good reason for us to believe that this is so. For example, if white holes are discovered in our universe, and if, theoretically, a white hole in one universe is just a black hole in another, then we should have a scientific case for believing that other universes exist. But, by the nature of this case, we could never say anything about these other universes except that they are governed by similar physical laws to ours, and that black holes occur in them. However, those who believe in other possible worlds certainly do not do so for any such reasons as these. They claim that every world which we can consistently imagine or describe exists, and that this can be known *a priori*. The other universes which might exist through black holes would not even *count* as other possible worlds. For, if we became convinced of their existence we should say that they *actually* existed.

The point can be generalized. If, for *any* reason, we became convinced of the existence of a plurality of physical worlds, occupying different spatial and temporal dimensions from our own, then we should consider their existence to be actual. We should say that there actually are these other dimensions of space and time in which worlds, which may or may not be like our own, exist. So, for something to count as another possible world, we must be convinced that it does not *actually* exist. Therefore, we cannot think of possible, but non-actual, worlds as ones occupying different spatial and temporal dimensions from our own. For we must also be convinced that these extra spatial and temporal dimensions do not actually exist. Thus, there appears to be an incoherence in the concept of a merely possible world. On the one hand, we are invited to think of such worlds as physical realms, more or less like our own, but occupying different spatial and temporal dimensions. On the other hand, if they are *merely* possible, there can be no actual spatial or temporal dimensions which they occupy. The spatial and temporal dimensions in which they exist cannot actually exist. For then, the supposed other world would be just a part, albeit an inaccessible part, of the actual world.

The argument to this conclusion goes through, whatever the nature of the argument for the reality of other physical realms. It may be an argument drawn from cosmological theories, or a transcendental argument. If it is any good as an argument, and it convinces us that other physical realms really do exist, then we should be convinced that they actually exist. A good argument for the existence of physical realms other than our own from which we happen to be physically isolated would have to be a good argument that they actually exist. But if they actually exist, then their existence would not be merely possible. These other physical realms would have to be considered to be parts, albeit isolated parts, of the actual world. Therefore, modal, or 'possible worlds', realism would appear to be defensible only in the absence of a good and convincing argument for it.

The reply to this would be that the point I am making is just a verbal one. No doubt, if we were convinced modal realists, we should, like anyone else, be inclined to say that *actually* there are all these other worlds which are inaccessible to us, because 'actually' is normally used in the sense of 'as a matter of fact' or 'truly'. In normal usage 'actually' is not an indexical, and cannot be equated with 'in the causally accessible parts of the world in which we live'. But, to defend their position, the modal realists have only to say that, for them, 'actually' *does* mean this. It *is* an indexical of this kind. The causally inaccessible realms are thus real but not actual.

But now a new difficulty arises. Suppose that according to our best cosmological theory there is another world which is just like this one, but it is a world of antimatter rather than matter. Suppose, moreover, that, according to the theory, it occupies different spatial and temporal dimensions from ours, and is totally inaccessible to us causally. Then, if by 'actually' we mean 'in the causally accessible parts of the world in which we live', we cannot say that anything in this antimatter realm actually exists. We must say that its existence is merely possible. But of course, if we accepted the cosmological theory, this is just what we should *not* think. We should think that this other world had just the same status as ours. And certainly we should want to distinguish it from any merely possible world. So if we accepted the realists' definition of what is actual we may be forced to make a threefold distinction. For it seems that we should now distinguish between what is actual (our world), what is real, but not actual (the antimatter world) and what is merely possible.

To deal with this difficulty modal realists have just two options. They can either move to include the antimatter world in the actual world by amending their definition of actuality, or they can defend the view that the antimatter world is just a possible world not to be distinguished in any way from other possible worlds. Taking the first of these options we might say that the actual world includes not only those physical realms which are accessible to us but any which we have good physical reasons to believe in. But why *physical* reasons? Surely a good reason is a good reason whether or not it derives from physical theory. It would appear to be quite arbitrary to pick out any particular *kind of reason* for the purpose of distinguishing between what is actual and what is not. If the qualification is dropped, however, then realists about possible worlds are forced into a hopeless dilemma. For they must now say either that they have no good reason to believe in the existence of the merely possible worlds, or that all possible worlds are parts of the actual world. And either way their position is untenable. On the other hand, if the modal realist takes the second of the two options, and maintains that the antimatter world is just another possible world, and is not to be distinguished ontologically from any other merely possible worlds, then he or she is effectively saying to the cosmologists who have laboured to produce the theory of the antimatter world, and convince the scientific community of its truth, that they have just wasted their time. For the modal realist could have told them *in advance* of any theory construction that this world existed. Indeed, if they are to be believed, they have a *much better* reason to believe that the antimatter world exists than any scientist (who has never studied semantics) could possibly have. For they claim to be able to show, not only that it does exist, but that it does so *necessarily*.

Those who believe in the reality of other possible worlds do so mainly because they think that all other accounts of the nature of possible worlds are unsatisfactory. It is almost common ground that possible worlds do, in some sense, exist. The only question, in the minds of most philosophers, is what sorts of things they are. They have to believe that possible worlds exist, because the semantic analyses of modals and conditionals require them. Every strong conditional, and every possibility claim, is, according to these analyses, an existential claim concerning possible worlds. And since at least some of these claims are true, the required possible worlds must somehow exist. So, nearly everyone is committed to the existence of possible worlds. The question for most philosophers is how this existential commitment is to be understood.

Nominalists about possible worlds are those who hope to be able to construe them as maximally consistent sets of sentences. There is, however, no agreed solution to how to do this, and several arguments that it cannot be done at all. First, and most obviously, since the actual world is not a set of sentences, it is not a maximally consistent set either, and so, in the nominalist sense, it is not a possible world. But it is surely a requirement on any theory of possible worlds that the actual world should turn out to be a possible one. So any nominalist reconstruction of possible worlds will require a nominalist reconstruction of the actual world. Second, a maximally consistent set of sentences must be a set of sentences of some language. So the sets of possible worlds must be relativized to languages. For, in general, the set of maximally consistent sets of sentences in one language is different from those in another. But our talk about possible worlds is not relativized to languages. So to interpret what we say about possible worlds nominalistically, we should have to specify the language with respect to which a possible world is a maximally consistent set of sentences, and nobody knows how to do this. Third, a language adequate to describe all possible worlds, relative to which a possible world could be defined, would have to have names for all possible particulars. For surely there must be possible worlds which have more things in them than this one. But relative to such a powerful language, a complete and true description of the actual world would not be a maximally consistent set, and so not a possible world. Fourth, if possible worlds are construed as maximally consistent sets of sentences, then we cannot use possible worlds theory to give an account of consistency. We cannot say that a set of sentences is consistent, iff they are all true in some possible world, because this must be equivalent to saying that it is consistent iff it is a subset of a *maximally* consistent set of sentences.

For these and other more technical reasons many philosophers prefer modal realism to nominalism, despite the former's intuitive implausibility. Of these reasons, the first is perhaps the main one. Whatever kind of thing a possible world may be, the actual world must be something of this kind. If possible worlds are rationally completed belief systems, then the actual world must be such a system of beliefs. If they are maximally consistent sets of sentences, then the actual world must be such a set of sentences – presumably the set of all the true ones. The realist account of possible worlds thus seems to be the only one that is compatible with a physicalist ontology for the actual world. The only other account that has any plausibility is that the world is the totality of all true *propositions*; that it is, as Wittgenstein maintained, everything that is the case. To accept this view of reality, however, is to accept that the world is an abstract entity, which is surely incompatible with a physicalist ontology.

Therefore, the argument goes, it is modal realism or the bush. We really do not have a choice. David Lewis has argued very effectively for modal realism in this way (Lewis 1986). Yet modal realism is really no better than the 'ersatz possible worlds' theories he is attacking. It does not have the same defects, but quite apart from the difficulties already raised, it is incompatible with a causal theory of knowledge, and hence with the view of man which science requires us to take. To suppose that we can have knowledge of the existence of other possible worlds with which we cannot causally interact, but which may nevertheless be physical worlds just like our own world is to postulate a capacity for knowledge which is incompatible with a scientific view of man. It is another case, like the reduction of properties to sets, of allowing our ontology to be determined by the requirements of logical theory rather than science.

4.6   RATIONAL BELIEF SYSTEMS

If we take science seriously as our guide to ontology, we cannot accept modal realism. That is, we must accept that worlds which are merely possible do not exist. Therefore, to give an adequate account of the truth conditions of modals and conditionals we must eschew possible worlds. But this evidently cannot be done. No one knows how to specify adequate truth conditions for modals or conditionals without quantifying over possible worlds – and surely not for lack of wit or effort. Given the enormous amount of work that has been put into the semantic analysis of modals and conditionals by the best minds in the business, it must now be reasonable to conclude that the required analyses do not exist. So that, if there are any true modals or conditionals, their truth cannot be shown to depend just on what the terms or predicates occurring in them denote or are satisfied by. But surely there are *some* true modals and conditionals. For some of the most fundamental laws of nature are properly expressed as impossibility claims (the second law of thermodynamics, the Nernst heat theorem, and the principle that light is a first signal), and most of our other laws of nature are universal conditionals. Therefore, it is reasonable to suppose that there are *some* true statements which cannot be given adequate semantic analyses that can be understood realistically. Therefore, the semantic theory of truth, for all its initial promise, must finally be abandoned.

Fortunately, we can reject the semantic theory of truth, and hence the programme of semantic analysis, without abandoning 'possible worlds' analyses. For the beautiful results which can be obtained using 'possible worlds' models can be achieved using the theory of rational belief systems, and the usefulness of these models for achieving these results can be explained. So anyone who is devoted to 'possible worlds' analyses can continue to use them with a clear conscience. But no one should pretend that merely possible worlds, or their analogues in the theory of rational belief systems, really exist.

In the theory of rational belief systems the analogue of a possible world is a rationally completed belief system. Such a belief system is a special kind of rational belief system. Now, a rational belief system is a *theoretical ideal*. It has a role in the theory of rationality which, for example, is parallel to that of a perfectly reversible heat engine in thermodynamics. There are no such belief systems or heat engines in nature. Nevertheless, it is useful to theorize about them, and use them as models of the ordinary physical systems whose structure or behaviour we wish to explain. Completed rational belief systems have a special role in providing such explanations. The explanations they provide, however, are *model theoretic* ones. So there is no need to suppose that these model systems or their elements exist. Their role is only to provide *frameworks* for causal questions, not answers to them. If the efficiency of a heat engine is less than the theoretical ideal, then the question is why this is so. And *this is* a causal question. Likewise, if a belief system is, or appears not, to be rational according to the theory, then a causal explanation of *this* fact is required.

The theory of rational belief systems takes a non-Tarskian approach to the analysis of languages, and to the foundations of logic. Instead of defining languages, in the Tarskian manner, by specifying (recursively in a metalanguage) truth conditions for their sentences, languages are defined in the manner of other abstract model theoretical entities in science. To define a Euclidean space, we must specify the laws (axioms) which relate the elements (points etc.) in such a space. To define an inertial system we must state the laws governing the behaviour of mass points in such a system. Likewise, to define a language it is sufficient for the purposes of logic to state the laws governing the structure of a rational belief system on this language (as it may be lexically or syntactically defined).

To do this, it turns out that we do not need to be able to say what would make any sentence of the language true or false. It is enough if we can say under what conditions a belief expressible in the language can occur in a rational belief system on it. Consequently, to understand a sentence of the language sufficiently for the purposes of logic, we need only to know its *acceptability conditions*. We do not have to be able to say what would make it true or false. We do not have to know its truth conditions. Indeed, the theory is compatible with a radically subjectivist theory of truth. In this respect it is like subjective probability theory. An objective calculus of probabilities can be founded on a subjectivist theory of probability by founding the logic of probability claims in a theory of rationality. Likewise, an objective calculus of truth claims can be founded on a subjectivist theory of truth by developing a suitable theory of rationality to deal with such claims. The theory of rational belief systems shows how this can be done.

I have no wish to defend a subjectivist theory of truth. And certainly, my theory of rational belief systems does not commit me to it. For the theory of rational belief systems commits me to no particular theory of truth. All it does is determine a logic of truth claims. If one could develop an adequate correspondence theory of truth, for example, then this could be accepted compatibly with the theory. Something similar is the case with subjectivist foundations of probability theory. If adequate truth conditions for probability claims could be specified, then there is no reason why they should not be accepted as part of a theory of truth for a language in which such claims can be made. But the rationality of a system of beliefs, which includes beliefs about what is probable or improbable, could still be explained on the theory of rationality which subjectivists have developed.

What I am committed to, though, is a programme of analysis in terms of acceptability conditions. Classically, an argument is valid iff there is no possible world in which its premises are true and its conclusion false. So to understand any proposition sufficiently for all of the purposes of logic we must know its truth conditions for all possible worlds. In the theory of rational belief systems, an argument is valid iff there is no rational belief system in which its premises are accepted (with the truth, falsity or probability evaluations assigned to them) and its conclusion is rejected (with the truth, falsity or probability evaluation assigned to it). Therefore, to understand any proposition sufficiently for all of the purposes of logic we must know under what conditions it can or cannot occur in a rational system of beliefs, i.e. we must know its acceptability conditions.

4.7   THE FAILURE OF ANALYSIS

The programme of analysis which derives from Tarski's semantic theory of truth is in serious trouble. For successful analyses have not been offered for any of the kinds of statements which we initially listed as being problematic. *Formally* satisfactory semantics do exist for some of these kinds of statements. But in no case can the semantics be interpreted realistically in accordance with the requirements of the correspondence theory of truth. We still don't know what makes it true that A causes B, or that A is probable, given B, or that A explains B. We do not have realistically interpretable semantics for conditionals, or for nomic necessity or possibility claims. The logicist and nominalist programmes for mathematics are defunct or in difficulties. We cannot yet define a Tarskian language adequate for expressing the basic laws or theories of science. Statements expressing propositional attitudes have also proved to be hard to analyse. And so we could go on. Of course, I do not expect everyone to agree with all of these claims concerning the failure of analysis. But I think that even the most optimistic semantic theorists will agree that there is still a lot of work to be done on most, if not all, of these problems.

Some of these problems could, quite reasonably, be considered too difficult to be solved at this stage in the development of the programme. But surely we should expect some progress, at least, in our understanding of the truth conditions of the connective 'if'. For this connective is basic to our understanding of all hypothetical reasoning, and has been the object of intensive study. Moreover, it ought to be a relatively simple one to understand. For it is one which a child must learn to use quite early in life. And, if to understand a statement sufficiently for logical purposes is to know its truth conditions, then those truth conditions should not be too hard to grasp. Any child who has learned to reason hypothetically should have at least an intuitive understanding of them. So, I see the problem of conditionals as being quite crucial for the programme of analysis, and hence for the correspondence theory of truth. If we cannot provide realistically interpretable semantics for such statements, then either conditionals are not genuinely true or false, or the correspondence theory of truth is false. For I see no prospect of developing a more powerful correspondence theory (than Tarski's) on which their truth or falsity could be explained.

Now there are some philosophers who have argued that conditionals are not genuine truth claims. Ryle, for example, defended the view that a conditional is really just an *inference licence* (Ryle 1950). The conditional 'if p then q' licenses the inference from 'p' to 'q'. As such, however, it says nothing that is true or false. And if we *say* it is true, then we can mean only that it is reliable – or something of the sort. We are not judging it as a statement *about* the world, but as a *mode of reasoning* concerning it. A similar view of conditionals was defended by J. L. Mackie. As he put it, a conditional is a '*condensed argument*' (Mackie 1962, p. 68). What he had in mind, I think, is this: to say that 'if p then q' is true is just to endorse the argument: 'p, so q', without commitment to either 'p' or 'q'. It is to endorse a mode of reasoning rather than any claim about the world – although, no doubt, some claims about reality must be accepted if this endorsement is to be rational. For example, it would not be rational to endorse this argument form if one believed that p, but not q.

In fact, I have sympathy with these analyses. For basically, they are analyses in terms of acceptability rather than truth conditions – and my own account of the acceptability conditions for conditionals is not so very different from theirs. Moreover, the 'condensed argument' theory explains a number of important properties of conditionals. For example, it explains why 'if p then q' and 'if p then $\sim q$' seem so evidently to be contraries in normal cases. For one could hardly endorse the argument from 'p' to 'q' and also the argument from 'p' to '$\sim q$' unless one thought 'p' to be self-contradictory. The theory also explains why the probabilities of conditionals are normally the same as the corresponding conditional probabilities. For 'probably, if p, then q' must be regarded as a 'condensation', or, as I should prefer to say, 'abstract endorsement', of the argument 'p, so probably q'. So naturally, the probability of a conditional will normally be given by the probability of its consequent given its antecedent.

However, I do not see how a correspondence theorist can draw much comfort from these analyses. First, the conditional 'If John lives in Melbourne, then he lives in Victoria', has as much right to be accounted true as any other truth claim. And if the theory requires us to say that it is not true, or true in some sense other than that in which its antecedent or consequent might be, then so much the worse for the theory. Second, since many of the most fundamental scientific laws have the form of universal conditionals, the theory requires us to say that these laws are neither true nor false. We can endorse the arguments which they license, but we cannot accept them as true statements about the world. Consequently, anyone who accepts the 'condensed argument' theory of conditionals must accept a form of instrumentalism in science. Third, if conditionals are not true or false in the ordinary sense, then in what sense might, say, the conjunction of an ordinarily true statement with a true conditional be considered to be true? Presumably, it is not true either in the correspondence sense or in the sense appropriate to conditionals. Fourth, if we have to operate with a different concept of truth for conditionals, shouldn't we also need a different concept of validity? A disjunctive syllogism might be valid in the sense that there is no possible world in which its premisses are true and its conclusion false. But *modus ponens* cannot be valid in this sense because of the conditional premiss. An argument of this form could only be valid in the sense that it would be irrational for anyone to accept its premisses and reject its conclusion. But the irrationality of this could not be explained in the usual way. Fifth, the theory does nothing to explain why we find it so natural to say some conditionals are true. On the face of it, endorsing an argument is quite different from saying that the things named in some statement have the properties attributed to them. How could we ever have confused the two? Sixth, if conditionals are just statements endorsing arguments, then in what sense can conditionals be said to be true? Obviously, not in any sense explicable on a correspondence theory of truth. Is the concept of truth appropriate to conditionals, perhaps, a coherence concept – such as ultimate rational acceptability? If so, are we to operate with a sort of mixture of coherence and correspondence concepts? The theories we are considering do not tell us how we are to understand the truth of conditionals.

For reasons like these, most philosophers have rejected mixed theories of truth. Correspondence theorists have sought to define realistically interpretable extensional languages in which conditionals can be expressed, and their properties explained. Coherence theorists have tried to articulate a concept of truth which will be applicable not only to conditionals, but also to the kinds of statements which seem evidently to be true in the correspondence sense. Neither has so far been successful.

Most philosophers distinguish between what they call 'indicative' and 'subjunctive' conditionals. The distinction is supposed to correspond fairly closely to a grammatical distinction of mood. An indicative conditional is (roughly) what is asserted when we say that something *is* or *will be* the case if some antecedent condition *is* fulfilled, and a subjunctive conditional is what is asserted when we say what *would be* or *would have been* the case if this condition *were to be* or *had been* fulfilled. There are reasons to think that this distinction is superficial, as V. H. Dudman has argued convincingly (Dudman 1983), and I should prefer to operate with his distinction between hypotheticals and true conditionals which cuts across the indicative–subjunctive distinction.[2] But most of the recent literature on conditionals makes use of the distinction between indicative and subjunctive conditionals, and we cannot avoid doing the same here.

For indicative conditionals, correspondence theorists accept a simple truth functional analysis: 'If p then q' is true iff 'p' is false or 'q' is true. For subjunctive conditionals they accept a much more complex analysis: 'If p then q' is true iff there is a possible world in which 'p' is true and 'q' is true which is nearer to the actual world than any world in which 'p' is true and 'q' is false.

The reason for making the distinction is that a simple truth functional analysis, like that accepted for indicative conditionals, is clearly not acceptable for subjunctive conditionals. For, in many cases, the antecedent conditions specified in such conditionals are not fulfilled (and known not to be so); but clearly this does not make all these conditionals true. Moreover, the change of mood, from indicative to subjunctive, appears to make a lot of difference to the sense of what is said. Compare, for example,

(1) If Oswald did not kill Kennedy, someone else did.

with

(2) If Oswald had not killed Kennedy, someone else would have.

The second statement is not just the first asserted after the event in the belief that Oswald did kill Kennedy, but an altogether different assertion.

These reasons for distinguishing between indicative and subjunctive conditionals are not convincing, however. First, we are no more inclined to consider an indicative conditional which *turns out* to have a false antecedent to be true, just on that account, than we are to consider a conditional, which is *already known* to have a false antecedent (and which we may express in the subjunctive mood) to be true just because of this. The falsity of the antecedent is not, in either case, considered a sufficient condition for the truth of the conditional. Second, *there is* an indicative conditional which has just the same sense as the subjunctive, 'If Oswald had not killed Kennedy, someone else would have'. It is the present/future tense

(3) If Oswald does not kill Kennedy, someone else will.

The subjunctive conditional (2) is just *this* indicative conditional asserted retrospectively in the belief that Oswald did, in fact, kill Kennedy. As it would ordinarily be understood, the past tense indicative conditional, (1), admits of evidence of a kind which is *irrelevant* to the acceptability of (2) or (3), viz. the evidence that Kennedy was assassinated by Oswald. The conditional prediction, (3), however, is *not* subsequently vindicated by the discovery that its antecedent is false. So what has to be explained is the difference between the two *indicative* conditionals, (1) and (3). The past tense indicative conditional, (1), appears to be the odd man out, not the subjunctive conditional, (2).

The reason why the sense of

(1) If Oswald did not kill Kennedy, someone else did

is different from that of

(2) If Oswald had not killed Kennedy, someone else would have

and

(3) If Oswald does not kill Kennedy, someone else will

is that (1) is naturally interpreted as a remark concerning the *identity* of Kennedy's killer. (1), so interpreted, is equivalent to

(4) If Kennedy's killer was not Oswald, then he was someone else.

So the subjunctive conditional which corresponds to (1) is

(5) If Kennedy's killer had not been Oswald, then he would have to have been someone else.

But (1) clearly *does* bear another interpretation. Imagine the following conversation:

(A) If Oswald did not kill Kennedy, then he is probably still alive somewhere.
(B) I don't think so. They would have killed him by now. You can be sure that *if Oswald did not kill Kennedy then someone else did*.

In the context of this conversation the indicative conditional, (1), has precisely the same sense as the subjunctive conditional, (2). So the difference in sense between (1), as ordinarily interpreted, and (2), is not due to the difference of mood. For the same difference exists between (1), as ordinarily interpreted, and (1), as it occurs in our imagined conversation.

The supposition that Oswald did not kill Kennedy is in fact open to several different interpretations, and the identity of any conditional having this antecedent depends on what interpretation is put on it. Which interpretation we adopt will normally depend on what we take to be at issue. In (1), standardly understood, what is at issue is the identity of Kennedy's killer. In (1), as it occurs in the context of the above conversation, and also in (2) and (3), what is at issue is what happens (happened, would have happened) if Oswald misses (missed, had missed). In the following context,

(6) If Oswald did not kill Kennedy, then he killed *someone very much like him*,

what is at issue is something different again. In this case, it is who was killed by Oswald. So my conclusion is this: the reason why the conditional normally expressed by (1) is so different from that expressed by (2) is that what is at issue is assumed to be different. If we imagine a situation, as in the above conversation, in which the issue can be assumed to be the same, then no important difference remains between the indicative and the subjunctive.

For these reasons, I am unimpressed by the usual arguments for distinguishing between indicative and subjunctive conditionals. On the other hand, there are good reasons for not distinguishing between them, except in those cases where the special implications of tense or mood are relevant. First, the acceptability of a conditional is not usually affected by the discovery that its antecedent is false. If we should judge an indicative conditional to be true or false or probable to some degree before the discovery, we should judge the corresponding subjunctive conditional to be true or false or probable to the same degree after the discovery. The Kennedy–Oswald case shows that we may have to exercise some care in constructing the *corresponding* subjunctive. But usually, a simple change of mood does the trick. Second, the unified theory of conditionals (Ellis 1978) explains simply how we may come to understand subjunctive conditionals. In the first place, we learn to make conditional predictions, and to express them as indicative conditionals in the present-future tense. We later learn to express them knowing or believing that their antecedents have not been fulfilled – using the subjunctive mood. There is, therefore, on the unified theory of conditionals, no great problem about how we come to understand them. The implications of the change of mood are no more difficult to grasp than of a change of tense.[3] On the standard theory of conditionals, however, subjunctives are quite different from indicatives. Their truth conditions are different. Indicatives are claims about the actual world, subjunctives are claims about the existence of other possible worlds related somehow to this one. On the usual theory it is a mystery how we could ever have learned to understand them. Third, the unified theory of conditionals explains the close epistemic relationship which holds between corresponding indicative and subjunctive conditionals. The usual theory does not. Fourth, the logic of conditionals is the same, whether they are indicatives or subjunctives. The validity of an argument involving indicative conditionals is not affected if we subsequently learn that the antecedents of some or all of these conditionals are false, and would, as a result, now express the argument as one involving subjunctive conditionals. Nor is the validity of an argument involving subjunctive conditionals affected if we come to believe that the reasons we had for using the subjunctive mood in expressing the premisses or the conclusion of the argument are unsound, and would now, as a result, use the indicative mood instead of the subjunctive.

I conclude, therefore, that the problem of conditionals is that of subjunctives. If realistically interpretable truth conditions for subjunctive conditionals cannot be provided, then they cannot be provided for indicative conditionals either. Therefore, in general, conditionals do not have truth values which are explicable on the correspondence theory of truth. But at least some conditionals do have truth values. Therefore, the correspondence theory of truth is false. It is not an extensionally adequate analysis of our concept of truth.

4.8 THE TRUTH ABOUT CORRESPONDENCE

Despite the failure of the programme of analysis, there is, as I said at the beginning of the chapter, something obviously right about the correspondence theory of truth. For it does give an account of what it is for some simple categorical statements to be true. For example, if I say that the cat is on the mat, then clearly what I say is true iff the cat and the mat both exist, and the cat stands in the appropriate relationship to the mat. I am not, of course, denying this. For this is precisely the claim that the statement makes, and I cannot see why anyone would wish to deny it. Yet those who do not accept a correspondence theory of truth are often accused of denying such obvious things, and opponents of the correspondence theory do sometimes get a bad press as a result. At any rate, this is not what I am doing. What I am saying is that there are many kinds of statements which we count as true or false which cannot be analysed in any such simple, straightforward way. They cannot be analysed truth functionally, and they cannot be expressed in an extensional language for which realistically interpretable semantics can be given. The programme of analysis has failed, and hence the theory of truth which gives rise to it cannot possibly be the whole truth about truth.

The reason why the statement of truth conditions for 'The cat is on the mat' is innocuous is that it is likely to be acceptable whatever one's theory of truth. The analysans differs from the analysandum only in that it spells out the ontological implications of the analysandum. But since nearly everyone thinks that cats and mats exist, and that cats can stand to mats in the relation of 'being on', nearly everyone could be expected to agree that the analysis is correct. If one grants the ontological implications of the claim, then one must accept that what would make it true that the cat is on the mat is precisely that these conditions are fulfilled. Hence, one cannot rationally accept that the statement is true, although the conditions are not fulfilled, or that the statement is not true, but the conditions are fulfilled. For correspondence, redundancy, coherence and pragmatic theorists alike, the analysis is acceptable, because *everyone* could agree that the analysans is logically equivalent to the analysandum. One's theory of truth need not come into it.[4]

What correspondence theorists believe (at least, those who would consider themselves to be scientific realists), which other theorists about truth do not believe, is that anything which we properly consider to be true can in principle be expressed in some language for which a formally correct, materially adequate and scientifically realistic truth theory can be defined; so that, in general, truth may be considered to be a complex semantic relationship, depending on the two primitive semantic relations of designation and satisfaction. But this, as we have seen, is untenable. The point is not the familiar one (made by Tarski in Tarski 1936) that truth cannot be defined satisfactorily for natural languages. It is, rather, that languages for which truth can be defined satisfactorily from the point of view of a scientific realist are not adequate, even in principle, for the purposes of science. This is what the failure of the programme of analysis shows.

Nevertheless, the correspondence theory of truth may be right about what truth *is*. That is, it may provide us with what Huw Price would call a correct *analysis* of truth.[5] For sentences may be the bearers of truth as most correspondence theorists believe, and true sentences may, as Tarski thought, be true in virtue of the fact that they designate actual states of affairs. Thus, Tarski may yet be right in thinking that truth is a relationship of designation holding between a sentence and a state of affairs, even if this relationship cannot be satisfactorily defined, in the way that Tarski hoped, for languages adequate for science.

5

The Bearers of Truth

Despite the failure of the programme of analysis to explain how any but the most elementary truths can correspond to reality, most scientific realists still accept some form of correspondence theory of truth. Indeed, they think that to be scientific realists they must accept such a theory, because their realism requires it. As realists, rather than idealists, they think they must believe in a mind-independent reality, and that they can do so only if they have a correspondence theory of truth.

However, I think this is wrong on at least three counts. First, the question whether there is a mind-independent reality is one of metaphysics, not specifically of truth theory, and one can believe in such a reality on many theories of truth, e.g. on a redundancy theory. Second, biological realism, which is part of scientific realism, implies that at least our *knowledge* of reality depends on how we process information, and therefore on the sorts of beings we are. Therefore, a theory of truth which makes truth relative to our nature as cognitive or rational agents seems not to be incompatible with scientific realism. On the contrary, scientific realism suggests that this is precisely the kind of theory we should be looking for. Third, if holism, rather than foundationalism, is true in epistemology, as the failure of the programme of analysis suggests, then, apart from some simple beliefs which, arguably, may correspond to reality fairly directly, the only kinds of semantic correspondence relationships which could exist must also be holistic, i.e. between whole systems of beliefs and the world. Therefore, if truth is a correspondence relationship, it must primarily be one which holds between belief systems and the world, and individual beliefs can be true only in the sense that they belong to true belief systems.

In this chapter, I will argue that no form of correspondence theory of truth, with the possible exception of a kind of holistic correspondence theory, is compatible with scientific realism. I shall begin by outlining the main argument to be presented.

5.1 THE FUNDAMENTAL INCOMPATIBILITY OF REALISM WITH CORRESPONDENCE THEORIES OF TRUTH

For scientific realists who want to hold a correspondence theory of truth, there is, firstly, a problem about *the bearers of truth*. These must exist, and therefore be the sorts of things which scientific realists can believe in. But since truths are timeless, if truth is a relationship between a bearer of truth and reality, then a bearer of truth cannot change in this relationship. It must, therefore, be either a Platonic entity, like an eternal sentence or proposition, a temporally circumscribed one, like an event of utterance, or a non-temporal entity, like a state of mind or belief. For a scientific realist, a bearer of truth cannot be a Platonic entity, because no such things exist. It cannot be an event of utterance, unless the identity of this event depends on the state of mind or belief of the utterer or audience. So, a bearer of truth could be an event of utterance only in a Pickwickian sense. For a scientific realist, therefore, the bearers of truth must be psychological states of some kind. Most plausibly, they are thoughts or beliefs.

Many scientific realists find this conclusion hard to accept, even though they hold a physicalist theory of mind, and so, presumably, have no ontological grounds for objecting to thoughts or beliefs as truth bearers. The reasons why they are reluctant to accept this conclusion are various, but the main ones are probably these:

(1) there could be at most only finitely many truths, because the number of thoughts or beliefs is finite;
(2) whatever the bearers of truth may be, they must also be the relata of logical relationships; therefore, if one accepts that the bearers of truth are thoughts or beliefs, one is committed to psychologism in logic, because logical relationships must be relationships between psychological states;

(3) it is inconsistent with the semantic theory to accept that the bearers of truth are psychological states, because the semantic theory requires linguistic items as truth bearers.

The conclusion that the bearers of truth are thoughts or beliefs thus has far-reaching implications in philosophy. The reluctance of many scientific realists to accept what appears to be a clear consequence of their philosophical position is therefore understandable.

The implication that there are at most finitely many truths is not very serious, and I imagine that if this were the only objection to a realist correspondence theory of truth, it would quickly be dismissed. If a truth is a true belief, then of course there are only finitely many of them. Scientific realism may imply belief in a mind-independent reality, but it does not imply belief in an infinite set of mind-independent truth bearers. The commitment to a psychologistic theory of logic is more serious, since it is contrary to the whole tradition of scientific philosophy, from Frege and Russell onwards. However, adequate foundations for all standard logical systems can be provided on a psychologistic theory (Ellis 1979), and most of the objections to psychologism in logic stem from a misunderstanding of the nature of scientific theory. There is no reason whatever why scientific realists should not accept that the laws of logic are laws of thought; on the contrary, this is precisely what they should believe.

The apparent conflict between scientific realism and the semantic theory of truth is also troublesome to many philosophers. Realism requires realistic truth bearers; the semantic theory seems to require that they be the eternal sentences of some ideal language or languages. Consequently, some philosophers have gone to considerable lengths to marry these two ideas, and show that the bearers of truth may, after all, be linguistic entities of some kind. It has been held, for example, that a truth bearer is a sentence of a language for a person at a time. But, in the end, identifying a truth bearer requires reference, either explicit or implicit, to what someone (or people in general) may intend or understand by something, and therefore, directly or indirectly, to what someone may think or believe. The semantic theory of truth therefore appears to be incompatible with scientific realism.

The semantic theory of truth might yet be saved if believing could be shown to be a relationship between believers and the right kinds of linguistic *objects of belief*; for then these objects of belief could be identified as the proper bearers of truth. But the relational theory of belief is also incompatible with scientific realism. The idea that there are languages which have sentences which have meanings which we can grasp, and that having grasped them, we can form attitudes of belief or disbelief towards them, sounds more like Popperian 'third world' philosophy, or even Platonic psychology, than scientific realism. A realist should say that there are just people interacting with each other verbally, causing some modifications in their belief and thought structures. There are no other kinds of things involved in the interaction.

If the semantic theory of truth is incompatible with scientific realism, then what remains? One possibility is that truth is a correspondence relationship between belief states and the world. For it is quite likely that we have certain inbuilt ways of mapping our surroundings, and it may well be thought that our true beliefs are just those which map them correctly. There are, however, several difficulties with this suggestion. First, while it is plausible that such a theory could account for the truth of some simple beliefs of ours, it is most unlikely to be generally applicable. No one believes that our beliefs about what is possible, what is necessary, what would happen if certain conditions were realized, what $2 + 2$ equals, and so on, all map reality in the same kind of way – even if they are all true. So the theory depends on the viability of a programme of analysis designed to show how and why some of our beliefs are true, even though they are not true in the sense in which some of our most basic beliefs may be. The failure of similar programmes of analysis in the past does not hold out much hope for this one.

However, there is a much more fundamental objection to any realist correspondence theory of truth. It is that truth cannot be identified with any physical property or relationship, unless it is one that has intrinsic epistemic value; and no such property or relationship could have the value it needs. If we know that a brain state possesses the property, or stands in the relationship, then we know that the belief it represents is true; so it must be accepted, whatever the evidence for or against it may otherwise be. Thus, the value of this property or relationship must decisively outweigh all other epistemic values. But I cannot believe that such a property or relationship exists. It would be more credible if it somehow incorporated all of our epistemic values, so that whatever is known to have the property, or satisfy the relationship, is necessarily what we ought rationally to believe. But then, we should no longer be dealing with a correspondence theory of truth. Such a theory would be an evaluative theory of the kind I shall later propose, and truth would be roughly what it is right to believe after taking all relevant evidence into account. I conclude, therefore, that scientific realism is incompatible with any form of the correspondence theory of truth.

To establish this conclusion, I shall present the detailed case in more or less the same order as the summary, beginning with a discussion of the bearers of truth. This leads naturally into a discussion of the objects of belief (for the bearers of truth and the objects of belief are generally assumed to be the same), and then into a more general discussion of the propositional attitudes. It is concluded that there are no proposition-like objects which could serve as the objects of the propositional attitudes (and hence as the objects of belief) nor any which could be the bearers of truth. In particular, there are no linguistic entities which could serve in these various roles. Relational theories of the propositional attitudes, including belief, must therefore be rejected, along with any form of the correspondence theory of truth which postulates the existence of propositional objects of this kind. The question then shifts to whether there is any viable form of the correspondence theory of truth in which our beliefs or thoughts are themselves regarded as the truth bearers. It is argued that there is not, and the general case that truth could not be a physical property or relationship is then elaborated.

5.2 TRUTH BEARERS

When I speak of 'a bearer of truth', I mean whatever is non-derivatively true or false. It is what the predicates 'true' and 'false' attach to most directly, i.e. not in virtue of their attachment to anything else. Thus, if a belief is true or false in virtue of the truth or falsity of what is believed, and this is something that exists independently of its being believed, then it is not the belief itself that is the bearer of truth, but what is believed, i.e. 'the object' of the belief. On the other hand, if the truth or falsity of a sentence derives from that of the belief or thought it expresses, or would be understood as expressing, then it is the belief or thought that is the bearer of truth, not the sentence. It is not always easy to tell which way the dependency runs, for there are no straightforward tests to decide the issue. In the end, it depends on what theory gives the best account of the relationships between the various candidates for the role of truth bearers. The best theory will have to be one that is ontologically acceptable. The question is then: what account of the bearers of truth can scientific realists accept compatibly with their ontology?

We require of any bearer of truth that it be a relatum of logical relationships. Since truth is supposed to be a timeless property, and logical relationships to hold timelessly between their relata, a bearer of truth must be an unchanging entity. It is, presumably, either: (1) an eternal entity, like a Platonic proposition, (2) an event, like an event of utterance, (3) a state, like a state of belief, or (4) a universal, like a sentence-type. Moreover, if a bearer of truth is required also to be an object of belief, i.e. the sort of thing that can be believed or disbelieved, then a bearer of truth must be something that is more or less publicly accessible – at least to the members of some language community. For it must be possible for the speakers of the language to agree by believing the same, or sufficiently similar, things, and to disagree by believing logically incompatible ones.

A bearer of truth must be something that is true or false without reference to time, place or circumstances. Thus, it cannot be the case that there is anything that is true at one time, but false at another, or true here, but not there, or true in one set of circumstances, but not in some other. It is true that we sometimes use phrases identifying times, places or circumstances in conjunction with the truth predicate, e.g. when we say such things as 'It is true today that . . .', but if we wish to identify the truth bearers for the classical concept of truth, these qualifications of the truth predicate must be seen as ways of identifying different truth bearers. Nor can a bearer of truth be anything that is true for one person, but false for another, or true on one interpretation, but not true on some other interpretation. For if any such qualification is needed, it shows that the item is not in itself a truth bearer, but something that is true or false in virtue of something else, e.g. how it is understood, or what interpretation is placed upon it. The truth or falsity of such an item is therefore derivative. The truth bearers, whatever they are, must have their truth values absolutely. For that is the nature of the concept of truth we are dealing with. A truth bearer cannot be something which is true on one description, but not true on some other description. If there is need for such a description, this is enough to show that the object of reference is not a truth bearer.

For scientific realists, the bearers of truth cannot be Platonic propositions, because there are no such things in their ontologies. This is a pity, because they are otherwise ideally suited to the role. Nor can they be sentence tokens, since these may endure, while the language, or the world around them changes; so that what is true today may not be true tomorrow. They cannot be sentence types, because sentences of the same type may be used to say different things on different occasions, or even, when one is being deliberately ambiguous, to say two or more different things on the same occasion. Nor can the bearers of truth be utterances, because the same utterance may mean different things to different people, and so be true on one understanding, and false on another. Moreover, the speaker may have intended the utterance to be understood differently by different people. Nevertheless, it is generally considered that the bearers of truth, and hence the objects of belief and the relata of logical relationships, must be linguistic entities of some kind; and most philosophers, including most scientific realists, suppose that sentences of some kind, or under some description, must be the bearers of truth.

Perhaps the main reason why philosophers have fixed on sentences as bearers of truth is that Tarski's truth theory, which seems to be the best theory available, requires them to be. According to the theory, truth is a relationship between the sentences of a language, on the one hand, and the world, on the other, which holds iff certain satisfaction conditions are met. Now there is no denying the convenience of making sentences the truth bearers when developing semantics for formal languages. But what is useful for formal semantics may not tell us much about what is really true or false. In mechanics, it is useful to represent massive objects as dimensionless points. But it does not follow that what is really massive is a dimensionless point. Likewise, if the bearers of truth were beliefs or thoughts, we might, nevertheless, choose to represent them, for theoretical purposes, by sentences of nicely regimented formal languages. Therefore, to discover what the truth bearers are, it is no good looking to see what is done in formal semantics. We must look to the natural languages in which our beliefs about the world are actually expressed; and if sentences, or certain kinds of sentences, are the bearers of truth, we should be able to show this by reference to the genuine sentences of these languages.

Another reason why many philosophers may prefer to have linguistic entities as the truth bearers is that they or their tokens are at least in the public domain. If the bearers of truth are not linguistic entities, the only alternative would appear to be that they are psychological states of some kind, e.g. beliefs or thoughts. But to many philosophers, including many scientific realists, this alternative does not bear thinking about. For at least a generation, around the turn of the century, scientifically minded philosophers struggled to liberate philosophy from the dominating influence of introspective psychology. Above all, they strove to be objective in their iquiries, as they imagined physical scientists were. Accordingly, they regarded as real, or at any rate as worthy of scientific study, only what was publicly observable, and had no use for subjective or introspective reports. They did not want to know what the observer thought or believed or felt. They were interested only in those observations which they supposed were intersubjectively testable, and they had no scientific interest in anything which could not be observed in this way.

This attitude of mind is clearly reflected in the writings of the logical positivists. It is to be found also in the works of Frege and Popper. Indeed it was the almost universal attitude of those philosophers who took their methodological cues from science to be anti-psychologistic. Many psychologists were themselves influenced by this flight from introspective psychology, and schools of behavioural psychology, which prided themselves on their scientific approach to their subject matter, began to flourish. As a result, 'psychologism' became a dirty word, and psychologistic theories were neither proposed nor defended again until quite recently. It is not surprising, therefore, that many scientific realists should be reluctant to accept that the bearers of truth are thoughts or beliefs. They are reluctant to do so because the bearers of truth must also be the relata of logical relationships; and if these should be thoughts or beliefs, then they must be the primary subject matter of logic, and the laws of logic must refer to them. Thus, the old psychologistic thesis that the laws of logic are laws of thought would be revived.

The arguments against psychologism in logic were never very strong. They depended in part on a misconception of the nature of scientific laws and theories, and in part on the very anti-psychologism they sought to provide grounds for. The main arguments were these:

(1) If the laws of logic were laws of thought, then we should no more be able to think illogically than to violate any other law of nature.
(2) The laws of logic are not descriptive, but prescriptive; they do not tell us how we actually think, but how we ought to think.
(3) Logic is the most exact and least dubitable of all of the sciences; psychology is one of the least exact and most dubitable. It is absurd, therefore, to suggest that logic may be a branch of psychology.

The first of these arguments reflects a certain naivety about laws of nature. In particular, it depends on the assumption that any instance of illogical thought would be in violation of the laws of thought. Not at all! If the laws of thought are like other laws of nature, then they will be laws governing the behaviour of certain kinds of idealized systems; they will not be generalizations about how people actually think. In this case, the idealized systems will presumably be ideally rational beings. Therefore, any instance of illogical thought is direct evidence only that the person involved is not ideally rational. Of course, this raises the question why the person thought illogically on this occasion; and this is a question of a kind we cannot afford to leave unanswered too often if we wish to defend our ideal of rationality. But there is nothing in the case so far to distinguish laws of thought from other laws of nature. Compare them, for example, with the ideal gas laws, or with those of black body radiation.

In general, theory construction in science nearly always involves abstraction from the imperfections of ordinary systems, and the enormously complex and variable forces which act upon them, to say how the unblemished systems would behave in an idealized environment free from the influence of all but the most tractable of these forces. And we should not expect our theories of rationality to be any different in this regard. The ways in which we think and reason are undoubtedly influenced by many non-rational forces, including, perhaps, some which are genetically encoded. We are subject to various social and moral pressures to believe things, and we sometimes have strong personal interests in doing so. Added to this we all have obsessions, or belief fixations, which prevent us from drawing appropriate inferences; moreover bad habits of reasoning have sometimes been reinforced, and sound ones extinguished. Therefore, to construct an adequate theory of rationality, we should have to abstract from this complex of forces to consider how an ideally rational being would think, and we should not expect the laws of thought for such a being to apply directly to ordinary people.

The second objection to psychologism in logic, viz. that the laws of logic are normative, is more interesting. For it is clear that there is a distinction between regulative ideals which generate normative principles, and theoretical ideals which normally do not. An ideal of social organization may give rise to a system of normative rules, and thus serve as a regulative ideal, but an ideal gas is not a regulative ideal, and the gas laws are not normative. Hence, to explain the normative force of the laws of logic, we require that our ideal of rationality should be a normative one. Therefore, even if there are laws of thought of the kind we have been discussing so far, there is a further question as to whether we should think as they say. However, the distinction between theoretical and regulative ideals is not as clear as it seems initially to be when the theoretical ideals are idealized people (e.g. ideally rational agents). For, given that people have desires and aspirations, there is no reason why a theoretical ideal should not also be a regulative ideal. If you aspire to be ideally rational, then the theory tells you how to proceed. There is, of course, a further question as to why anyone should aspire to be ideally rational; but it would be extraordinary if the ideal of rationality which most naturally appeals to us as a regulative ideal had not been effective in generating and structuring our belief systems. Therefore, we should expect the theoretical ideal of rationality required to *explain* the structure and dynamics of our belief systems to coincide with the ideal of rationality which *appeals* to us most fundamentally as a regulative ideal.

The third argument against psychologism has been included as much to give the flavour of the early dispute as to make a serious point. For there is no doubt that psychologism in logic was ridiculed in this kind of way. This can be seen, however, to be a rather cheap debating point. There is very good reason to suppose that human beings have been rigorously selected over tens of thousands of generations for their abilities to think; so it should not be at all surprising to find that certain thought patterns have become genetically encoded, including their basic logical structure.

Let us, therefore, approach the question of what the truth bearers are without prejudice in favour of linguistic entities, or against psychological ones. If we do, we shall see there is good reason for thinking that a truth bearer is not a linguistic entity at all, but a psychological one, such as a thought or belief. So logic does, after all, appear to be a branch of psychology, viz. the formal theory of human rationality.

The first argument that the truth bearers are psychological states is from the *indeterminatenesss of meaning*. I suppose it will be agreed that what I believe when I believe that an A is a B depends on my concepts of A-hood and B-hood. However, there is no epistemologically significant way of distinguishing between those beliefs concerning As and Bs which determine my concepts of A-hood and B-hood, and those which are merely about As and Bs. For example, is it part of my concept of a whale that it is a mammal, or is this just something I happen to believe about whales? Any answer I gave to this question would be more or less arbitrary, for there are plausible arguments leading to opposite conclusions, and no decisive arguments either way. Therefore, no epistemologically valid distinction can be drawn between what is true in virtue of meaning, and what is true as a matter of fact; that is, the analytic–synthetic distinction cannot be sustained. This being so, there is no way of determining precisely what a sentence of a language means. But whether a sentence is true depends on what it means. Therefore, if a *sentence* can be said to be true, it can only be so in a derivative sense – when, for example, it would be considered to be true *whatever it might reasonably be taken to mean*. Therefore, sentences as such cannot be the bearers of truth – only sentences under some interpretation, or as understood in a certain way.

We might, perhaps, be able to escape this difficulty by making the bearers of truth the sentences of formal languages, in which the meanings of all sentences are determined precisely by appropriate truth theories. For the purposes of formal semantics, this is certainly a sound strategy. But it is not much good to anyone looking for a concept of truth which is compatible with scientific realism and applicable to the judgements we make about the world in the languages we speak. The sentences of formal languages are highly idealized, abstract entities which scientific realists can no more believe in than they can in Platonic propositions. Scientific realists have enough trouble in understanding what the sentences of ordinary languages could be. In any case, the sentences of these abstract, formal languages are not the bearers of the scientific truths upon which scientific realists rely so heavily for their ontologies.

The second argument for psychological entities as truth bearers is from *context-dependence*. All natural languages contain demonstratives, token reflexives and ambiguous terms, and sentences involving such terms say different things in different contexts of utterance. But their truth is dependent on what they say. So these sentences, at least, cannot be bearers of truth. Nevertheless, when I say, for example, 'He is not here', I may well be saying something that is true or false, depending on the context, or the occasion. Therefore, it cannot be the sentence I utter which is true or false – it must be something else. It might, perhaps, be some eternal, non-ambiguous sentence which says what this sentence says on the occasion of its utterance, or it might be the utterance itself. It cannot in general be an eternal sentence, however, because often there is no eternal sentence which says the same thing as a given occasion sentence. If I say, 'I am now at home', then what I say is true. But there is no eternal sentence which says just this. The sentence 'Brian Ellis was at his home at the time he wrote "I am now at home" for the first time in the first draft of his chapter "The Bearers of Truth"' does not say this, because it says both more and less than the sentence in question, and it could be false, even though the other is true, and conversely.

Perhaps it is the utterance itself which is the bearer of truth. No, because utterances may occur in multiple contexts. My friend, Mr Alfred Duplex, has two telephones on his desk. Two women he knows, both called 'Mary', rang him simultaneously wanting to know where their respective husbands were. Alfred picked up both receivers and said: 'Hello Mary, I think he has gone to the bank. Sorry I cannot stop and talk to you now. I hope you find him.' And then he hung up. Alfred intended one Mary to understand that her husband had gone fishing, and the other to understand that her husband was at the trading bank. In this case, there was only one utterance, or sequence of utterances, but there are at least two, and possibly as many as four different truth bearers. There are the two things Alfred intended the women to believe, and there are the two things the women understood Alfred to be saying – and conceivably they are all different. Therefore, if utterances are the bearers of truth, a bearer could be both true and false.

To meet this objection it might be supposed that a bearer of truth is *an utterance in context*, or an ordered pair consisting of an utterance and a context of utterance. This proposal would allow one to say that, since the utterance of Mr Duplex occurred in the contexts of two different conversations, there are really two truth bearers here, not one. But surely we need more than two contexts, because there are more than two things which are true or false involved. There are the two things Mr Duplex intended to say to the two Marys, and there are the two things the women understood him to say.

If one did not have a strong aversion to psychological entities as truth bearers, the conclusion would surely be that this is what they are. But most philosophers are evidently reluctant to draw this conclusion. I suspect this is because they do not wish to be committed to psychologism, which is what the conclusion must lead to; so they seek to retain at least the trappings of the theory that the bearers of truth are really sentences. Thus we have Donald Davidson's suggestion that a truth bearer is an ordered triple consisting of a sentence, a person, and a time.[1] On this theory, what the person understands by the sentence does not seem to be involved. But clearly it is. For suppose the person does not understand the sentence, because, for example, he or she does not speak the language. Does the truth bearer in this case lack a truth value? Suppose it is understood as being ambiguous. Might it then have two truth values? If a truth bearer is simply an ordered triple of this kind, then it will exist whether or not there is any understanding, and it should be the same, since the ordered triple is the same, however it might be understood. I do not see that there is any way to escape the conclusion that it is what a person uses or understands a sentence to say that is true or false, not the sentence itself.

5.3 OBJECTS OF BELIEF

It is generally thought that the bearers of truth are also the objects of belief. The objects of belief are supposed to be those things to which we may stand in a relationship of believing. It is thus assumed, by those who speak of 'objects of belief', that believing is a relationship between a believer and a thing believed; they hold what is called 'a relational theory of belief'. The objects of belief are normally taken to be mind-independent entities, i.e. things which exist independently of their being believed, or indeed, even of their being entertained or considered. The usual candidates for the role of objects of belief are the same as those for the role of truth bearers, viz. such linguistic or quasi-linguistic items as sentences, propositions, and the like. The objects of belief are, of course, also assumed to be the relata of logical relationships.

Many of the arguments against sentences, propositions, and

other abstract particulars as truth bearers also count against such things being the objects of belief. For if these things do not exist, or are not the bearers of truth, then they are not the objects of belief. But there are other arguments against them as well. First, a scientific realist is committed to a causal theory of knowledge. By the causal theory of knowledge, we cannot have contingent knowledge of anything that is not part of the causal network. Consequently, if the bearers of truth were abstract, mind-independent entities of the kinds postulated, they could not impinge upon us, and so we could not know anything about them other than what is ultimately true or false by definition. Hence, contingent knowledge would be impossible. The objects of belief cannot, therefore, be abstract particulars.

Second, the relational theory of belief, which we require to make sense of the idea of an object of belief, is untenable. To show this, it is enough to show that there are beliefs, which undoubtedly have truth values, but which cannot be construed as relationships between believers and objects of belief. Conceivably, someone may wish to argue that this would only show that there are two kinds of beliefs, viz. those which have objects and those which do not. But anyone who holds this must also allow that there are two kinds of truth bearers, viz. the objects of belief, where these exist, and otherwise the beliefs themselves. However, a partially relational theory of belief like this is not satisfactory. For if we have two kinds of truth bearers, then we shall also need two kinds of truth, one for the abstract particulars which are the objects of belief, and one for the neurophysiological states which are the beliefs themselves. It is hard to imagine what these two very different kinds of things could possibly have in common. The only way to restore coherence to the theory of truth would be to make our beliefs uniformly the truth bearers. But in that case, we should have no need for any objects of belief, since their *raison d'être*, which was to externalize the truth bearers, would have disappeared.

There is a general argument that the objects of belief, if they exist, are not always propositional, and hence cannot always be identified with any abstractly considered linguistic constructions. For, as David Lewis has shown (Lewis 1979), we must recognize the existence of beliefs *de se* as well as *de dicto*. Roger Appleby's belief that he is David Hume, for example, is a belief *de se*. His is not the belief that Roger Appleby is David Hume. Nobody believes that, not even Roger Appleby. Nor is it the belief that David Hume is David Hume. Everyone believes that. What Roger believes, he is alone in believing. His belief is just that *he* is David Hume. It is an example of what Lewis calls *de se* belief; and there is no proposition which can be said to be its object. There is no way of construing it as a belief *de dicto*.

Lewis' analysis of such *de se* beliefs is given in terms of *property self-ascription*. In the above case, for example, Roger Appleby is ascribing to himself the property of being David Hume. He holds that all beliefs *de se* can be similarly construed. But more interestingly, he holds that *every* belief can be construed in this way; *de se* beliefs cannot be analysed as beliefs *de dicto*, but all *de dicto* beliefs can be interpreted as beliefs *de se*. For, anyone who believes that *p* can be thought to be ascribing to himself the property of inhabiting a *p* world. Therefore, according to Lewis, believing is property self-ascription. To believe something is not to stand in a relationship of believing to an object of belief. It is just to ascribe (or at least to be disposed to ascribe) a certain property to oneself.

Now I do not agree with Lewis about the general point, because I do not want to admit all these properties into my ontology. First, it is no property of me that I inhabit a world in which quasars exist, because there are no other worlds which I could have inhabited. There is only the one world and it is one in which quasars exist. Hence, if it is a property of me that I live in such a world, then it is one which I have simply in virtue of existing. However, I am reluctant to count anything as a property if a thing can have it simply in virtue of existing. For such a property must either be possessed by absolutely everything, irrespective of ontological category, or by nothing at all. If atoms, forces, spatial relationships and properties exist, then they all exist in a world in which quasars exist. Even the property of existing in a world in which quasars exist would exist in a world in which quasars exist, if it were indeed a property. It is, of course, a contingent fact that quasars exist. That is not being denied. It is also a contingent fact that I exist. The point is that, given these facts, it follows that each exists in a world in which the other exists. But neither, I should say, has the property of existing in such a world. Co-existence is no more a property than existence is.

Nevertheless, I think that Lewis' analysis of *de se* beliefs is correct; and if it is correct, then it follows that not all beliefs have propositional objects of the kind required as truth bearers. This is enough to show that believing is not in general a relationship between a believer and an external, propositional object of belief. At least *de se* beliefs are not like this. But in general *de se* beliefs are true or false. So, either they are themselves the truth bearers, or the truth bearers for them are states of the individuals who hold them. If we must say that the bearers of these truths are the beliefs themselves, then we might as well abandon the relational theory of belief altogether. The theory is in enough trouble without having its scope restricted to *de dicto* beliefs. Also, with such a restriction we should be forced to place a similar restriction on our theory of truth. For it is hard to see how a belief, which is a state of the central nervous system, could be true or false in the same sense as a propositional object of belief. My hunch is that philosophers would have abandoned the relational theory of belief long ago if they had not been so worried that the alternative was too psychologistic.

There is, however, an argument in favour of a relational theory of belief which much be treated with respect, viz. that unless one has such a theory one cannot give a unified and coherent account of the propositional attitudes. This must now be considered.

5.4 THE PROPOSITIONAL ATTITUDES

The propositional attitudes include believing, intending, hoping, fearing, knowing, remembering, and so on. To express a propositional attitude it is usual to say something of the form 'I X that p', where 'X' is the appropriate case of the attitude verb, and 'p' is a declarative sentence. The standard view is that by saying such a thing one is expressing an attitude that one may have in virtue of standing in a certain relationship to a proposition, or proposition-like object. The different attitudes reflect different relationships with these propositional objects; the declarative sentences which may be substituted for 'p' either are or express the various objects of these relationships.

This theory is neat and coherent, and is reflected in the language we use; it is the natural theory to hold. But everything we have said about linguistic and quasi-linguistic truth bearers as objects of belief applies with as much force to the supposed objects of these other propositional attitudes. What then could the common objects of these various propositional attitudes be?

It has been suggested by Jerry Fodor that the objects of belief, and the other propositional attitudes, are mental representations – internal sentences written in the language of thought. His idea is that if one believes that *p* then one is standing in a certain relation to a mental representation; if one hopes that *p* then one is in a different relationship to this representation. The relationship in question is said to be a disposition to calculate with the mental representation in some way. Fodor puts it this way:

> ... having a propositional attitude is being in some computational relation to an internal representation. The intended claim is that the sequence of events that causally determines the mental state of an organism will be described as a sequence of steps in a derivation if it is describable in the vocabulary of psychology at all. More exactly: Mental states are relations between organisms and internal representations, and causally interrelated mental states succeed one another according to computational principles which apply formally *to the representations*. (Fodor 1975, p. 198).

He also says that:

> ... for each of the (typically infinitely many) propositional attitudes that an organism can entertain, there exist an internal representation and a relation such that being in that relation to that representation is nomologically necessary and sufficient for (or nomologically identical to) having the propositional attitude.(Fodor 1975, p. 198)

Thus, according to Fodor, the propositional attitudes are to be distinguished as different ways of computing with mental representations. His idea is that believing, hoping, fearing, intending, supposing, and so on, are to be thought of as different ways of operating with the common objects of these attitudes. Thus, if I believe that p, then I am disposed to compute belief-wise with some mental representation r of which 'p' is a verbal expression. If I hope that p, then I am disposed to compute hope-wise with r. If I intend that p, then I am disposed to compute intention-wise with r. If I suppose that p, then I am disposed to compute suppositionally with r.

Fodor views the brain as an instrument like a computer. It is endowed with a certain hardware, and must have some kind of initial programming. It has, or somehow acquires, a capacity to make mental representations of reality. These mental representations are thought of as sentences written in a computer language which the brain understands. The propositional attitudes are then supposed to be like sets of computational instructions. If a brain has a propositional attitude to a sentence written in the language of its thought, it is disposed to compute with this sentence in accordance with the appropriate set of instructions. The display of the propositional attitude, including what the individual says or thinks, is then just the outcome of the brain operating with these instructions on the sentence in question.

Fodor's theory of propositional attitudes is an outline of a genuine causal explanatory theory of mind, and mental representations have the status of theoretical entities within it. Moreover, the theory is clearly compatible with a physicalist ontology. So a form of the relational theory of belief may yet be tenable for a scientific realist. If Fodor is right, then perhaps believing is a relationship between a believer and a mental representation. Leaving aside belief for the time being, I am inclined to think that Fodor is basically right in his analysis of the propositional attitudes, but that the theory he offers is not really a relational theory in the sense I have defined it. My hoping (fearing, intending, supposing etc.) that p may be nomologically equivalent to my standing in some computational relation to a mental representation. But the relationship in question is *not* one of hope (fear, intention, supposition etc.). What I hope is that p *is true*. My attitude is not to any supposed neutral object of the propositional attitudes. My hope is that p will turn out to be the case. Now in fact Fodor does not explicitly identify the propositional attitudes with the computational relations he supposes to be necessary and sufficient for them. What he identifies is having the hope that p with *being in* a kind of computational relationship with something. So the argument does not show that Fodor is wrong in what he says. What it shows is that having the hope that p cannot be construed as being in the relationship *of hope* to the mental representation which 'p' expresses. A woman who hopes that p might, in fact, be in some kind of relationship to a mental representation r. Her being in this relation to r might even be nomologically necessary and sufficient for her hoping that p. But r is not the object of her hope. It cannot literally be *what* she hopes when she hopes that p.

Fodor admits, quite rightly, that his theory of the propositional attitudes does not apply to all of them. It does not apply, for example, to knowing, remembering or seeing. My knowing that p cannot be just a matter of my standing in a certain computational relation to a mental representation, because whether I know that p depends on whether 'p' is true. Similarly with remembering and seeing. I cannot remember that p unless I once knew that p, and I cannot see that the cat is on the mat unless the cat is on the mat. But his theory does, or at least is intended to, apply to the *pure* propositional attitudes, i.e. those we can have independently of whether their objects are true.

The pure propositional attitudes include hoping, desiring, intending and believing. If Fodor's theory applies at all, it must surely apply to these. However, these propositional attitudes can all be *satisfied* in some way by events or states of affairs. My hopes can be *fulfilled*, my intentions *carried out*, my desires *satisfied*, and my beliefs *true*. And whether they are satisfied or not does not depend on what the computational programme may be. It depends only on what occurs or exists. Thus, the following condition appears to hold generally of these attitudes:

G: If x has the propositional attitude A that p,
   then x has an A which will be satisfied iff p.

In particular, if x hopes that p, then x has a hope which will be fulfilled iff p; if x desires that p, then x has a desire which will be satisfied iff p; if x intends to do y, then x has an intention which will be carried out iff x does y; and if x believes that p, then x has a belief which will be true iff p. Consequently, the identity of the propositional attitude A that p must depend on its satisfaction conditions. The identity of a hope, a belief, a desire or an intention must depend on what in the world would satisfy it. Therefore, the propositional attitudes cannot be characterized *purely internally* – so something important seems to be left out in Fodor's account.

On Fodor's theory, the propositional attitude A that p is a computational relationship between an organism and a mental representation. But there is nothing in Fodor's theory about the satisfaction conditions for such computational relationships, and it is hard to see how they could be introduced into his theory without destroying its purity. I think Fodor wants to say that to have a particular belief, desire, intention or whatever *is* to be in a particular mental state, which can be characterized independently of anything else that might exist or occur. But this cannot be right. To ascribe a particular belief, desire, intention or hope to someone is to imply that they have an attitude of a kind which will be satisfied by certain *external* states of affairs or happenings. It cannot be just to say that they are disposed to compute with something in a certain kind of way. There may in fact be some common mental representation r with which I am disposed to compute when I hope, believe, desire or intend that p, but what these attitudes have in common is really that they have the same satisfaction conditions, and the postulate that there is a common mental representation involved does not fully explain this fact.

So, I suppose my main worry about Fodor's theory is that it does not adequately account for what similarly directed propositional attitudes most obviously have in common, viz. the same satisfaction conditions. The hypothesis that the hope, the belief, the desire and the intention that p are similar, in that they are directed towards the same internal representation, does not fully explain why these various attitudes have the same (presumably external) satisfaction conditions. But this is surely just what we should expect any adequate theory of the propositional attitudes to do. Therefore, Fodor's theory is not adequate as a theory of the propositional attitudes – at least, not as it stands. However, the thesis I want to advance here does not really depend on whether

Fodor is right. If he is, and there are mental representations which are, in some sense, the objects of belief, then these are *not* mind-independent things. They are psychological states of some kind. And even if we should describe these states as 'sentences written in the language of thought', we do not turn them into publicly accessible linguistic entities as opposed to private psychological ones. They are linguistic only in the sense that our brains compute with them, and so bear a certain analogy to sentences written in a computer programme. But they are not sentences which can be inscribed anywhere other than in our heads. So they are not objects of belief in the ordinary sense. They fail the test of public accessibility.

Now it is required that the objects of belief, if there be any, should also be the bearers of truth and the relata of logical relationships. Therefore, there seems to be no escaping the conclusion, drawn earlier, that the bearers of truth are psychological states, and that the primary subject matter of logic is psychological.

In reaching this conclusion I have allowed that there may be objects of belief of the kind that Fodor postulates. I am sceptical about Fodor's theory on a number of counts. First, I don't think that the postulation of common objects of the propositional attitudes fully explains what they most obviously have in common, viz. the same satisfaction conditions. Second, the propositional attitude of believing seems to be more basic than the others. A being incapable of understanding what it would be for the belief that p to be true would appear to be incapable of having any of the other propositional attitudes to p. But a being could have the belief that p without understanding what it would be for the hope, fear or desire that p to be fulfilled. Fodor's theory offers no account of this asymmetry. Finally, Fodor's theory is essentially a dualist one. It is not, of course, dualist in the ontological sense. It is dualist only in the sense that it retains the language and categories of ontological dualism. He speaks as though people may operate with their mental states as one might operate with a string of symbols written on paper, performing certain computations. But I am profoundly sceptical of this analogy. I think that this dualistic mode of speaking is just a relic of an outmoded theory, and has no place in a scientific theory of mind. I am therefore of the opinion that there is no satisfactory relational theory of belief – that believing is not a relationship between a believer and an object of belief.

5.5 BELIEFS AS TRUTH BEARERS

I assume that the only alternative to a relational theory of belief is a property theory according to which a belief is not a relationship between a believer and a thing believed, but is a property or state of mind. On a relational theory, we express beliefs by saying things which somehow indicate what the objects of our beliefs are. We name or express the entities to which we stand in the appropriate relationship of believing. On a property theory, however, the verbal expression of a belief does not point to an object of belief, it *displays* one's belief, much as crossing oneself displays one's piety. When I say that *p*, I show you *how* I believe, rather than *what* I believe.

If one adopts a property theory of belief, then the only possible truth bearers are the beliefs themselves. But beliefs are presumably states of mind. Therefore, if truth is a relationship between a truth bearer and reality, the first term in this relationship must be a state of mind. For any scientific realist, a state of mind is a state of the central nervous system. Therefore, if truth is a relationship, it must be one between a state of the central nervous system and reality. Third, if truth is such a relationship, then it is plausible to suppose that it is some kind of mapping relationship, and that when we know a great deal more about the neurophysiology of belief, we might reasonably expect to discover what this relationship is. If there is a unique mapping relationship $\emptyset$ in virtue of which a belief B is true, then presumably we should be able to determine whether a given belief is true by showing that it bears this relationship $\emptyset$ to reality.

The properties or states of mind which are our beliefs cannot, of course, be simple properties. If I believe that some particular thing is red, then I must, in some sense, have that thing and the property of redness in mind, and be classifying it as having that property. Just what this amounts to I am not yet in a position to say, and, if Fodor is right, then no one will be until we know a great deal more about how our brains work. So I cannot, as yet, fully articulate a property theory of belief. Nevertheless, I am hopeful that a scientifically acceptable theory of what it is for someone to have something in mind, and to think that it has a certain property, can be given.

Note that it is not a theory of *reference* that is required here, but a theory about how our beliefs are related to the things or properties they are about. Reference is another matter; for referring is something we do in the process of communicating with each other. I may, for example, have the belief that a particular thing is red. In order to communicate this belief to you, I have somehow to focus your attention on the thing I have in mind. To do this, I may have to use a number of *referential focusing expressions*, which I could only use if I had sufficiently many other beliefs about the thing in question. Thus, I may have to say: 'The biggest Jonathon apple in the bright green basket is red.' But what I say, when I say this, is much more than the belief I intend to communicate, and the belief I have to express to convey what I have in mind could well be false, though what I have in mind is true. My belief is just that *that* is red, where 'that' refers to what I have in mind.

Let me just assume that a satisfactory theory of the relationship between our beliefs and what they are about can be developed, and go on to consider some of the consequences of adopting a property theory of belief. First, the adoption of a property theory introduces a whole new perspective. For now we are required to say:

(a) that there are no objects of belief,
(b) that if there are any truth bearers, then they are the beliefs themselves, and
(c) that beliefs are the relata of logical relationships.

We are thus forced into a psychologistic conception of logic, and, if we wish to retain a correspondence theory, we must accept a psycho-physicalist conception of truth. I have argued at length elsewhere (Ellis 1979) that a psychologistic conception of logic is viable. Let us here concentrate on the theory of truth.

There are some immediate consequences of adopting this position which most scientific realists will find disturbing (although, I think, they shouldn't). First, since there is at most a finite number of beliefs, there is at most a finite number of truths (or true beliefs). Second, since the number of beliefs varies from time to time, we must suppose that the number of truths (i.e. true beliefs) also varies. Third, while beliefs cannot change in truth value, they may, nevertheless, cease to exist: true beliefs may also come into being. Therefore, there may be truths which existed yesterday which do not exist today, and truths which do not exist today which will exist tomorrow. Fourth, while there may be things we do not know about, or properties we are ignorant of, there cannot be any truths apart from what people know or believe. If truth is a relationship between belief states and reality, and a truth is a true belief, then there cannot be any truths which exist independently of beliefs. I think that most philosophers, including most scientific realists, will find these conclusions unpalatable. But, if one considers a truth to be a true belief, and truth to be a property of beliefs, I do not see any way of avoiding them.

The reason I think scientific realists should be willing to accept these conclusions is that they are compatible with all of their beliefs *qua* scientific realists. They must reject the idea of there being a kind of Platonic heaven of truths which are there, so to speak, waiting to be discovered, and reinterpret some of the things they want to say. But the changes they must make do not affect their ontology. If there were no beliefs, then of course there would be no truths, but the world would contain the same stars, planets, streams, mountains and subatomic particles, and would be governed by the same laws. No scientific realist can accept that the existence of such things, or of their properties, is in any way dependent on what anyone may believe. Therefore, scientific realists should believe that if there were no truths the world would be much the same – it would just be a world in which there were no true beliefs.

Many philosophers are persuaded by a number of 'ordinary language' arguments of the existence of truths which are independent of our beliefs. Indeed, it is said to be just commonsense that there are such things, and, if my reasoning leads me to the opposite conclusion, then either my physicalist premises are false, or my reasoning is unsound. I normally do not put much store by such arguments, particularly if there is reason to think (as there is in this case) that our ways of thinking about things, and the linguistic expressions we use, reflect the very philosophical biases I am arguing against. Nevertheless, such arguments for the independent existence of truths and falsehoods are important just because they are so influential, and I shall shortly consider some of them in detail. But let me return to the main line of argument.

If beliefs are truth bearers, and truth is a relationship of correspondence with reality, and beliefs are states of our central nervous systems, then the truth relationship must be one between states of our central nervous systems and reality. It is presumably some kind of mapping relationship. Let us call it ø. Then we must say that a belief B is true iff B bears ø to reality. So far, so good. Any scientific realist should, as first sight, be delighted with this conclusion. However, on closer inspection, it appears to be not so good.

First, it is highly implausible that all of our true beliefs map reality in the same kind of way. It has some plausibility if we limit our attention to simple attributions of properties to things. But our beliefs are formed into highly complex integrated systems, and it loses all plausibility if we have to suppose that all of our true beliefs bear just the same kind of relationship to reality. What kind of map of reality is my belief that probably p? How does the true belief that it is logically possible that p map reality? And what about my true belief that if this piece of ice had been out in the sun for half an hour it would have melted? If the correspondence theory of truth is to retain any plausibility, the truth of these more complicated beliefs must somehow be shown to be dependent on that of more elementary ones. And this, as we have seen, has been the project on which logical empiricists have been engaged, without much success, since the thirties.

Second, and more importantly, it is demonstrable that truth is not a physical relationship. For if it were, then the belief that it is *true* that bananas are yellow would be quite distinct from the belief that bananas are yellow. The first is the belief that the (as yet unidentified) state of mind or brain which constitutes believing that bananas are yellow bears the (as yet unidentified) relationship ø to reality. The second is a belief about the properties of bananas. Now it is clear that these two beliefs are not logically equivalent. There might be no such relationship ø. It is also clear that they are not epistemically equivalent. An epistemic justification for the second belief is by no means an epistemic justification for the first. They may indeed be materially equivalent. But what we have to explain is not a contingent equivalence. For, any epistemic justification for the belief that p is *necessarily* a justification for the belief that it is true that p, and conversely. But this cannot be explained on the assumption that truth is a physical relationship of correspondence.

Further to this point, suppose that we have identified some physical relationship ø which we suppose all and only true beliefs to bear to reality. Suppose, moreover, that neuroanatomy and physiology have developed to the point where we can study people's heads, identify the beliefs they contain, and decide which stand in this relationship to reality. Now, either we have to establish in the ordinary non-physiological way that 'p' is true *in order to* establish that the belief that p bears ø to reality, or we don't. If we do, then that is the end of the matter. The belief is true however it might be related to reality. If we don't, then the fact that the belief bears ø to reality is just some further evidence that we must take into account in evaluating the belief as true or false. For, let us suppose that the belief that p, which we had previously thought, on good evidence, to be false, turns out to be true by this criterion. Would it, now, not be quite rational for me to say that although it is true that p, I don't believe it. Certainly, the discovery that a particular belief bears ø to reality would give us some reason to accept it, if sufficiently many other beliefs that we count as true do so. But if truth were such a relationship, then the truth of a belief would be just one factor, among others, that we should have to take into account in deciding whether to accept it.

It may be objected that the processes of establishing that the required physical relationship holds between our belief states and reality might involve all of the normal processes of investigation and epistemic evaluation, so that there could never be any conflict between establishing whether p, and establishing whether p is true. But even if demonstrating that ø holds essentially involves demonstrating that p, the converse surely could not be true. For, to show that ø holds, we must find out what is going on in people's heads when they believe that p, as well as what is happening elsewhere (unless, of course, 'p' happens to be about what is going on in people's heads). Suppose, for example, that we have a certain belief about whales. Then it must be possible for this belief to turn out to be false, because a brain scan reveals that it does not bear ø to reality, even though we had the very best of zoological evidence for it. Therefore, if there were such a property ø it would need to have intrinsic epistemic value – sufficient to outweigh all other epistemic considerations.

I think this shows that there is something radically wrong with the suggestion that truth is a mapping relationship between brain states and reality. For even if there were such a relationship which all and only true beliefs bore to reality (which seems very unlikely), it would not be truth. *For truth cannot be identified with any property or relationship which lacks intrinsic epistemic value.* Whatever we know to be true must be belief-worthy, whatever the evidence may otherwise be. There is, therefore, something essentially evaluative about our concept of truth, which makes any identification of truth with any property or relationship which lacks intrinsic epistemic value invalid. When I say that a belief is true, I am *endorsing* it in some way, giving it my stamp of epistemic approval, which is not at all the same as saying how it is related to reality. To identify truth with a correspondence relationship is thus to commit the epistemic equivalent of the naturalistic fallacy. It is to treat an expression of epistemic approval as though it were the attribution of a property to the object of approval. But it is not, and cannot be, that; although there may be properties of beliefs which are correlated with our epistemic evaluations.

Of course, our concept of truth might change. And if sufficiently many of our best accredited beliefs turned out to bear a particular relationship ø to reality, then this would be an important discovery; and we might wish to distinguish between those of our beliefs which bear ø to reality and those which don't. To mark the distinction we might come to say that those which do bear ø to reality are true, and the others false. But then the predicate 'is true' would be a descriptive, classificatory one which was not *necessarily* associated with epistemic approval. And, if that were the case, one could quite rationally deny what one believed to be true.

Thus, a crucial weakness of the correspondence theory of truth, in the only form in which it can be accepted by a scientific realist, is that it seeks to identify truth as a physical relationship. For if it is that, then to say that something is true is not necessarily to endorse it epistemically.

The same argument tells against all ontologically objective theories of truth. Truth cannot be any property or relationship which holds independently of our epistemic values, because if it were, we should have no explanation of why rationally we should seek to discover what is true, rather than, say, round or married. We might happen to think that this is a particularly useful thing to know, but if there is no necessary connection between what we think is true, and what we think we ought rationally to believe, i.e. no necessary connection between truth and epistemic evaluation, then there would be nothing essentially *rational* about seeking to know what is true. If what we think is true is not necessarily what we should judge to be worthy of our belief, which it would not be if truth were a relationship which held independently of our epistemic values (and hence independently of what anyone might find belief-worthy), then truth is just another property in which we may or may not happen to have a special interest. Jorge Borges, in his brilliant satirical essay, 'Tlon, Uqbar, Orbis Tertius' (1962), describes a nation in which the philosophers are more interested in what is *astounding* than what is true. If truth is just a property which things may have, independently of what we think we ought to believe, then we have no more reason to believe true theories than astounding ones.

Let us assume, therefore, that truth is not any kind of property or relationship which holds independently of our epistemic values. Then, either truth is not a property or relationship at all, or it is one that is dependent on our epistemic values. We shall consider these possibilities in turn in the next two chapters.

5.6 SUMMARY OF THE CASE AGAINST CORRESPONDENCE THEORIES

The main reasons for rejecting correspondence theories of truth are the following.

(1) *The failure of the various programmes of analysis.* Many things we believe to be true, including most scientific theories, cannot be

expressed in languages for which realistically interpretable truth theories exist. To interpret realistically the semantics for the sorts of languages we require for science, we should at least need a reality which consisted of an infinity of possible worlds. But possible worlds realism is incompatible with scientific realism, because it is incompatible with a causal theory of knowledge.

(2) *The variety of kinds of truth.* If truth is any kind of relationship between a truth bearer and reality, it is not a simple one. There are too many kinds and categories of truth claims for it to be plausible that they all correspond to reality in the same sort of way. Some way of reducing complex truth claims to truth functional compounds of simple ones (which just plausibly are all true in the same sense) is therefore required. The failure of the various programmes of analysis which attempted such a reduction is therefore a failure for the correspondence theory of truth.

(3) *The lack of adequate truth bearers for a semantic theory.* The semantic theory of truth, which is the most sophisticated form of the correspondence theory, identifies the bearers of truth as the sentences of certain formal languages. However, the sentences of such languages are idealized entities of a kind which scientific realists cannot believe in. They might well believe in sentence tokens or in the events of utterance which produce them. But such entities as these lack the properties they need to be truth bearers. In any case, their truth or falsity is derivative from that of the beliefs they purport to express.

(4) *If beliefs or other psychological states are the bearers of truth, then they are also the relata of logical relationships, and the subject matter of logic is psychological.* This is not incompatible with scientific realism, since psychological states are physical states, but it is certainly incompatible with the views of most scientific realists, and with the correspondence theories of truth they hold.

(5) *The lack of epistemic value in correspondence relationships.* Truth cannot be identified with any property or relationship which lacks intrinsic epistemic value. For a rational person must believe what he or she believes to be true. Moreover, the epistemic value of truth must be sufficient to override all other epistemic considerations; otherwise, it might be rational both to believe that p is true, and not believe that p, or to believe that p, but not believe that p is true.

Therefore, if truth is any kind of property or relationship, it must be one which somehow incorporates our most important epistemic values. However, there is no plausible relationship between beliefs (or sentences, for that matter) and the world (unless it be one which is specifically defined in terms of our epistemic values), which, if known, would always, and by itself, establish their belief-worthiness, and render all other epistemic considerations irrelevant.

6

Redundancy Theories

Many scientific realists have now abandoned the attempt to discover any genuine property or relationship of truth, and have joined those who think there is no such thing as truth. It is not a natural property, in any case, because the truth bearers, whether linguistic or psychological, did not exist before people (or other animals capable of forming beliefs), and would not exist now if we did not exist. The problem, as they see it, is to explain how the word 'true' functions in our language, given that the predicate 'is true' does not ascribe a property to anything. Various answers are possible, ranging from the view that it is a grammatical device, used for emphasis or expression of agreement, to the theory that it functions as a prosentence (which is something like a pronoun, except that it stands for a sentence). I myself once held the view that 'is true' is an assertion operator used to incur a particular kind of epistemic commitment, viz. the kind we normally incur when we make an assertion. I call all of these theories 'redundancy theories' (although the differences between them may be quite substantial), because their proponents are agreed that there is no genuine *property* of truth designated by the predicate 'is true'.

In the following sections of this chapter, I will examine some of these theories to see whether any can be sustained. In the end, I do no think they can be; nevertheless the theories are often attractive to scientific realists, and some may prefer them to the evaluative theory I shall later propose. The theories are attractive because they arise from genuine attempts to understand how words like 'true' and 'false' function in language, rather than from ancient metaphysics, or from an empiricist preoccupation with judgements of observation (which are about the only kinds of judgements for which a correspondence theory of truth seems plausible). Moreover, the theories are mostly compatible with scientific realism. One does not have to believe in truth bearers, because there is no need for them. One only needs people with views and opinions, who are interacting with each other, assenting, asserting, denying, and so on.

There are some general difficulties which must be faced by anyone who wishes to maintain a redundancy theory of truth. First, if there is no such thing as truth, and hence there are no truth bearers, then what is the subject matter of logic? What do logical relationships relate? Are they, perhaps, relationships between objects of belief? If so, what is their nature, and what is supposed to be preserved by valid arguments? Second, what sense can we make, on a redundancy theory, of principles like that of bivalence which seem to presuppose the existence of a class of truth bearers, i.e. things that are either true or false? If there are no truth bearers, and there are no properties of truth or falsity, how can there be a class of things which are necessarily either true or false? Third, knowledge of the truth is often thought of as one of the principal aims of inquiry, and therefore, presumably, as something worth pursuing. But if there is no such thing as truth, what sense can we make of these claims about the value of truth?

I shall not discuss all of these objections to redundancy theories of truth. In particular, I shall not take up the first set of objections concerning the impact of such theories on accepted views of the nature of logic, because I think these views are mistaken in any case, and so do not provide a sound basis for criticism. I mention them only because they are difficulties many scientific realists would have to face if they wished to accept a redundancy theory of truth. I shall, however, discuss the second and third objections as they apply to various redundancy theories, i.e. the objection that there is a class of truth bearers for which bivalence holds, and the point that redundancy theories cannot account for the *value* of truth. I shall consider only a selection of redundancy theories, but I shall argue that it is doubtful whether there is any form of redundancy theory which can escape these objections. Moreover, I claim that the failure of redundancy theories to give any adequate account of the value of truth points to the need for some kind of evaluative theory of truth.

6.1 TRUTH AND INDIRECT ASSERTION

If truth is not a property, then what are we doing when we say that something is true? One possibility is that 'is true' is a device for making indirect assertion possible, i.e. the assertion of named, definitely described or ostensively indicated beliefs which we cannot, or do not wish to, assert directly. Thus, ' "*p*" is true' might be held to assert indirectly what '*p*' asserts directly. This, roughly, is the view taken by F. P. Ramsey in his famous paper, 'Facts and Propositions' (Ramsey 1927). It is, initially, a very plausible theory, which explains a great deal that is difficult to explain on property theories.

First, the theory explains the irrationality of asserting that '*p*' is true, while denying that *p*, and of claiming that '*p*' is false, while asserting that *p*. Doing these things is irrational, according to the theory, because it is either asserting indirectly what one is directly denying, or denying indirectly what one is directly asserting. The theory therefore allows the straightforward deduction of all the Tarski T- sentences, i.e. sentences of the form:

'*p*' is true if and only if *p*

The theory also explains the equivalence of 'It is true that *p*' and '*p*'. For, following Donald Davidson (1969), we may interpret the 'that' in the phrase 'it is true that' as a demonstrative pointing to the sentence that follows it; then what we have is that what the first sentence ostensively indicates and says is true, and therefore indirectly asserts, is what the second sentence asserts directly. The theory therefore allows the deduction of what we may call the Ramsey T-sentences, i.e. sentences of the form:

It is true that *p* if and only if *p*

It is a requirement on any theory of truth that it should yield these two equivalences.

A satisfactory theory of truth must also account for the pragmatic equivalence of saying that *p* is true and claiming to believe that *p*. The two are pragmatically, rather than logically, equivalent because there is no necessity that they should have the same truth value. It might be true that *p*, although I do not believe it, and conversely. Nevertheless, one cannot rationally claim to believe that *p* while denying that *p* is true, or disavow belief that *p* while asserting that *p* is true. This fact is difficult to explain on the assumption that truth is a property or relationship, as we saw in our discussion of correspondence theories. But it is well accounted for on the theory that 'is true' is an indirect assertion operator. For, anyone who asserts that *p* is true is asserting indirectly that *p*, and so is expressing the belief that *p*. So, if one then denies that one has this belief, one is both expressing the belief and denying that one has it. Likewise, if anyone claims to believe that *p*, yet says that *p* is false, then one is explicitly claiming to believe what one is implicitly disavowing. The theory that 'is true' is an indirect assertion operator thus gives a good account of the pragmatic equivalence between the truth claim that *p* and the claim to believe that *p*.

This version of the redundancy theory of truth appears to be compatible with scientific realism. Certainly, I know of no good arguments to the contrary, and it seems unlikely there could be any. To accept the theory, we have only to believe that our language contains a device for indirect assertion, that one such device is the predicate 'is true', and that this assumption is sufficient to account for the various uses we have for this predicate in English. Therefore, if there are any objections to the theory, they are likely to be that the assumption does not account for the grammatical or linguistic facts of the case, not that the assumption is incompatible with the ontology of scientific realism.

The redundancy theory is usually associated with the thesis of *eliminability*, i.e. that what can be said indirectly, using the predicate 'is true', can in principle be said directly, without using this, or any equivalent, predicate. In this form, however, the redundancy theory can easily be defeated, as Herbert Heidelberger (1968) has shown. But there is no need for a redundancy theorist to accept the thesis of eliminability; Ramsey himself rejected it right from the outset. Commenting on the sentence, 'He is always right', Ramsey remarked:

. . . there does not seem to be any way of expressing this without using the word 'true'. But suppose we put it thus: 'For all p, if he asserts p, then p is true', then we see that the propositional function p is true is simply the same as p, as e.g., its value 'Caesar was murdered is true' is the same as 'Caesar was murdered'. We have in English to add 'is true' to give the sentence a verb, forgetting that 'p' already contains a (variable) verb. This may be made clearer by supposing that only one form of proposition is in question, say the relational form aRb; then 'He is always right' could be expressed by 'For all a,R,b, if he asserts aRb, then aRb', to which 'is true' would be an obviously superfluous addition. (Pitcher (ed.) 1964, p. 17)

While those who regard 'is true' as an indirect assertion operator are not thereby committed to the view that this phrase is wholly superfluous, one would expect them to argue that this is because direct assertion is not always possible, or because we are able to say, by means of the truth predicate, things we could not otherwise say. Thus it has been argued, e.g. by Stephen Leeds (1978), that the point of having a truth predicate is that it extends the range of things we can say in a finitary language. This is the kind of argument we should expect, since it explains why we need a truth predicate, even though there is no such thing as truth, and does so compatibly with the idea that the truth predicate is an indirect assertion operator. Ramsey's argument, by contrast, is that we need a truth predicate to preserve the grammatical structure of English – in particular, when quantifying over claims we wish to endorse, or otherwise assert indirectly. For example, if we wished to endorse everything that Socrates said, it would be no good just uttering the words, 'Everything Socrates said', because this is not a complete sentence of English.

However, it is doubtful whether this adequately explains why we have a truth predicate. Why not just say 'I endorse' or 'I agree with' whatever it is we wish to endorse? Why invent a predicate, and why make it look as though we are ascribing a property to what we are endorsing – especially if we do not believe there is any such property? Why, for that matter, should we be bound by the conventional grammar of English? Why not, after all, say things like: 'Everything Socrates said'; 'Something Plato said'; 'Your last remark'; 'What is written on the other side', if these are things we want to assert; or 'Not everything Socrates said'; 'Nothing Plato said'; 'Not your last remark'; 'Not what is written on the other side', if we wish to deny them? People would soon understand what we were doing, and if enough people adopted the same strategy for making indirect assertions and denials, there would be nothing grammatically incomplete about such remarks. The grammar of the language would just be different.

The fact that we can do this trick with 'is true', and eliminate the predicate by modifying the grammar of the language, does not, however, support a redundancy theory of truth; nor does it count against such a theory. Consider the predicate 'is orange'. If people had an overriding passion to know what is orange, and most of the claims we made were orangeness claims, this predicate might also be made to seem superfluous. For, instead of saying that something is orange, we might get into the habit of simply naming it, or otherwise just referring to it. For it would readily be understood, in this strange society, that to use a name or referring expression *by itself* is always to make an orangeness claim. But this has no tendency to show that orangeness is not a property. On the contrary, unless we understood what the objects referred to were supposed to have in common, we could not know what was being said about them.

The predicates 'is true' and 'is orange' are not logically similar. Nevertheless, it might be the case that the relative redundancy of the truth predicate is due to our overriding interest in truth claims. If, every time we wished to make a truth claim, we had to flag it in some way to indicate its status, i.e. say something like '". . . ." is true', or 'It is true that. . . .', then our language would be much more cumbersome. So, perhaps the reason why the predicate 'is true' is more or less redundant is that we have learned to do without it (wherever we can) in the interests of economy of thought and expression. That is, the predicate 'is true' may be mostly redundant, not because it is logically superfluous, *but because, in the absence of any contrary indication, every claim is assumed to be a truth claim.* In other words, '". . . ." is true' may be just the default mode of assertion, reflecting our overriding interest in making truth claims. Any unflagged assertion is assumed, by default, to be of this form. If this is the case, then the equivalences:

'p' is true if and only if p

may hold only because '"p" is true' says just what 'p' says by default.

Imagine a nation of gamblers in which there is such a thing as a standard bet (say, \$10 to \$1). We may suppose that it is understood by all that whenever anyone says that p, a standard bet is being offered on p, unless the speaker says otherwise. For example, if someone says; 'It is true that p', or 'It is probable that p', then it is understood that a truth or probability claim is being made, and that no bet is being offered. Likewise, if someone says; 'I'll bet you \$100 to 50c that p', then this is taken to be the offer of a non-standard bet. But if someone just says that p, then everyone understands this to be an offer of \$10 to \$1 that p. To accept the bet, one need only put down \$1. (All bets are adjudicated by the Betting Tribunal, whose decision is final.) Now in this nation, the phrase 'it is true that' and the predicate 'is true' are clearly *not* redundant, for they are needed to distinguish truth claims from offers of standard bets. What *is* more or less redundant is the performative, 'I'll bet you \$10 to \$1 that', for it is seldom used, except when talking to foreigners.

The fact that '"p" is true' is roughly equivalent to 'p' in English tells us very little about truth, except perhaps that it is important enough, or that truth claims are made commonly enough, for it to be tacitly understood that when we assert 'p', we are claiming that 'p' is true. This fact is consistent with truth being some kind of property with intrinsic epistemic value; it is also compatible with the view that 'is true' is an indirect assertion operator, as it is held to be on the version of the redundancy theory of truth we are considering.

6.2   THE CASE AGAINST THE INDIRECT ASSERTION OPERATOR THEORY

The following are the main difficulties with the view that truth is an indirect assertion operator.

(1) *The predicate 'is true' often occurs in non-assertoric contexts*, i.e. contexts in which it cannot reasonably be interpreted as an indirect assertion operator. For example, in the sentence, 'If the premises are true, then the conclusion is true', there is no assertion of either premisses or conclusion; hence there is no indirect assertion. An indirect assertion of this claim would say that the whole conditional is true. The predicate also occurs in various questions, commands and other non-assertoric contexts, where it is clearly not being used as an indirect assertion operator. However, its use in the context of conditionals is a more persuasive argument against this form of the redundancy theory. For a question whether something is true may reasonably be interpreted as an invitation to make an indirect assertion or denial in response – compatibly with the theory in question.

(2) *In many contexts 'is true' appears to be predicative.* The above conditional is such a case; for it seems to be saying that if the premisses possess the attribute of truth, the conclusion will also have it. Any other interpretation of what it says seems forced. The same is true in many other cases where truth and falsity claims are conjoined, disjoined, negated, or otherwise formed into truth functional compounds. For example, the claim that it is either true or false that p is not properly analysable as a sort of disjunctive assertion and denial of 'p'. It seems to be just the claim that 'p' possesses one or other of two mutually exclusive attributes, viz. truth and falsity.

(3) *The principle of bivalence must be abandoned on this form of the redundancy theory*; therefore, the concept of truth it yields is *non-classical*. There are many things we should be unwilling to assert or deny, although they are clearly things which might be asserted or denied. Let us call anything that anyone may ever wish to assert or deny, 'a proposition'. Then it follows that there are propositions which we should not be willing to assert or deny. Concerning some

of these propositions we may be willing to make indirect assertions and denials disjunctively by saying, for example, that it is either true or false that p, where the commitment is to defend one or other of these two claims, but we don't say which. But such a disjunctive assertion is not the same as the assertion of a disjunction. To defend the disjunctive assertion, we should have to defend one of the disjuncts. To defend the assertion of the disjunction, however, it would be sufficient to cite the law of excluded middle. Therefore, if 'is true' and 'is false' are indirect assertion and denial operators, the claim that every proposition is either true or false is not sustainable. Hence, the principle of bivalence must be rejected, and the concept of truth is non-classical.

(4) *The principle of bivalence should not be rejected just for the reason that there are propositions we are unwilling to assert or deny.* For there is an important difference between the case where something is genuinely indeterminate, e.g. whether the electron went through this or that slit in a 'two slit' experiment, and the case where we just do not know what happened. To reject the principle of bivalence simply on the ground that there are some questions which remain, and perhaps will always remain, undecided, is to confuse two very different kinds of cases. It may be neither true nor false that the electron went through slit A, but there is a truth of the matter whether Caesar winked as he crossed the Rubicon. Any adequate theory of truth should be able to mark this difference; the indirect assertion theory cannot.

(5) *The indirect assertion theory cannot account for the value of truth.* If the predicate 'is true' is just an indirect assertion operator, its value is, presumably, that it makes indirect assertion possible – although perhaps it has the added value of making it possible for us to say certain things which we could not otherwise say. Why then should we seek the truth? According to the theory, if there is such a thing as truth, it must be what we should assert indirectly, and so, presumably, what we happen to believe. Hence, the theory suggests that seeking the truth must be synonymous with seeking beliefs – *any old beliefs*, apparently, because it is being denied that there are any such things as true beliefs. Moreover, it would seem to follow, from the indirect assertion theory, that truth is *radically subjective*. For what is true for me is what I should assert to be true; and what

is true for you is what you would assert to be true. And, there should be no question who is right, for, if there *were* any objective standards for the evaluation of truth claims, the judgement that something is true would at least be the judgement that it met these standards. Truth would then be an evaluative concept of some kind, perhaps like that of rightness in ethics, and 'is true' would not be merely an indirect assertion operator.

The last of these grounds for rejecting the indirect assertion theory of truth is also a ground for rejecting most other variants of the redundancy theory. Consider, for example, the idea that '". . . ." is true' is just a device for semantic ascent (from the object language to a metalanguage), which enables us to say certain things about the language, and how it functions, which we could not say otherwise. The idea is that, although ' "p" is true' says in the metalanguage exactly what 'p' says in the object language, we often need to speak metalinguistically, e.g. when talking about logical relationships, and the truth predicate is one of the devices we need to do this. For example, we need to be able to say such things as; 'In a valid argument, if the premisses are true, then the conclusion is true'. And this is something which can only be said in a metalanguage. Tarski's theory of truth is sometimes interpreted as being a redundancy theory like this. My point is that whatever truth may be, it cannot be just a device for semantic ascent, although it may indeed have this role, for the value of truth does not derive from this source. The truth has to be something worth pursuing.

6.3 THE PROSENTENTIAL THEORY OF TRUTH

One of the latest variations on the theme that 'is true' is not an attributive predicate, but a linguistic device of a quite different kind for increasing the expressive power of our language, is the prosentential theory of truth (Grover, Camp and Belnap 1975). According to this theory, 'is true' is 'a syncategorimatic part of a prosentence', a prosentence being, roughly, a sentence of the form:

X is . . . true

where 'true' may (or may not) be negated or modally qualified, and X names or otherwise refers to some sentence or class of sentences. Prosentences satisfy the following conditions:

(1) they may occupy all grammatical positions that can be occupied by declarative sentences;
(2) they are generic, in that any declarative sentence can be the antecedent of a prosentence;
(3) they can be used anaphorically in the two kinds of ways that pronouns can be used;
(4) they have anaphoric antecedents which determine the classes of admissible sentential substituends for them.

The two kinds of ways referred to in (3) are 'the lazy way' and 'the quantificational way', as in

(a) If Mary saw it, she would have been surprised,

and

(b) If anything is red, then it is coloured.

In (a), the anaphoric antecedent of 'she', namely 'Mary', can replace the pronoun without meaning change. In (b), the apparent anaphoric antecedent of 'it', namely 'anything', cannot replace the 'it' without changing the sense of what is said. However, (b) is equivalent to an infinite conjunction of sentences of the form:

(c) If x is red, then x is coloured,

where x ranges over all the things that can be referred to in the language. So the anaphoric antecedent of 'it' in (b) is the set of all such things. Consider now the sentences:

(a′) If Mary said that $7+5=12$, then it is true,

and

(b′) Everything Mary says is true.

In (a′) the prosentence is 'it is true', and its anaphoric antecedent is '7+5=12'. In (b′) the prosentence is (b′) itself, and its anaphoric antecedent is an infinite conjunction of conditionals of the form:

(c′) If Mary says that *x*, then *x*

where *x* ranges over all of the sentences of the language. In the simplest case, viz.

(d) '*p*' is true

the prosentence, (d), displays its own anaphoric antecedent, namely '*p*'. Hence the Tarski equivalences.

The main difficulties with the theory are seen as being technical, e.g. to explain how a 'not' or a modal qualifier inserted between 'is' and 'true' changes the class of admissible sentential substituends for the prosentence. I shall ignore these difficulties, however, for my objections to the theory are more elementary.

First, the theory is strongly counter-intuitive, at least grammatically. It is more plausible to suppose that '*p*' does duty for '"*p*" is true' than the other way round, since this is the direction of economy of thought; and it is highly implausible that '. . . is true' has no grammatical structure, as the theory implies, because this expression behaves grammatically just like any other predicate. For example, it can be negated, qualified, conjoined with other predicates, and so on. The theory would, therefore, need some solid linguistic evidence in its favour before it could be accepted.

Second, if '". . ." is true' is just an operator which transforms a sentence into its own prosentence, then to say that something is true is just to assert it, but in a less direct way. And, if I say that something is true, and you say that it is false, then you are denying indirectly what I am indirectly asserting. However, for a prosentential theorist, there can be no question which, if either of us, is right. For this question presupposes another *quite different* concept of truth, namely, that of what is right in the way of belief. I am assuming that a prosentential theorist can have no other concept of truth like this to fall back on. For such a concept of truth would allow us to classify beliefs as objectively true or false, and any such concept of truth would inevitably be of much greater interest to philosophers than any mere grammatical device. With such a concept of truth in the background, 'is true' would just be a normal predicate, meaning roughly, 'is the right thing to believe'. Defenders of the prosentential theory of truth must therefore deny that there is any such thing as what it is right to believe. Their position is, therefore, incompatible with epistemic objectivism.

Third, the prosentential theory, like the other redundancy theories we have considered, does not motivate the search for truth. It will be agreed, I suppose, that it is rational to want to have only true beliefs. But how should we put this on the prosentential theory? I want it to be the case that if I have a belief, then it is a true belief. So what I want is that an infinite conjunction of conditionals of the form, 'if I believe that x then x', should be true. But how can I eliminate 'should be true' from the statement of what I want? It is not that if I believe that x, then I want it to be the case that x, because I might not like what I believe; in any case, this would not eliminate the predicate 'is true' in the way required, because the conditionals now contain the predicate 'is the case'. Nor is it true that if not x, then I do not want to believe that x, because what I want or don't want is not so particularized. I do not want to have any false beliefs, but that is not to say that I am actively wanting to disbelieve what happens to be false. It is like hunting tigers. One can be hunting tigers, although there are no particular tigers one is hunting. Similarly, one can be wanting to rid oneself of false beliefs, without having any particular false beliefs in one's sights.

This may be just a technical difficulty to which I cannot, at the moment, see a solution. However, I suspect that it is more deep-seated than the word 'technical' suggests, and that the programme of the prosentential theory was bound to run into difficulties with truth in intensional contexts. Be that as it may, the general criticism that I have of redundancy theories, that they do not explain the *value* of truth, stands. What is crucially wrong with redundancy theories, generally, is that they fail to explain why the truth matters.[1] For truth cannot be anything of epistemic value if 'is true' is just a linguistic device of some kind – an operator which may be of interest to grammarians, perhaps, but hardly to epistemologists.

Redundancy theorists may be right to deny that there is any semantic property or relationship which the truth predicate designates, but they are wrong to conclude that truth is *nothing*. They need to recognize the essentially *evaluative* nature of truth.

6.4   TRUTH AS OBJECTIVE CERTAINTY

In 'An Epistemological Concept of Truth' (Ellis 1969), I proposed a theory of truth which, though not strictly a redundancy theory, is like one in that it treats ' "..." is true' as a kind of assertion operator. However, it is unlike redundancy theories in other ways, because it is not suggested that ' "..." is true' is just a grammatical device needed only for special purposes. On the contrary, the truth predicate is theoretically nearly always present, although it may be suppressed in normal discourse for reasons of economy of thought or expression. The truth predicate, according to this theory, is just one, and indeed the most important, of a family of assertion operators. And, if it is redundant, it is only so because it is the mode of assertion we assume in default of any other assertion operator being supplied. To explain the theory, a certain view of the nature of assertion needs to be understood.

There are obvious differences between assertions and sentences. In uttering a sentence, we may or may not be making an assertion, depending on the sentence, the context, and even the tone of voice. We make an assertion if and only if our action incurs certain kinds of epistemic commitments; and, quite plausibly, the identity of the assertion we make depends on what commitments we incur. By this criterion, different sentences can be used to make the same assertion, and the same sentence to make different assertions. Hence, there is not even any extensional equivalence between assertions and the sentences we use to make them. Yet to make an assertion, it is usually sufficient just to utter a declarative sentence in an appropriate context. There is no need for any sentential operator like, 'It is true that ...', or performative like, 'I hereby assert that ...'. One can usually incur the epistemic commitment involved in making an assertion just by uttering the appropriate sentence. Of course, what one asserts by doing this may be an open question; for this may depend on the context, on what one is intending to say, and also on what one may reasonably be interpreted as saying. However, it is conventional that assertions can be made in this way; and this is an important fact about our language. It is because of this fact that it is often convenient to represent assertions just by declarative sentences, or their formal counterparts, and otherwise simply ignore the distinction.

To understand the theory to be explained here, it is important to keep the distinction between assertions, and the sentences we use to make them, clearly in mind. Assertions are already statements or claims; but the sentences we use are not, and some actions of epistemic commitment are required to make assertions out of them. I shall therefore distinguish between assertions, on the one hand, and declarative sentences, or their idealized, disambiguated formal counterparts, viz. propositions, on the other. The latter may be asserted or denied, or said to be probable to some degree, but they are not themselves assertions. They define the contents of our assertions, perhaps, but the epistemic commitments made by asserting a proposition depend also on the mode of its assertion.

To explain this: if you assert that p, and I deny that p, then we may take the view that there is just the one proposition here which is being asserted and denied, viz. p. This contrasts with the standard view that there are really two propositions, p and $\sim p$, being asserted, one by you, and the other by me. On the first view, there are two modes of assertion, T and F, but only the one proposition; on the second view, there are two propositions, but only one mode of assertion, say A, which is supposed to be the same for both. Logicians have generally preferred the second description of this situation, because it is more economical, for their purposes, to represent any differences of mode of assertion as assertions of different propositions. However, it is important here to think of T and F as contrary modes of assertion, and of propositional negation as something different from either. If we represent a proposition by the sentence letter 'p', then we should represent the truth and falsity claims made in respect of this proposition by 'Tp' and 'Fp', respectively. It is important to be clear, however, that Tp and Fp are strictly not propositions, and therefore cannot be asserted or denied. This is not to say, of course, that they cannot be agreed or disagreed with, or accepted or rejected. It is just that, since they are already assertions, they are not themselves assertable.

The truth and falsity claims that we may make in respect of p are not the only kinds of assertion we can make. If the evidence we have regarding p is favourable, but inconclusive, we may wish to make only a probability claim, Pr, in respect of p. Such a claim would then be represented by 'Pr(p)'. Like Tp and Fp, Pr(p) is an assertion, and therefore not the sort of thing that can be asserted or denied. Consequently, expressions like 'TTp', 'TFp', 'TPr(p)', 'Pr(Tp)', and so on, are all ill-formed. To make sense of them, the inner predicates 'is true', 'is false', 'is probable' etc. must be given *de re* interpretations. The *de dicto* modalities of necessity and possibility must, of course, also be regarded as modes of assertion.

With this theory of assertion in mind, let us return to the suggestion that the truth predicate may be mostly redundant because truth is the standard mode of assertion of English; so that any assertion which is not otherwise labelled may be assumed, by default, to be a truth claim. The idea is appealing, because it promises to explain both the importance of truth as well as its usual redundancy. If 'It is true that . . .' and '". . ." is true' are the default assertion operators of the language, then this is presumably because we are more interested in truth claims than other sorts of claims; and the reason why these operators are not often needed may therefore be that any unflagged assertions are automatically assumed to be truth claims. In the nation of gamblers I described earlier, the default operator was 'I'll bet you $10 to $1 that', and the truth assertion operators were clearly needed here for ordinary conversation.

The theory has several other attractive features. First, the suggestion that every claim that has no attached assertion operator is assumed, by default, to be a truth claim has a high degree of initial plausibility, and it explains the usual equivalences between 'p', 'It is true that p' and '"p" is true' at least as well as any redundancy theory. Second, it explains the incongruity of predicating truth or falsity of probability claims (and sometimes of other modalized assertions). For example, to make sense of 'It is true that it is improbable that p', the theory requires that the predicate 'is improbable' be given a *de re* interpretation; and, if the judgement is clearly a subjective probability claim, any such reading is implausible. It is true that there is nothing odd about saying that something is 'probably true' or 'necessarily false', as there should be according to the theory; these are quite normal expressions of probability and impossibility claims respectively. But perhaps this is just because the classical concept of truth, which allows such expressions, is deeply entrenched in our language. The theory is not, after all, being proposed as an 'ordinary language' theory.

The theory has the further attraction that it makes possible some unification of our truth and probability theories. Many philosophers have thought that truth and probability are in the same line of business. The difference between 'That's true' and 'That's probable' is intuitively not very great; it reflects, perhaps, some difference in degree of conviction, or maybe caution on the part of the speaker, but both are expressions of epistemic support for what has been said. Therefore, we should expect the accounts we require of truth and probability to be fairly similar. Certainly, we should not expect them to be such radically different concepts as they are classically represented as being. However, if truth and probability are both modes of assertion, the close links between these concepts can easily be explained. For what distinguishes the performatives 'It is true that . . .' and 'It is probable that . . .' can only be the different epistemic commitments their use involves.

Making an assertion always involves some kind of epistemic commitment; in particular, to defend what we have said in a manner appropriate to the mode of assertion. The commitment is made to those to whom we are answerable, i.e. to those who are considered to be in a position to evaluate what we have said, and whose opinions are therefore worth considering. In practice, we may not often be called upon to fulfil the epistemic commitments we have made. Most of our statements go unchallenged. But this does not imply that there is no commitment made. Those to whom we are answerable normally form a consensus, in the sense that they are mainly agreed about what is evidence for what, and what is a conclusive case. Moreover, the members of the consensus are disposed to agree, non-collusively, about what is true or probable. If these conditions were not usually satisfied, then realistic epistemic commitment, and therefore assertion, would be impossible.

When we make truth or probability claims, we become committed to defending our assertions appropriately before a relevant consensus. Depending on the nature of the propositions we are assert, and the modes of assertion we adopt, we may commit ourselves in one or more of the following ways: (1) we may stake our reputations for honesty as observers or competence as language users on the genuineness and accuracy of our observational judgements and introspective reports; or (2) we may place our reputations for rationality or theoretical competence at stake by committing ourselves to accepting the normal logical and theoretical consequences of our assertions; or, if we should not accept these consequences, then to developing some alternative logical or theoretical system, and defending its adequacy.

In terms of the commitments incurred, what distinguishes a truth from a probability claim is the kind of backing one is committed to providing. In the case of the truth claim that p, one is committed to arguing:

(1) that there are excellent grounds for asserting that p, and no good grounds for denying it;

and

(2) the case for asserting that p is conclusive, so that there is no need for further inquiry.

If the claim that is being made is a judgement of observation or introspection, and there are no contrary testimonies, or special circumstances which would impugn such a judgement, then the conditions (1) and (2) are presumed to be satisfied, and the claim epistemically justified.

In the case of a probability claim that p there is normally no commitment to either (1) or (2). To justify $\Pr(p)$ epistemically it is usually sufficient just to show:

(3) the case for asserting that p is better than the case for denying it.

Therefore, this must be the extent of the epistemic commitment that is usually made by asserting that '*p*' is probable. Where this is so, let us, at the risk of some confusion, say that the claim is 'subjective'. I say there is a risk of confusion, because a subjective probability claim is often assumed to be a claim that one has a certain degree of belief in something. Now what I am calling a subjective probability claim should certainly be the *expression* of an appropriate degree of belief; but, by the epistemic commitments incurred in making the claim, this is clearly distinct from the claim that one has this degree of belief. For the latter is a truth claim which would, presumably, be justified epistemically by a combination of introspection and psychological testing. The former is a probability claim which we should justify by considering the available evidence concerning the proposition said to be probable.

I call the claim, where the epistemic commitment is only to (3), a 'subjective' probability claim to distinguish it from the kind of probability claim (usually quantified) where there is a commitment to conclusiveness. The latter is what I should call an 'objective' probability claim. Anyone who claims that it is *objectively* probable to degree i that *p*, i.e. that $\Pr(p) = i$, is committed to arguing that:

(4) On the basis of the evidence available, it is rational to believe to degree i that *p*;

and

(5) there is no further evidence to be had which might upset this conclusion.

An objective probability claim is thus quite like a truth claim; and may indeed be represented as such. For the condition (5) is like the commitment to conclusiveness that is involved in a truth claim.

Conditionals, especially so-called 'counterfactuals', are often the subjects of objective probability claims. For example, it is objectively probable to degree (approximately) 1/2 that if I had tossed this coin on to the table an hour ago it would have landed heads. For the coin is a fair one, and there is no reason to suppose that further evidence may show that it is not. It is, of course, also objectively probable to degree 1/2, or thereabouts, that the coin would have landed tails if it had been tossed an hour ago – for precisely the same reasons. Some philosophers (e.g. David Lewis) would say, counter-intuitively, that these conditionals are both false, and known to be so, since this follows from the account they give of the truth conditions for such conditionals.[2] Others (e.g. Robert Stalnaker) would say that while one or other of the two conditionals must be true, we may never know which;[3] probably, all we shall ever be able to say is that they are equally probable. However, it is just as implausible to suppose that there is a truth of the matter here, which we can never know about, as it is to say that both conditionals have zero probability, since both are known to be false. What is needed, apparently, is a theory which will allow us to say that these conditionals are both objectively probable to degree 1/2, but neither is true or false.

The theory that truth and objective probability are comparable modes of assertion, which are to be distinguished from each other only by the epistemic commitments their users incur, allows us to do just this. For, according to the theory, objective probability should not be interpreted as probability of truth. On the contrary, $\Pr(\ldots) = 1/2$ should be regarded as a modality, just like T and F. Indeed, in terms of the epistemic commitments made, $\mathrm{T}p$ should be identified with $\Pr(p) = 1$ (where this is understood to be an objective probability claim), and $\mathrm{F}p$ with $\Pr(p) = 0$, as comparison of (1) and (2) with (4) and (5) shows. For, epistemically, truth and falsity are just the extreme cases of objective probabilities. Using the Stalnaker corner '$>$' for 'if . . ., then . . .', 'p' for 'the coin was tossed an hour ago' and 'q' for 'the coin landed heads', we should clearly accept $\Pr(p > q) = 1/2$, but reject both $\Pr(p > q) = 1$ and $\Pr(p > q) = 0$, and hence both $\mathrm{T}(p > q)$ and $\mathrm{F}(p > q)$.

Two points should be made here to avoid misunderstanding. First, rejection of both $\mathrm{T}(p > q)$ and $\mathrm{F}(p > q)$, and hence conditional bivalence, does not involve rejection of conditional excluded middle, which is the characteristic Stalnaker thesis. On the contrary, the theory suggests that we may identify the objective probabilities of conditionals with the corresponding conditional probabilities, and hence accept both

$$\Pr((p > q) \text{ v } (p > \sim q)) = 1$$

and

$$\Pr(p > q) + \Pr(p > \sim q) = 1$$

as theorems of a new probability logic. Indeed, it was with the development of such a probability logic in mind that I proposed the epistemic concept of truth in the first place.[4]

Second, the identification of truth with objective certainty was not an attempt to capture the classical concept of truth (which I considered hopelessly metaphysical). At the time, I wanted a concept of truth which would allow us to say whatever we might be epistemically justified in saying, but nevertheless was a kind of limiting probability concept which we could use to develop a comprehensive logic of truth and probability claims. I had three main reasons for seeking such a concept.

(1) Truth and probability seemed to me to be similar in many ways. To say that something is probable is like saying that it is true, but hedging one's bets a bit. It is a way of reserving some room for doubt, rather than expressing full belief. Now it had already been shown that the probability calculus could be interpreted subjectively – as a logic of probability claims, expressing various measured degrees of belief. Therefore, a logic of certainty (suitable for gods, and others who never have any doubts), should be derivable from this system by limiting the range of possible probability values to 1 and 0. Hence, if truth can be considered to be objective certainty, this system of logic should be identical with the logic of truth claims. In fact, as I argued in Ellis (1973), the sentential calculus is derivable from the classical probability calculus by restricting the range of possible probability values in just this way. However, *only the absolute fragment of the probability calculus is needed for the derivation to go through.* The sentential calculus is therefore a restricted logic of certainty, and hence of truth. It is a logic without conditionalization, and hence without genuine conditionals.

(2) I was convinced that the conditionalization, or 'given', operator of probability theory was a far better representation of 'if'

than the material conditional used by logicians. Within the context of probability claims, the latter gave quite absurd results, while the former yielded intuitively sound conclusions about what combinations of beliefs were rational. Even in the limiting cases, where the probabilities were restricted to 1 and 0, the conditionalization operator seemed to yield much better results. For it led to the discovery of many convincing counter-examples to standard argument forms – ones which had previously been held by nearly everyone to be valid. On the other hand, there were no convincing counter-examples to the use of the conditionalization operator to represent 'if'.

(3) The main stumbling block to the development of a satisfactory system of logic for both truth and probability claims thus seemed to me to be our concept of truth; since this was clearly not an epistemic concept, and therefore not comparable to the required concept of probability as degree of belief. I argued, wrongly I now think, that an epistemic concept of truth as objective certainty would serve all of our legitimate purposes. There were other difficulties, some of them quite formidable, in defining a conditional connective with the right properties; and an early attempt of mine to define such a connective proved to be unsatisfactory.[5] However, the main difficulties were conceptual.

The reasons why I now think the epistemic concept of truth is inadequate are somewhat similar to those I have for rejecting redundancy theories. First, the predicate 'is true' often occurs in non-assertoric contexts, where it is difficult to interpret it as an assertion operator. A *de re* interpretation of 'is true' seems to be required for many such contexts. Second, if truth is to be equated with objective certainty, as the theory requires, then bivalence must be abandoned. This, in itself, would not matter, if we could say everything we wanted to using the new concept of truth. However, it is doubtful whether this is so. For it does not seem possible to distinguish between undecidability and indeterminacy on such a theory of truth. If I cannot know whether p, because any possibility of finding out has been destroyed, then I am obliged to reject both Tp and Fp, just as though p were indeterminate. But there is a world of difference between a case of genuine indeterminacy, and one where knowledge has become impossible because the evidence is no longer available.

However, the epistemic concept of truth, as objective certainty, is less flawed than the redundancy concepts we have been considering. For at least it gives us some explanation of the importance of truth. According to the theory, the value of truth lies in the certainty and finality it offers us. Knowledge of the truth is objective knowledge – knowledge of what is objectively certain – and valuable for just this reason. It is with some reluctance, therefore, that I have abandoned this theory. I have done so because I am now convinced that we need a concept of truth which will allow us to distinguish between truth and epistemic justification. The concept of truth as objective certainty does not do so. However, the idea that a truth claim involves a commitment to certainty and finality concerning some aspect of our knowledge is an important insight. For it suggests that truth may be identified, not with what is certain and final in the current state of our knowledge, but with what would be so if our knowledge system were perfected. The advantages of the epistemic concept of truth may thus be retained in some form of pragmatic theory.

Part III

Epistemology

Part III

Epistemology

Naturalistic Truth and Epistemic Evaluation

The only kind of theory of truth which promises to be able to account adequately for the *belief-worthiness* of true beliefs is one which somehow builds belief-worthiness into the concept of truth. It has been demonstrated that truth is not an objective relationship between beliefs and the world which is independent of our epistemic values, as the correspondence theory says it is, and that it is not just a grammatical device for semantic ascent, or for making indirect assertion or expression possible, as it is according to the redundancy theory. For, among other things, these theories fail to explain why we ought rationally to seek the truth, or believe what we know to be true. They fail to account for the *value* of truth. To account for its value, we have to suppose that truth is *essentially* connected with epistemic evaluation – that it is *necessarily* what it is *right* epistemically to believe. Any theory which makes this supposition I call *an evaluative theory of truth*.

Belief-worthiness may depend on either (1) the properties of the individual beliefs to be evaluated, (2) the properties of the systems of beliefs to which they belong, or (3) some combination of these. A theory which claims that epistemic value derives just from the properties of beliefs, e.g. from their observationality or intuitiveness, is a *foundationalist theory of truth*. Empiricists, for example, often seem to hold theories of truth of this kind. A theory of truth according to which epistemic value derives from a whole system of beliefs, and so depends on such systemic values as comprehensiveness or consistency, is a *coherence theory of truth*. F. H. Bradley's theory, for example, was a coherence theory in this sense. The theory of truth which I think a scientific realist ought to hold is an evaluative theory which recognizes the importance of *both* foundationalist and systemic considerations for epistemic evaluation. I call it *the naturalistic theory of truth*.

The naturalistic theory of truth is an evaluative theory similar in some ways to the pragmatic theories of C. S. Peirce and William James, as well as to F. H. Bradley's coherence theory. It is like Peirce's theory in that it relates truth to an ideal of perfection of knowledge and understanding. It is like James' theory in that it assumes truth to be an evaluative concept, like rightness in ethics. And, like Bradley's theory, it admits the importance of coherence and comprehensiveness as epistemic values. However, the naturalistic theory of truth is not to be identified with any of these ealier theories. It differs from Bradley's theory in that it assumes our concept of truth to be firmly grounded in human nature. Bradley was too much influenced by Hegel to have accepted such a view. It differs from James' theory in at least three respects. First, James made no clear distinction between epistemic and other values, and so laid himself open to the criticism that something could be true, according to his theory, just because it is *pleasing* or *comforting* to believe. Secondly, his theory is not tied to any ideal of *perfection* of knowledge or understanding, as it is in the naturalistic theory. Thirdly, the naturalistic theory is not pragmatic in the sort of way that James' theory is. The truth is what it is *right* to believe (in a sense to be explained), but it is not necessarily what *works* as a belief, or what it *pays* to believe.

Peirce's theory of truth is perhaps the most similar to the naturalistic theory. However, while truth is related to an ideal of knowledge and understanding on the naturalistic theory, it is not my view that this ideal will ever be realized, or even that it *would* be realized if scientific inquiry were to continue forever. So the naturalistic theory of truth is also importantly different from Peirce's theory.

However, the most important difference between the naturalistic theory and these other evaluative theories – the one which really sets it apart from them – is the nature of the epistemological theory on which it depends. Every theory of truth which identifies truth with what it is right to believe depends on some epistemology. For it depends on one's theory of right belief. Thus an empiricist epistemology will yield an empiricist theory of truth; a rationalist theory of knowledge will yield a rationalist theory; and a coherentist epistemology will yield a coherence theory of truth. What is distinctive about the naturalistic theory of truth is that it derives from a *naturalistic values-based* epistemology, i.e. an epistemology which makes rationality depend on a complex system of natural epistemic values. To my knowledge, no other epistemology gives such a central role to a system of natural epistemic values. The usual assumption in epistemology is that there are just two basic epistemic values, viz. truth and avoidance of error, and the task of epistemology is seen as being to formulate a reliable system of inductive rules for acquiring knowledge of what is true. On the naturalistic theory, however, truth is not itself an epistemic value, but rather what it is right to believe in relationship to our epistemic values. Hence truth itself does not play the key role in this epistemology.

The naturalistic theory also differs from most other epistemologies in being a *values-based,* rather than a *rules-based* theory. Writers on ethics are familiar with the distinction between values-based and rules-based ethical theories. Ideal act-utilitarianism, for example, is a values-based ethical theory, and to understand what rightness is for such a theory, we must know the value system with reference to which rightness is defined. On such a theory, the right act is that which maximizes moral value. However, there are no rules, other than strategic rules (or 'rules of thumb' as they have misleadingly been called), for maximizing moral value. Kant's ethics, on the other hand, is a rules-based theory; and to do what is right, on Kant's theory, we must act dutifully in accordance with these rules.

The distinction between values-based and rules-based epistemologies is much less familiar. Epistemologists in the empiricist tradition have usually seen their main task as being to discover an adequate system of inductive rules which we may justifiably use to obtain knowledge of what is not directly known. Epistemological holists have generally denied that there is any system of inductive rules which has more than heuristic value. But they have not tried to construct a values-based epistemology to replace the inductivist theory. Rather, they have shown an increasing tendency to move towards positions of epistemological anarchism and relativism. However, we can abandon rules-based epistemologies without adopting either of these alternatives. For we can construct a values-based epistemology which is neither. It is true that a values-based epistemology will not have exact principles of induction or theory construction, but nor will it be the case that anything goes on such an epistemology. On the contrary, it can be as objective as any consequentialist or other values-based ethical system. Indeed, we may expect it to be somewhat more so.

Objectivists in ethics distinguish between what is morally right and what is morally justified. What is morally right, they say, is an objective matter, which is independent of the circumstances or values of any particular individual. What is morally justified, on the other hand, may depend on what beliefs or attitudes are reasonably held by a person at a time. Now when I say that the truth is what it is epistemically *right* to believe, I do not mean that it is, necessarily, what anyone is epistemically *justified* in believing. What it is right to believe, I want to say, is an objective matter which is independent of what any individual may actually believe or be justified in believing. The naturalistic theory of truth is thus an objectivist theory.

7.1 ABSOLUTE AND NATURALISTIC THEORIES

There are two kinds of ethical objectivism – an *absolute* version, and a *naturalistic* one. On an absolute theory, moral properties, such as rightness, exist independently of human values; so that it is possible that what is morally right may, in fact, be morally repugnant to us. Moreover, this repugnance may be *essentially ineradicable*, since it may stem, not from any lack of appreciation of the circumstances, or consequences, of our actions, but simply from the fact that we, *qua* human beings, have the wrong values. On a naturalistic theory, however, the objectivity of moral properties derives from the possibility of non-coercive agreement being reached about what is right or wrong – an agreement made possible by the fact (if it is a fact) that human beings all have the same basic moral values.

There are, correspondingly, two kinds of epistemic objectivism –

an absolute kind of theory, and a naturalistic one. On an absolute theory, the truth is independent of human epistemic evaluation; so that what is true may be something we should all say was certainly false, or conversely. Moreover, this may not be through any lack of information we could possibly obtain, or have obtained, but just because we are forever precluded from knowing certain things, or because we are the victims of Evil Demons, or because we all have the wrong epistemic values. As a result, what is true absolutely may be false for us, and conversely. For example, those who think we might all be brains in vats, so manipulated by super-beings that we are forever condemned (or blessed) to remain in ignorance of the truth about ourselves, are epistemic absolutists. On a naturalistic theory, however, the truth is necessarily what it is right *for us* to believe, and the brain-in-vat hypothesis is necessarily false.[1]

The kind of necessity involved in this claim is not logical necessity, but what I call 'pragmatic necessity'. The claim that something is pragmatically necessary is always relative to some person or class of people. It is the claim that it cannot rationally be denied by them. A person cannot, for example, rationally deny that they exist, or that they have beliefs, although it is not a matter of logical necessity that a person should exist or have beliefs. The claim that something is logically necessary, by contrast, is the claim that its denial is a contradiction, and so cannot occur in any rational belief system, human or otherwise. Now what I want to say about the brain-in-vat hypothesis is that it cannot be right for any *human being* to believe it. If there are other kinds of beings with belief systems structured like ours, it is logically possible that it should be right for *them* to believe it. But as the case is described it cannot rationally be accepted by any of *us* that we are just brains in vats. The claim is, therefore, from the perspective of human beings, necessarily false.

7.2 EPISTEMIC NATURALISM

Ethical naturalists typically hold that there are certain properties of things of which human beings naturally approve, and therefore think are good. These properties, they say, are not *constitutive* of goodness; nevertheless, things are good in virtue of them. An epistemic naturalist likewise holds that there are certain properties of beliefs which naturally meet with our epistemic approval, and accordingly, beliefs which have these properties are judged to be true or probable in virtue of their having them. This applies most obviously to beliefs with the property of having been acquired directly by perception or introspection. For there is a strong natural tendency in all of us to accept such judgements as true, or at least as very probable.

According to one version of ethical naturalism (which it is not my purpose to defend), there are certain features of actions, or traits of character, which naturally tend to create certain attitudes of approval or disapproval in people. Those of which we naturally approve are said to be good; those of which we naturally disapprove, bad. According to this theory, all correct judgements of right and wrong, and good and bad, derive from these basic attitudes of approval and disapproval. Consequently, if we are wrong about a moral judgement, it can only be because (a) we have acquired some unnatural attitudes, or (b) we are wrong about whether the actions or persons of which we approve (or disapprove) have the properties we think they have.

This form of ethical naturalism is epistemically an objectivist meta-ethical position, because it makes questions of right and wrong, and of good and bad, objective questions which are in principle able be settled by empirical investigation (assuming that the distinction between what is natural, and what is not, is ultimately an empirical one). Naturalism in ethics is to be contrasted with moral absolutism, according to which what is good or bad, or right or wrong, is independent of any human tendencies to approve or disapprove of things. On the absolutist theory, goodness is supposed to be a *non-natural*, or perhaps a *second order*, property which things may have independently of human attitudes. Such a theory is *ontologically objectivist*, but *epistemically sceptical*. It is ontologically objectivist, because it posits goodness as a *natural kind*, and supposes that the question whether something is good is just whether it is a thing of this kind. It is sceptical, however, because it is possible, given the theory, that even the best possible moral theory, from a human standpoint, may be wrong.

Epistemic naturalism is the meta-epistemic position parallel to this form of ethical naturalism. It is the view that truth is epistemic rightness, and is to be understood in the same sort of way as the ethical naturalist understands moral rightness. First, truth must be considered to be an epistemically objective concept. That is, while questions of truth and falsity can, in principle, be settled to our satisfaction by methods we can agree to be rational, and appropriate for their settlement, the explanation for this is that we are basically similar kinds of beings, similarly programmed to gather and evaluate evidence, to draw inferences, to construct, test and evaluate hypotheses, and we are all responding to the same world. Secondly, truth must be supposed to be an ontologically subjective concept if we accept epistemic naturalism. That is, there cannot be any ontologically objective property or relationship of truth which holds independently of our epistemic values; i.e. truth cannot be a natural kind. To suppose otherwise, as metaphysical realists do, is to adopt the epistemically sceptical view that even the ideally best theory about the nature of reality, from a human standpoint, may not be the true one.

7.3   THE DESIRABILITY OF PARALLEL META-THEORIES

Whatever kinds of epistemology and ethics we eventually adopt, it is desirable that they should similar; i.e. our means of deciding what we ought rationally to believe should be similar to those we need for deciding what we ought morally to do. I say this, firstly, because it seems unlikely that we should have two fundamentally different mechanisms for decision making. If we have the capacity to intuit basic moral rules, so that the natural morality for human beings is rules-based, then it is plausible that we should also have the capacity to intuit basic inductive rules, and that the natural epistemology for human beings should also be rules-based. On the other hand, if the natural morality is values-based, we should also expect to find that the natural epistemology is values-based. Secondly, inductive and moral rules seem to have the same kind of status; and we seek to improve them in the same kind of way. Inductive rules seem to be strategies for increasing our knowledge and understanding of things; moral rules seem to be strategies for promoting human happiness, dignity and so on. We criticize these rules by considering particular cases where they seem to give the wrong results, and by trying to find principled ways of restricting their application to areas where they are more successful.

According to George Pugh (see Pugh 1978), we are, biologically speaking, value-driven decision systems, i.e. systems with inbuilt mechanisms which systematically determine basic preferences. Pugh claims that these inbuilt systematic preferences, or values, were acquired by natural selection, and that, in addition to some basic personal and social values, we also have some primitive intellectual or epistemic values, which have a role in the formation and development of our belief systems. If he is right about this, then we need a values-based epistemology to explain how we think, and values-based personal and social psychologies to explain our personal and social behaviour.

The kind of values-based epistemology we need to explain our scientific inductive practices will be developed in the next chapter. For the remainder of this chapter, I shall continue to develop the analogy between epistemology and ethics, and elaborate on the concept of truth as epistemic rightness, i.e. as the epistemic parallel to the concept of moral rightness. I shall argue that there is a fundamental value of objectivity, which explains how our epistemic and moral preferences become objectified, and so interpreted as properties of the objects of our preferences – in particular, as the properties of truth and rightness.

7.4   ETHICAL AND EPISTEMIC EVALUATION

The terms of ethical and epistemic evaluation are logically similar to each other, although there are differences which make the parallel less than perfect. The epistemic equivalents of 'right' and 'wrong' are 'true' and 'false', but there are no distinctive terms for 'good' or 'bad' in the field of epistemic evaluation. Good theories and explanations are just good theories and explanations. In Ellis (1980), I made the mistake of comparing truth with goodness, and arguing that 'true' is a term of epistemic approval having a role in epistemology like the term 'good' has in ethics. But the correct ethical parallel is *rightness* rather than goodness. For 'true' and 'right' both have connotations of ultimate *correctness* of belief or action which are not implied by any weaker commendations or expressions of approval.

Compare the following pairs of sentences:

(1) (a) X is right
    (b) I prefer X

and

(2) (a) 'p' is true
    (b) I believe 'p'

The relationship between 1(a) and 1(b) is that between *evaluating* an action (state of affairs, attitude, or whatever) as right, and preferring it to anything else which might be done (be the case, adopted, etc.). From the speaker's point of view, it seems that the two are always the same, if the modes evaluation and preference are the same. Thus, if X is said to be right *morally*, and the preference expressed is for X *morally*; or if X is said to be right *prudentially*, and the preference is for X *prudentially*; or, in general, if X is said to be right in respect of U, and the preference expressed is for X in respect of U, then the evaluative judgements and the preference statements are apparently the same. For to evaluate an action as being morally right, and at the same time not to think it morally preferable to do it, or conversely, to prefer an action morally, but think it is not morally right to do it, is incoherent. However, the two statements do say something different, and so are not logically equivalent. For there is no reason why anyone *other than the speaker* should not accept the one and reject the other. The two statements are said to be only *pragmatically equivalent*. For a *logical equivalence* we require a pragmatic equivalence which is not speaker-relative.

The distinction between logical equivalence and pragmatic equivalence is important in this context. According to the epistemic semantics developed in *Rational Belief Systems* (Ellis 1979, ch. 2), two sentences of a formal language L are logically equivalent iff there is no rational belief system on L in which the sentences occur with opposite T and F evaluations. However, the object languages considered in this book were idealized to the extent that different speakers uttering the same sentence were assumed to be expressing the same belief. For object languages which include token reflexives, such as first personal pronouns, this assumption is obviously false. Different people using the same sentence of such an object language may express different beliefs. Moreover, they must sometimes use different sentences to express the same belief. And since beliefs, not sentences, are fundamentally the bearers of truth, and hence the relata of logical relationships, we must, for such a language, change the definition of logical equivalence. Two sentences P and Q of a language with first personal pronouns may be said to be *pragmatically equivalent* for a rational agent A iff they cannot occur with opposite T and F evaluations in A's belief system: they are *logically equivalent* iff there is no rational belief system on the language in which sentences expressing the same beliefs as P and Q do for A receive opposite T and F evaluations.

To illustrate the distinction that is being made between logical and pragmatic equivalence, consider the sentence 'All of my beliefs are false'. Clearly, we do not want this sentence to come out as being logically equivalent to a genuine contradiction, just because there is no rational belief system in which it is given a T evaluation by an evaluator who is evaluating his or her own beliefs. For the kind of contradiction expressed by 'All of my beliefs are false' is not a logical one. There is, for example, no *a priori* reason why *you* should not believe that all of my beliefs are false; it is just that this is something that *I* cannot rationally believe. Two sentences which are pragmatically equivalent for any given speaker can be said to be logically equivalent only if the sentences that any other speaker would need to use to express *the same beliefs* are also pragmatically equivalent.

Now the relationship between 2(a) and 2(b) is evidently like that between 1(a) and 1(b). If an object language L includes a truth predicate (with the usual properties), ' "p" is true' and 'I believe "p" ' could not occur with opposite T and F evaluations in a rational belief system on L.[2] However, the equivalence is not a logical equivalence, because what is asserted by 2(b) is speaker-relative, whereas what is asserted by 2(a) is not; although it would be incoherent for me to assert 2(a) and deny 2(b), or assert 2(b) and deny 2(a), there is no reason why you should not make opposite T and F evaluations of the beliefs I should express by asserting these two propositions. The equivalence of 2(a) and 2(b) is therefore only a pragmatic equivalence, just like that of 1(a) and 1(b).

What then is the nature of the relationship between ' "*p*" is true' and 'I believe "*p*"'? Why are these two logically distinct claims nevertheless pragmatically equivalent? The best explanation of this would appear to be that the relationship between these two claims is just like that between 1(a) and 1(b), and that the pragmatic equivalence holds for an exactly parallel reason. To see this, we have to appreciate the difference between *expressing* a belief or preference, and *stating* that one has this belief or preference. If I say that '*p*' is true, I am *expressing* my epistemic preference for believing '*p*', rather than, say, '~*p*' (or anything else incompatible with '*p*'). But if I say that I *believe* '*p*', I am *stating* that I have this epistemic preference. The belief I purport to be *expressing* is a meta-belief, viz. my belief that I believe '*p*'.

Any adequate theory of truth should be able to account for the pragmatic and logical equivalence relationships which hold between the three expressions '*p*', ' "*p*" is true', and 'I believe "*p*"'. The first and second are logically equivalent; the third is pragmatically equivalent to each of the other two. We have seen how the theory that truth is epistemic rightness can account for the pragmatic equivalence of ' "*p*" is true' and 'I believe "*p*"'. The pragmatic equivalence of '*p*' and 'I believe "*p*"' then follows from the normal redundancy of the truth predicate. For, on the evaluative theory of truth, ' "*p*" is true' is equivalent to '*p*' because '*p*' expresses what ' "*p*" is true' evaluates as being right to believe. Therefore, anyone who accepts the one, but rejects the other, has an incoherent system of beliefs. Note, however, that the equivalence of '*p*' and ' "*p*" is true' is not speaker-relative. Therefore, the relationship between these two claims is stronger than just pragmatic equivalence. It is one of *logical equivalence*, in the sense in which I have defined this relationship.

The account I have given also explains the pragmatic equivalence relationships between 'X is right' and 'X is good', on the one hand, and 'I prefer X' and 'I approve of X' on the other, where these are all judgements of the same kind (e.g. all moral judgements). But a deeper puzzle remains: the account does not explain why we need evaluative concepts, like rightness, truth and goodness. Why can we not just *state* what we prefer, believe, approve or disapprove of? Why do we have to express our beliefs, preferences and attitudes as though we were attributing mysterious properties to their supposed objects? I think we do so because we are naturally disposed to think about things in this sort of way. There is a value, I suggest, which lies behind this disposition. I call it *objectivity*.

7.5   THE VALUE OF OBJECTIVITY

The value of objectivity is a social value which has particular relevance to epistemology; although it is also important in ethics and aesthetics. It is the value of reaching an accommodation with others in matters of opinion, attitude and preference. I speculate that this value derives from the needs of primitive peoples to co-ordinate their activities and to pool their resources of knowledge and wisdom. But whatever its origin, it seems that we do naturally seek to adjust our belief and value systems to each other; if possible by persuading others to change their views, if necessary by adapting our own views to accommodate theirs. If we did not naturally seek such an accommodation, disagreements between us would not often matter very much. For we should have little interest in reconciling our differences of opinion, attitude or preference, if these were not likely to affect us more or less directly. But many of the things we argue about most intensely have no obvious bearings on our lives, and the passion with which we argue them is often disproportionate to any direct consequences. My speculation is that the reason for this lies in a primitive urge to construct a common, objective system of beliefs, values and attitudes.

To say that X is good or right or true (or, where X is a sentence, just X), is to express oneself in what I call the *objective mode*. But if I say that I approve of X, or that I prefer X morally, or that I believe

X, then I express myself in the *subjective mode*. This is not to say that the expression in the objective mode *means* the same as the corresponding one in the subjective mode. It does not; the two expressions are not even logically equivalent. Nevertheless, I may convey exactly the same information about my attitudes, priorities or beliefs, whichever form of expression I choose. Consider an expression in the subjective mode, such as 'I approve of X', which I use to state my attitude of approval. This statement is simultaneously the objective expression of a belief, viz. my belief that I have this attitude of approval. If I use the objective mode of speech, saying that X is good, I am *expressing* the same attitude of approval, although I am not *stating* that this attitude is mine. However, by making the evaluative statement, I should certainly be *implying* that the attitude is mine, and hence that I believe it is mine. Therefore, the implications overall are just the same whichever mode of speech is used. This is why the corresponding objective and subjective expressions of beliefs, attitudes and priorities are always pragmatically equivalent.

The difference between expressing a belief or attitude, using the objective mode of speech, and stating, using the subjective mode, that one has this belief or attitude is a difference of level of abstraction. Any statement I make is an abstraction of sorts from the totality of my knowledge; but to say that X is good or 'p' is true is to make a particular kind of abstraction from what I must know if I am making this claim sincerely, viz. that it is *my* belief or attitude I am expressing. In speaking in the objective mode, the belief or attitude I express is thereby disembodied, and put forward neutrally for discussion (or action or information) as though it was a thing which had some independent existence. It is presented as though it was not particularly *my* belief or attitude, but *the* belief or attitude, which is not anyone's in particular, which is up for consideration.

I call the process which enables us to consider beliefs, attitudes and priorities in an abstract way, and to evaluate them without reference to any individuals who may hold them, the process of 'objectification'. It results, I believe, from the value we all naturally put on objectivity, which I postulate to be one of our fundamental epistemic values. There is nothing wrong with objectification, I hasten to add. On the contrary, it is a process which has a vital role in concept formation, since it is the main process by which our abstract concepts are formed, and it is probably necessary for developing the common stock of beliefs, attitudes and priorities which any community needs for co-ordinated and co-operative activity. It may also be necessary for hypothetical reasoning, and therefore for all planning activities, because if beliefs could not be considered in abstraction from those who held them, we could not consider hypotheses which are not held as beliefs.

The value of objectivity is fundamentally the desire to reach agreement within one's tribe, or sub-group, on beliefs, values and priorities. Given the large amount of disagreement about these things which exists in the wider community, it may be doubted whether this value is a significant one. However, there is a sense of urgency with which disagreements on these issues are pursued within any close-knit social group, and sharing the basic beliefs, values and priorities of such a group is at least a large part of what is involved in belonging to it. I cannot show that this is universally the case, or that the value of objectivity which I postulate as a basic epistemic value is genetically encoded, as I think it probably is. But it is plausible that this should be so, and it would certainly be explicable if it were. For we are social animals, and our ability to survive has long depended on our ability to co-operate with each other – at least within the tribe. The ways we act, however, depend on our beliefs, values and priorities. It is plausible, therefore, that we should have acquired, by natural selection, a basic desire to co-ordinate our belief and value systems, and natural ways of thinking, speaking and acting adapted to this end. Objectification, I suggest, is a natural strategy for the construction of objective knowledge.

Linguistically, the desire for objectivity is manifested in the ways we speak. Our language is one which enables us to express our beliefs and attitudes without referring to ourselves as the holders of these beliefs or attitudes. It allows us speak neutrally, as it were, using sentences which could equally well be used by others to express the same beliefs or attitudes. Thus we can say, in the objective mode, 'X is good', or 'It is probable that p', or 'It is possible that p', or 'That was a very dramatic and moving play, although it ended rather badly, and left one feeling that the issue it raised had not been resolved.' The objective mode of speech is important for the following reason: it focuses attention on the substance of our beliefs, on the objects of our approval, and so on, rather than on us as the holders of these beliefs and attitudes, and so puts these objects forward for public discussion. It is therefore a mode of speech which is tailor-made for the construction of communal systems of beliefs and attitudes.

When we use the objective mode of speech in argument or discussion, we inevitably give the impression that we are presenting for consideration various propositions which are the objects of our beliefs; and because we make no reference to ourselves as the holders of these beliefs, we may be led to suppose that these propositions are independently existing entities – things which have truth values, which can contradict each other, carry entailments, have implications, serve as evidence for this or that, and so on. Consequently, our discussions often seem to involve abstract third world particulars, and to be carried out just by drawing attention to their implications. The propositions, and their implications, are all there, so to speak, needing only to be properly arranged and presented. Yet surely the reality is that there are just people saying things, to each other. The propositions are just illusions created by our ways of speaking.

7.6   OBJECTIVE KNOWLEDGE

The idea that there is objective knowledge which may exist without a knowing subject may be attributed to the existence of the objective mode of speech. For what is supposed to be characteristic of objective knowledge is just that it contains no token reflexive reference to the speaker, or to the time or place of the speaker's utterance, i.e. it is knowledge expressed in the objective mode. But the knowledge is the same however it may be expressed; and no special significance attaches to the manner of its expression. Therefore, to claim, as Popper does, that objective knowledge exists independently of knowing subjects, and that its generation is the sole concern of scientific inquiry, is unwarranted.

It is true that scientific inquiry is not much concerned with what individuals may believe, except perhaps in the context of some sociological or psychological investigations. And even in these contexts, the individuals studied are just like other objects of investigation, and no special significance attaches to their identities. It is also true that science is a co-operative enterprise concerned with the generation of knowledge for the human community, and hence with what may reasonably be called objective knowledge. Moreover, there is a great deal of material stored in libraries and other places recording the knowledge of previous generations. But to speak of any of this as objective knowledge which exists in some kind of third world, as Popper does, is to be misled by our use of the objective mode of speech.

There is no third world of numbers, theorems, propositions, problems etc. which are the objects of human knowledge or study. There are only books, papers, records, recordings, inscriptions, etc. which have been made by men and women in the past, conveying what they then knew or believed or were puzzled about. To suppose that they somehow furnished the third world by their efforts with abstract particulars such as these is fanciful, and quite contrary to the spirit of scientific realism.

8

The Problem of Induction

The problem of induction is to show that our scientific inductive practices are more or less rational.[1] To do this, we need a theory of rationality on which the various canons of induction may be evaluated. The kind of evaluation that is needed is an epistemic evaluation; i.e. the canons of induction must be evaluated as strategies for improving our knowledge and understanding. To improve our knowledge and understanding is the same thing as to increase the epistemic value of our belief systems. Therefore, to justify induction, it is necessary and sufficient to show that the various canons of induction we use are good strategies for increasing epistemic value. My aim in this chapter is to elaborate the epistemic value system required for this task, and to show how it might be used both to justify our inductive practices, in so far as they are rational, and to explain them.

The theory to be developed is one which takes certain epistemic values to be natural and fundamental, and construes inductive rules as being just more or less useful strategies for promoting these values. It is thus a naturalistic *values-based* epistemology. The theories sought by empiricists have usually been *rules-based*. For their aim has usually been to show that some particular inductive rule, e.g. the straight rule, is intrinsically rational, and hence that its use is rationally justified. However, for reasons given in Ellis (1965b), it is not enough to show that some abstractly considered rule has intrinsically desirable properties. What has to be justified is the way we actually use the rule; and this cannot be done without appeal to our epistemic values.[2]

The hope of many philosophers is that the problem of induction can be solved by developing a naturalistic theory of rational competence adequate to explain and justify some of our inductive reasoning. I share this hope; but I think such a theory will have to be a values-based theory within which rules have only the status of epistemic strategies, or rules of thumb – like the status of rules in act-utilitarianism. First, the inductive rules we use appear to have precisely this character. For there are no inductive rules which can be used indiscriminately, or where the subject matter is theoretically isolated. (See Ellis 1965b.) Secondly, it has now been well established empirically that the inductive principles we find most intuitive are often not rational, and that the inductive practices we think are most rational are often not intuitive.[3] There is some reason to doubt whether the experimental findings warrant all of the conclusions that have been drawn about the shortcomings of intuitive reasoning (see Cohen 1986). Even so, the prospects for developing an adequate epistemology which appeals to intuitively valid *principles* of inductive reasoning do not appear to be good.

Ultimately, the justification of our scientific inductive practices must depend somehow on our intuitive judgements of rationality, as Jonathan Cohen has successfully argued (see Cohen 1981 and 1986). But the appeals to intuition we make when we evaluate inductive rules or strategies are generally to the rationality or otherwise of *particular inferences*, and so, presumably, to the perceived, epistemically valued, *properties* of these inferences. The appeal is not to any more intuitively evident *principles* which may serve as a basis for criticism. Therefore, if our theory is to reflect our practice, what we need is a values-based epistemology rather than a rules-based one. Compatibly with the particularism of our practice of epistemic evaluation, I suppose one could have a kind of Rossian epistemology (cf. Ross 1939), in which inductive rules had the status of being *prima facie* rational. But I wish to put greater emphasis on the role of epistemic values in epistemology than Ross did on moral values in ethics.[4]

8.1 CONSTRUCTING A NATURALISTIC VALUES-BASED EPISTEMOLOGY

To construct a theory of the kind we need to explain and justify our scientific inductive practices we must set out to define an ideal of rationality which may serve as a *theoretical ideal* as well as a *regulative ideal*. It must be capable of serving as a theoretical ideal, because, on any naturalistic epistemology, it is basically irrationality, not rationality, which needs to be explained. Therefore, we need the concept of an ideally rational being to define how people would think if they were ideally rational, and so, by contrast, to determine what remains to be explained. But the theoretical ideal must also be capable of serving as a regulative ideal, because the theory is needed to tell us how we ought rationally to think.

The kind of theory we need is a model theory of a sort which is very common in science. The requirements on the model are:

(1) The ideal of rationality contained in the model should appeal to the normal intellect as a rational ideal.
(2) We should be able to use the model successfully to explain our inductive practices, i.e. our inductive practices should be more or less rational, as this is defined in the model; and in so far as they are not, we should be able to explain why.
(3) The model should be biologically realistic, i.e. it should be explicable biologically why we should have the basic epistemic values we do.

A theory of rationality which had all of these features would provide an adequate solution to the problem of induction. For it would explain both why we think inductively as we do, and how and why rationally we ought to think inductively.

I assume that, biologically, we are value-driven decision systems, and accordingly that the mechanism which shapes our belief systems is value-driven.[5] That is, I suppose that we have certain inbuilt values which together determine our belief preferences. Among these, I assume that there are certain rational, or epistemic, values which are distinguishable, although perhaps not sharply, from our personal and social values. Our *epistemic* values determine what we ought *rationally* to believe, as opposed to what is otherwise in our interests, or in the interests of society, or is pleasing or comforting to believe.

It is important to distinguish our epistemic values from the biological ends they serve. To flourish, people need reliable, economical, accurate and efficient belief systems which are well adapted to their environments, and applicable to most new situations which may arise. They also need to share many of the beliefs and attitudes of their tribe. Presumably, our epistemic values have been selected to make it possible for us to construct and maintain such belief systems. However, these biological needs are not our epistemic values, and it is not possible to justify our inductive practices with reference to them without circularity. For such ends refer beyond ourselves to our environments, and hence we must have knowledge of our environments if we are to use them for this purpose. Moreover, they may change or disappear as our circumstances change, but our epistemic values are not so externally dependent.

Our most basic epistemic values must be internally assessable things like consistency in our belief systems, beliefs that are empirically certified, well-corroborated beliefs, established beliefs and concepts, beliefs about what is universally the case, and theories establishing certain kinds of links between beliefs or systems of beliefs. Our biological needs have no doubt determined our epistemic values, but we must pursue them for their own sakes, without regard to this fact. It will be argued here that the values just listed are among those which motivate and explain our inductive practices. They are not all equally fundamental, and the list is certainly not complete. But they are all, I think, more or less basic human values which are independent of our social and personal values.

In pursuing knowledge and understanding, we seek to maximize the satisfaction of our epistemic values. And, to the extent that our inductive practices are effective means to this end, I claim that they are rational. For rationality is just the pursuit of epistemic value by appropriate means. Of course, many philosophers will want to define knowledge as knowledge of the truth, and to define truth in some way independently of our epistemic values. To such philosophers, I can offer no prospect of a solution to the problem of induction, because their position is essentially sceptical. But to those who think, as I do, that the truth is what it is right epistemically to believe, a naturalistic solution to the problem of induction may be possible. For the attempt to improve our knowledge and understanding in accordance with our epistemic values, and the quest for truth, are one and the same thing.

8.2 THE EMPIRICIST MODEL

The problem of induction is a problem of empiricism, and cannot be solved in an empiricist framework. To solve the problem, we must recognize that there are basic considerations which are relevant to the question of what we ought rationally to believe, which empiricists do not regard as fundamental. For empiricists, there are fundamentally only two kinds of consideration relevant to whether a proposition is rationally acceptable: (1) whether it is certified directly by experience, and (2) whether it is inferrable by logically justifiable rules from propositions which have been certified in this way. I believe that the problem of induction can be solved, but only if this restraint on what constitutes a justification is removed.

Empiricists, like most other philosophers, consider *empirical certification* and *consistency* to be basic criteria for rationally evaluating beliefs and belief systems. I call these our *empiricist values*. According to many empiricists, these values are derivative. They are not innate, as I should say, but derive from the supposedly primary values of truth and avoidance of error.[6] Thus, consistency is to be valued, not for its own sake, but because it is a necessary condition for truth. Empirically certified (i.e. perceptually and introspectively acquired) beliefs are generally to be given epistemic priority, not because we have an inbuilt disposition to do so, as I would suppose, but because they are assumed to be known most directly to be true, and hence least prone to error.

According to many empiricists, truth and avoidance of error are the only genuinely primitive epistemic values. So that, on their view, if anything else has epistemic value, its value is derivative. The values of comprehensiveness, verisimilitude and validity, for example, are all said to be explained in terms of these fundamental values. Thus, a more comprehensive theory is generally to be preferred to a less comprehensive one, if neither has been falsified, not because it unifies and makes comprehensible a wider range of phenomena, but because, potentially at least, it contains more truth. As Popper would say, it says more. Verisimilitude, however it is to be measured, is to be valued, not because the criteria we use to gauge it refer to properties which have any intrinsic worth, but because it is supposed that theories possessing these properties are nearer to the truth. Likewise, valid arguments commend themselves for no reason other than that they are necessarily truth-preserving, so that if we start with truths we shall never be led into error – although it is not explained why we should prefer to argue validly when we are dealing with ethical propositions, or subjective probability judgements, which, on many empiricist theories, are neither true nor false.

The problem of induction is one that arises within this empiricist framework. For inductive arguments are, by definition, not necessarily truth-preserving, and hence they are invalid. The problem, then, is to explain why an ideally rational being, whose only primary concerns are with truth and avoidance of error, should accept such arguments. The conclusion reached by Hume, and never subsequently overturned, is that there is no rational justification for doing so. Consequently, it is now widely accepted by empiricists that our general beliefs about the world – those which do more than just summarize their known instances – are not rationally held. We hold them, it is said, not because we are rationally entitled to, but because we are creatures of habit, or have found them useful instruments for prediction, and have nothing better to put in their place, or because we have found them unifying, elegant or aesthetically pleasing – at any rate not for reasons which would, in themselves, justify us in believing them to be true.

Some empiricist philosophers continue to hope that induction, by which they usually mean the straight inductive rule, can be *vindicated* by showing that its use is a rational strategy. Reichenbach had argued that, if our aim is to obtain knowledge of probabilities (defined as long run relative frequencies), the straight rule is a rational strategy to adopt, since it guarantees long run success (provided that the probabilities exist). For if probability is estimated by this rule it must eventually converge to the true probability, if there is one. However, the straight rule is only one of infinitely many convergent rules. Hence, people whose only primary epistemic values are truth and avoidance of error would not be bound to use the straight rule. But even if they were, there would be a problem of the short run. Why, rationally, should we apportion degrees of belief to probabilities, when probability is defined as long run relative frequency? For our only real concern is with relative frequencies in the comparatively short run.

Wesley Salmon attempted to deal with the first of these two problems by requiring that a rationally acceptable rule should yield probabilistic conclusions which are independent of any arbitrary features of the language used to describe the evidence. The only such rule, he argued, is the straight rule. He attempted to deal with the problem of the short run by offering a vindication of the 'straight short run' rule: 'Infer that the relative frequency in the short run approximates the limit of the relative frequency as nearly as possible'. I do not think that Salmon's vindication of the straight short run rule was successful, however, since all it showed was that the policy of adopting this rule must pay off in the long run. But what he needed to show is that it is a rational policy for the short run.

Be that as it may, the Reichenbach–Salmon attempts to vindicate induction do not justify our scientific inductive practices. First, we do not use inductive rules in a theoretical vacuum, and we think our theories do, and ought rationally to, influence our probability judgements. For inductive rules cannot be straightforwardly applied where there are relevant theoretical considerations involving other kinds of evidence than evidence of relative frequency (see Ellis 1965b). If they have any straightforward application, therefore, it can only be where the subject matter of the inference is theoretically isolated, i.e. where we have no prior rational expectations about the behaviour or properties of the entities we are dealing with, or where the evidence we do have is so clearly contrary to these expectations that we feel they must be put aside, and our probability estimates made independently of them.

On the other hand, if we assume we have no relevant background information at all about the subject matter of the inference, no prior knowledge about the kind of world in which these things occur, or of our relationship as observers to them (e.g. whether they are objective or subjective phenomena), no beliefs about their possible causes – in other words, if we assume a state of total theoretical ignorance, then I do not see how we could even describe the phenomena sufficiently to apply inductive rules. For, in the process of learning a language, we must acquire some kind of world-view, involving a complex integrated system of beliefs about the world and our relationship to it. Consequently, we cannot idealize to a state of total theoretical ignorance without destroying the theoretical basis of language, and hence that of description too. We are given, as it were, a more or less ordered world of continuing objects with more or less stable properties interacting with each other in more or less predictable ways. We have, therefore, a kind of base level theoretical model of reality acquired in learning the language and necessary for its understanding.

But perhaps we can discount the influence of our background theories, including our base level ones, in thought, if not in practice, so that we can say what the correct inductive inference would be if the relative frequency evidence were strictly the only evidence we had. However, to do this we should have to suppose that the terms and predicates we used to describe phenomena were completely uncommitted theoretically, like the symbols of the predicate calculus, for example. And this leads us straight into the Goodman paradoxes. For if the terms 'grue', 'bleen', 'green' and 'blue' were genuinely theoretically uncommitted terms, there would be no reason to prefer the description of emeralds as 'green' rather than 'grue' and hence no reason to prefer the straight inductive inference from 'All observed emeralds are green' to that from 'All observed emeralds are grue'. For the pairs of predicates 'grue' and 'bleen', and 'green' and 'blue' are symmetrically interdefinable, and there is nothing formally to choose between them.

Hence we are forced to conclude that some theoretical commitment of the terms used to describe events is a necessary condition for the possibility of sound inductive argument. But we have already seen that, where there is theoretical involvement of the terms we use to describe events, it is rational to be guided by our theories, and not just by evidence of relative frequency, in making our probability estimates. Therefore, no vindication of our scientific inductive practices of the kind sought by Reichenbach and Salmon is possible. If there is theoretical involvement, inductive rules can only be used rationally in conjunction with our theories; if there is no theoretical involvement, almost any inference can be justified on the basis of any given inductive rule if we choose to conceptualize the phenomena appropriately.

Now a good theory always accounts for most of the facts in its domain. It may alter somewhat our perception of the facts, and hence our judgement about what a good theory in the area should do. But if a theory restricts the domain of the facts too much, or leaves unexplained most of what it was designed to explain, then this is reason to think that the theory is unsatisfactory. A planetary theory which explained only the motions of the outer planets would not be a good theory. It might be acceptable as a step in the direction of understanding planetary motion, but the research programme it defined, of accounting for what the theory left unexplained, would have to be fruitful for it to remain so.

The empiricist theory of rationality, which purports to explain what we may rationally believe, is not a good theory by this criterion. For it leaves most of what it set out to explain, viz., the rationality of science, to be explained in other ways, although no satisfactory explanations have been forthcoming. It can, perhaps, explain our preference for empirically certified beliefs, and certain general facts about the structure of our belief systems. But it does not explain why, rationally, we should accept what most of us would regard as scientifically established. On the contrary, it implies that most of our scientific beliefs are not rationally held, and if nevertheless we hold them, then an empiricist is committed to explaining this fact as due to the influence of non-rational forces, e.g. force of habit, aesthetic preference, or perceived instrumental value. The failure of empiricists to solve the problem of induction is, therefore, a powerful argument against empiricism.

8.3   IMPROVING THE EMPIRICIST MODEL

To construct a more adequate theory of rationality, we must replace the empiricist model by a better one. To do this, we must try to retain those features of the empiricist model which have explanatory power, or replace them by others capable of doing the same job. Specifically, the values of consistency and empirical certification must be retained, whether or not they are regarded as fundamental.

I think the first step towards improving the model is to reject the assumption that our primary epistemic values are truth and avoidance of error. For we need to break away from the traditional restraints, and there is reason to think that these are not in any case genuine epistemic values. If we reject them, however, we must somehow retain our empiricist values as features of the model, for otherwise we shall just be throwing away the baby with the bath water. My proposal for keeping the baby is that we should regard our empiricist values as primary ones, which are not to be justified in terms of other values, epistemic or otherwise. For, in this way, we can retain those features of the empiricist model which are explanatory without importing the metaphysical concept of truth into the foundations of our theory.

One reason I want to say that truth and avoidance of error are not fundamental epistemic values is that on any theory of truth, other than a subjectivist one, they are not internally assessable, and cannot therefore be the epistemic values which form and shape our belief systems from the start. It might well be biologically necessary for us to have beliefs which are mostly true, and so likely that our epistemic values are adapted to this end. But given any objectivist theory of truth, truth cannot be a fundamental epistemic value.

But I want to go further than this. In my view, truth and avoidance of error are not epistemic values at all. We use various criteria to evaluate beliefs as true or false, but we do not use truth or falsity as criteria for the evaluation of beliefs in any other respect. 'True' and 'false' are terms which function in epistemology as 'right' and 'wrong' do in ethics. They are what I have elsewhere called 'modes of evaluation' (Ellis 1980). Now moral rightness is not a moral value, but something that has to be cashed in terms of our moral values, which are things like justice, happiness, considerateness, honesty, and so on. If we want to understand what moral rightness is, we must understand the value system with respect to which our judgements of right and wrong are made. Likewise, I should say, truth is not an epistemic value, but a mode of evaluation for a system of epistemic values. And if we want to know what truth and falsity are, we must understand the system of epistemic values with respect to which our judgements of truth and falsity are made.

Having made this move, the question then becomes: what are

our epistemic values, and how are they interrelated? To retain the virtues of empiricism, I assume that consistency and empirical certification must certainly be two of them, and that both have high priority. Indeed, I should suppose that the value of consistency always overrides. It is clear, however, that we need other values besides these to explain our belief preferences, and hence our judgements of truth, falsity, probability, and so on. For example, the assumption that the world did not exist before people existed is compatible with our empiricist values, as is the assumption that the sun will not rise tomorrow. Hence, if it is irrational to believe such things, as it surely is, it cannot be because it would be contrary to our empiricist values to do so. Therefore, the irrationality of such beliefs must be explained in other ways, or the appearance of irrationality dispelled. I assume that the latter cannot be done. Therefore, to explain the irrationality of such beliefs on the kind of model we are looking for, we must suppose that there are important epistemic values which underlie our judgements of truth and falsity besides the empiricist ones.

I postulate that we are innately disposed to value those kinds of beliefs and systems of beliefs which are biologically useful to us. Perceptually and introspectively acquired beliefs clearly fall into this category. No doubt having a consistent belief system does too. But our survival also depends on our ability to anticipate nature; and this depends largely on our general beliefs and theories. It is to be expected, therefore, that we should attach a good deal of value to our store of such beliefs and theories. We should be reluctant to abandon them, especially those that are well entrenched or have served us well in the past; and if forced to do so, it is to be expected that we should try to salvage what we can from them.[7] It is also to be expected that we should strive to increase our general knowledge and theoretical understanding, and hence that we should have some epistemic values adapted to these ends.

In the following sections of this chapter, I shall describe a number of processes which are evidently involved in the construction, establishment, integration and maintenance of general knowledge – in particular, the processes of generalizing, normalizing, testing and reconceptualizing. I shall not discuss the processes involved in theory construction, or the criteria by which theories are evaluated. My aim is just to describe the basic strategies, and to identify the epistemic values they serve. I shall argue that there are four basic epistemic values which are served by these processes: viz. regularity, epistemic conservatism, corroboration and connectivity. The first provides motivation for the strategies of inductive generalization and normalization, and for assuming a kind of 'uniformity of nature' principle. In the area we are concerned with, epistemic conservatism exercises control over what inductive generalizations we may make. It also helps to motivate the normalization strategy. Corroboration is the value most involved in testing general knowledge, and is therefore fundamental to the process of establishing it and determining its scope. Connectivity is a value concerned with the establishment of conceptual connections, and hence with the integration of knowledge. It motivates conceptual changes, and thus serves as a counter to our natural, and proper, epistemic conservatism.

8.4 INDUCTION AND EPISTEMIC CONSERVATISM

Induction is the primitive strategy we use to arrive at generalizations. Roughly, if something holds in a number of cases without exception, we are naturally disposed to think it will hold generally. What holds in most cases we know about, we are inclined to believe will continue to hold in most cases. What has rarely happened in certain circumstances, we naturally suppose will continue to happen only rarely in such circumstances. I do not think we can be much more precise in our description of the primitive strategy than this, although we are at liberty to theorize that an ideally rational being would generalize according to some more precisely defined inductive rule, such as the straight rule.

The strategy is primitive in the sense that it is unlearned. We could not have discovered it for ourselves, for we should have to have used it to do so. We were not taught it orally, because we needed it to learn at least the vocabulary of the language. For without it we should not know what any term meant, or if we did, that it would continue to mean the same. Nor is there any reason to think that we were ever conditioned to think this way. A crude disposition to generalize like this seems, therefore, to be a natural tendency. Yet, there are some generalizations we might have arrived at in this way which we should not accept, and others we find quite acceptable. So, however the process of inductive generalization may be articulated, an important question remains concerning the evaluation of inductive generalizations.

The general principle must be that we tend to value, and therefore seek, generalizations of the kinds that proved useful to us as language and thought evolved. These generalizations will naturally be concerned with the sorts of things we think there are, and therefore, historically, with the sorts of things which were included in our primitive ontologies. Now, we seem naturally disposed to think of our environments as consisting of objects in space and time, possessing various properties, doing various things, and having various effects. Consequently, we are likely to value generalizations concerning any of the sorts of things we think belong to any of these basic ontological categories.

I assume that the ontology we intuitively work with is reflected in the language we use to describe the world. Therefore, since we have names for certain *kinds* of objects and their properties, and verbs describing certain *kinds* of actions and events, our primitive ontologies must include kinds of things, actions and events, as well as individuals of these kinds. Therefore, given the general principle that our epistemic preference should be for the sorts of generalizations that have been useful to us in the past, and the presumed utility of our ontologies, we should prefer beliefs about recognized kinds of things to generalizations which are not about recognized kinds, i.e. we should prefer generalizations which derive from conceptually and ontologically conservative descriptions of things. There is nothing sacrosanct about our intuitive conception of reality, as physics has taught us, but it is the natural base from which we must begin; and any change to it needs to be established, and its worth demonstrated, before it can be used as a basis for inductive inferences.

Normally, the logical complements of things, or kinds of things, do not belong to the same ontological categories as the things or kinds they complement – if, indeed, they exist at all. For 'Crows exist' and 'Non-crows exist' are very different kinds of claims. The first is just the claim that things of a certain kind, viz. crows, exist.

The second is a much more complicated claim, because, in the sense in which it is true, it implies that there are kinds of things other than crows, and that there are things of at least some of these kinds, i.e. it is doubly existential. Interpreted straightforwardly, in the same way as the claim that crows exist, the claim is simply false. For there is no kind of thing which consists of all kinds of things which are not crows – at least not in my ontology. Likewise, the claim that non-Brian Ellis exists is, if true, just a very odd way of saying that there are individuals other than me. But if it is interpreted as the claim that there is *an individual* who consists of everything which is not me, then the claim is false. For there is no such individual.

I do not know how to distinguish between complementary terms which name genuine individuals or kinds from those which do not. I think it is a question of which we think name entities that are required for causal explanations. Certainly, causal involvement is one of our main criteria for what is physically real. But, however the distinction may be made, we all certainly make it, and it is essential to sound inductive reasoning that we should be able to. For inductive arguments must proceed from epistemically pre-ferred descriptions if they are to provide good reasons for their conclusions. And the preferred descriptions are those which, given our current understanding of the world, are conceptually and ontologically most conservative. The irrationality of arguing induc-tively from the existence of white swans or yellow bananas to the conclusion that all non-black things are non-ravens derives, not from the form of the inference, which is sound, but from the irrationality of the conception of such things as non-black non-ravens.[8] It is irrational because it violates the requirement of epistemic conservatism.[9]

The epistemic values of conceptual and ontological conservatism likewise rule out the Goodman inferences. Their irrationality stems from the irrationality of the conceptions from which they proceed. To conceive of emeralds as grue is already to admit into one's ontology a property of grueness, which we could not accept without doing a great deal of violence to our conceptual framework – thus abandoning much of what we think we know for a concept of no proven worth. Our intuition, which, I suggest, derives from the value we attach to established conceptions, is to reject this description along with the inference. Obviously, we cannot reject the description of emeralds as grue on empiricist grounds alone. For the description is compatible with everything that is empirically certified. It does not, however, employ established concepts. Therefore, before we could use such descriptions as bases for inductive inferences, we should need some argument to show that such descriptions were preferable to the established ones. In the absence of such an argument, the requirements of epistemic conservatism rule them out as acceptable bases for inductive inferences.

Epistemic conservatism is not to be equated with dogmatism, or with blind adherence to traditional ways of looking at things. It is neither of these things to refuse to accept the Goodman inferences, or the existence of a white horse as evidence for the generalization that all ravens are black. Nor is it incompatible with adventurous theorizing. If someone can produce a theory with a different ontology from the usual, which is demonstrably superior, by the criteria relevant to theory evaluation, then this theory should be accepted. What it does is establish the onus of proof. Those concepts, laws and theories which have been useful to us are to be retained in the absence of compelling reasons otherwise.

8.5 CORROBORATION

The values of epistemic conservatism restrict the range of inductive generalizations which are *prima facie* acceptable. The value of corroboration contributes to their entrenchment as beliefs and to determining their scope. I think Sir Karl Popper was right to recognize its importance as a value, and that he correctly perceived its role in the development of scientific theory (see Popper 1959).

However, Popper was wrong to distinguish, as he did, between corroboration and confirmation, because he left himself without any adequate explanation of the rational preferability of well corroborated beliefs. He cannot say that it is rational to be guided by them because they are most likely to be true. Nor can he say that having been well corroborated they are likely to continue to be.

Indeed, on his own theory, we have no reason to believe that falsified theories will not always be corroborated in future, and hence no more reason to trust corroborated theories than uncorroborated ones. In my view, Popper needs corroboration as a basic epistemic value, and a theory of rational belief which recognizes this value. The more often, and the more widely varied the circumstances in which a law, theory or generalization has been corroborated, the more rational it must be to believe it, and hence the greater its epistemic probability.

The value of corroboration, like that of epistemic conservatism, derives from the proven utility of corroborated beliefs. It is not that we know in advance that corroborated beliefs will continue to be corroborated. What we know is that they have, or would have, been successful predictors. Now the general principle from which our epistemic values may be derived is that the *sorts* of beliefs which have been useful to us in the course of evolution are the ones we are likely to value epistemically, and therefore to consider belief-worthy. So, by this principle, we should expect corroborated beliefs to be considered worthy of belief – the more so, the more often, and the more varied the circumstances in which they have been corroborated.

The point of varying the circumstances of corroboration is to test a hypothesis more widely. If the hypothesis is that all As are Bs, and if all instances of this generalization that have been observed are of As that are Cs, and if it is plausible, on background information, that an A's being a C is relevant to its being a B, then the corroboration we have obtained may only be for the more restricted hypothesis that all As that are Cs are Bs. So, to remove this doubt about the scope of the corroboration, we must examine some As that are not Cs to see whether they too are Bs. Background information is thus obviously relevant to corroboration. For we need to know what sorts of factors might limit the scope of a generalization to know what tests to perform. Blindly repeating tests under more or less similar circumstances is not a good way to corroborate a hypothesis; for it leaves open the possibility that the generalization holds only in these circumstances.

On the other hand, if we thought that observation itself, or time or place of observation, might be a factor limiting the scope of any generalization, then strong corroboration of unrestricted generalizations would be impossible. For while observing As that are Bs may make it reasonable to believe that all As that have been or will be observed are Bs, or that all As in our spatio-temporal region are Bs, we should not be able to corroborate strongly the more general hypothesis that *all* As are Bs. I assume, however, that strong corroboration of hypotheses of unrestricted scope or generality is possible, for otherwise the laws and theories of science could not be well corroborated. Therefore, we must be strongly disposed to believe, independently of corroboration, that what holds for us in our own spatio-temporal region holds generally. That is, we must operate with a sort of 'uniformity of nature' principle. Why this should be so will be considered presently.

It is impossible to say, without reference to our background theories, how strongly a hypothesis is supported by corroborative evidence. It depends how unequivocal the evidence is, how plausible the hypothesis is given our background understanding, how probable we should take the evidence to be independently of the hypothesis, how broad the scope of the hypothesis being tested, and whether there are reasons for thinking that some scope restrictions on the hypothesis being tested may be necessary.

If the degree of corroboration provided by the evidence e for the hypothesis h is measured by $P(h/e) - P(h)$, normalized to a zero to one scale[10] then

(1) $S(h/e) = P(h/e) \times P(\sim e/\sim h)$

That is, the more probable the hypothesis, given the evidence, and the more improbable the evidence, given the denial of the hypothesis, the greater the degree of corroboration. Thus, the strongest corroborations of our hypotheses are to be obtained from their least probable consequences.

Also, if h entails g, and g entails e, then the following *chain rule* holds:[11]

(2) $S(h/e) = S(h/g) \times S(g/e)$

Consequently, if the evidence we have all corroborates g, and g has been sufficiently corroborated, there is no point in seeking further evidence of this kind. To increase support for h, we must seek evidence of a different kind, viz. evidence for some consequence of h which is not a consequence of g. If h is the hypothesis that all swans are white, it is not to the point to go on examining European swans, once the hypothesis g that all European swans are white has been sufficiently corroborated. For the maximum degree of corroboration for h obtainable this way is $S(h/g)$, which, given our background knowledge of bird colour variation with geographical location, may be quite low.

These two results define and explain the importance of test severity and test variety in the process of corroboration. If a hypothesis survives sufficiently many and various tests of enough severity, it will be well-corroborated. And a well corroborated hypothesis, I hold, is one which, other things being equal, we ought rationally to believe. Hence, there may come a point, in the process of corroboration, when the evidence for a hypothesis becomes compelling, and if it is contrary to anything else we believe, it may be necessary to revise this belief. The claims of epistemic conservatism may thus be overcome by the corroboration of hypotheses.

8.6 UNIFORMITY OF NATURE

It is often held that induction depends on the assumption that nature is uniform, i.e. that all things are governed by strictly universal laws. However, no principle of the uniformity of nature can be formulated which will justify our inductive practices. For it cannot be used to validate any inductive inferences, unless we can identify those local regularities which instantiate universal laws. Moreover, the assumption itself needs justification, since it is not *a priori*, nor even generally accepted. The Ancient Greeks, for example, expected to find perfect regularity only in the heavens, and in the abstract world of the Forms. And many people today would exempt human actions from the ambit of universal laws. So the assumption is not justified either way. But even if it were, we do not appear to need it. The Ancient Greeks argued inductively, though they did not make this assumption.

Nevertheless, there is something to the suggestion that belief in the uniformity of nature supports our inductive practices. For we seem naturally to be disposed to search for regularities or uniformities in nature, and to see any deviations from the regularities we think we have discovered as being superimposed by extraneous forces. It is not that nature, as we find it, is uniform, even within the range of our observations. But we are inclined to assume it is, nevertheless, and to conceive of things as instantiations of general regularities, distorted though they may be by their peculiar circumstances or histories. We seem thus to be natural *regularity seekers*. We are not content with local generalizations. Whatever holds locally, we are naturally inclined to suppose holds generally, unless there are special reasons (such as those the Greeks had, or libertarians have) to think otherwise. Newton summed up the attitude in the third of his 'Rules of Reasoning in Philosophy': 'The qualities of bodies which admit neither intensification nor remission of degrees, and which are found to belong to all bodies within the reach of our experiments, are to be esteemed the universal qualities of all bodies whatsoever' (Thayer (ed.) 1953, p. 3).

To explain this attitude, which presupposes the uniformity of nature, I assume that the drive to discover regularity is primitive. It is not that our inductive reasoning is justified by our belief in the uniformity of nature. It is rather that the epistemic values which determine the patterns of our inductive reasoning naturally incline us towards this belief. Belief in the uniformity of nature cannot justify our inductive inferences; nor can that belief be justified inductively. But there is an underlying attitude, which does much to explain both, viz. the primitive desire to discover regularity in nature.

The value of regularity manifests itself in a number of ways. Most obviously, it inclines us to believe that generalizations which are found to hold locally also hold generally. But more importantly, it drives us to search for deep or *underlying* regularities in phenomena, where no such regularities are apparent, or if apparent, then not unblemished. The search for regularity has led to the development of a number of strategies. Of particular importance are the strategies of *normalization* and *idealization*. The first of these is a primitive strategy for concept formation; the second, a basic strategy for theory construction. The normalizing strategy is primitive, at least in the sense that it is pre-verbal. For without it we could not acquire knowledge of the concepts or grammar of a language. The strategy of idealization is probably not primitive in this sense. It appears to be an extension of the strategy of normalization – one which is useful when the conditions for the applicability of the normalizing strategy are not satisfied.

To normalize is to distinguish between normal and abnormal cases in order to formulate or defend some generalization, and to isolate any real or apparent counter-examples. A normalized generalization is then seen as being the statement of some *underlying* regularity; and the counter-examples are seen as being more or less superficial distortions produced by special conditions or circumstances.

Philosophers have not paid much attention to the strategy of normalization which is standardly used in connection with empirical generalizations. Yet the normal/abnormal distinction, and its many variants, is as fundamental and pervasive as any in our language. We apply it to people, stars, modes of behaviour, speech patterns, chemical reactions, circumstances, samples, and just about everything else. Indeed, to conceive of things in terms of norms and exceptions is normal practice, and it seems to come quite naturally to us. No theory of human rationality can be satisfactory, therefore, if it gives no account of it.

Evidently, the disposition to normalize is primitive. For without a readiness to distinguish between normal and abnormal cases, and thus maintain generalizations in spite of exceptions, we could never learn to speak. Most of our empirical concepts depend for their identity on the set of normalized generalizations we accept concerning them. Thus our concept of man is not defined by the set of strictly universal generalizations we accept about men. There are too few such generalizations, and they are not specific enough to distinguish men from many other animals. What distinguishes men at the perceptual level, which is the level at which our concept is acquired, is what they *normally* look like, what capacities they *normally* have, what features are *normally* present, and so on. And the identity of our initial concept of a man must depend on these. The same is true of most of the other empirical concepts we need in

order to acquire a knowledge of language. Therefore, the normalizing strategy must be primitive enough for us to be able to operate
with it at this level.

8.7 CONNECTIVITY

The desire to understand things is the main motivation for scientific inquiry, and we should expect there to be several primary
epistemic values concerned with this activity. Here I shall focus on
one which I think is important. I call it the value of connectivity,
because it is concerned with the establishment of conceptual connections, and hence with the theoretical integration of knowledge.

The inductive practices I have considered so far have been more
or less straightforward inferences from samples to populations.
Those involved in the establishment of conceptual connections are
much less straightforward. Indeed, they include the full range of
strategies described by Imre Lakatos in his 'Proofs and Refutations' (Lakatos 1963).

The strategies of normalization and idealization enable us to
identify certain underlying regularities in nature, and to define the
irregularities which remain to be accounted for. The acceptability
of the norms and ideals we thus arrive at depends on how well we
can explain what is not normal or not ideal relative to these
concepts and principles. Hence our normalizing and idealizing
strategies cannot in themselves satisfy our desire to discover
uniformity or regularity in nature; they merely set an agenda for
doing so.

To explain why some As are Bs, given that As are not normally
or ideally Bs, we must try to discover some characteristics of the As,
or the circumstances in which we find them, which are sufficient to
account for their B-ness. So, minimally, we must look for generalizations of the form, 'All As that are Cs are Bs'. However, not every
acceptable generalization of this form is explanatory. For example,
'All As that are Bs are Bs' is not. To be explanatory, the condition
C cannot be more than *contingently* sufficient for the B-ness of As.

There may, however, be several contingently sufficient conditions for the B-ness of As. Thus, all As that are Ds may be Bs, as

well as all As that are Cs. Moreover, there may be As that are Bs which are neither Cs nor Ds. So we may have to say that some As are Bs for other reasons. Furthermore, the explanatory hypotheses we arrive at may themselves turn out to have exceptions, and so have to be normalized. For example, we may find that C is only normally a sufficient condition for an A being a B. And then, no doubt, we should want to know what sometimes prevents C from having its normal effect. The search for explanations of the exceptions to our normality generalizations, or to the framework principles postulated as governing the behaviour of the idealized theoretical entities of science, may thus lead to many complications.

Proliferating subsidiary explanations in this kind of way is intrinsically unsatisfying, and if it seems that there are too many reasons why an A may be a B, then we are likely to think that we have not got to the heart of the matter. For example, we may think that the appearance of diversity amongst the reasons for B-ness is superficial, or that the allegedly similar effects are fundamentally dissimilar. In extreme cases, we may think that the problem is generated by the norms or ideals we have adopted, and so seek some other way of conceptualizing the subject matter of our inquiry.

Our search thus appears to be for conditions which are not only sufficient for the effects we wish to explain, but also, if possible, necessary. And persistent failure to discover conditions which are both necessary and sufficient for a given effect can be a powerful incentive to re-evaluate the conceptual framework within which the problem arises. The discovery of such conditions for things is evidently intellectually satisfying. So, presumably, some epistemic value attaches to the knowledge of them. This is the value I call 'connectivity'. The source of this value, I suppose, is that such knowledge forges the conceptual links we need to build up an adequate conceptual framework for interpreting reality, i.e. it is an important contribution to our *understanding* of things. If we know that A is a necessary and sufficient condition for B, then the knowledge that something is a B is not isolated, but linked to the knowledge that it is an A. Hence, if we can discover what makes something an A, we may also find out what makes it a B. Or perhaps we shall find that there is some common cause for both A-ness and B-ness. Either way, the knowledge that something is a B may be located in a systematic framework, and so better understood.

The biological advantage of establishing such connections between items of knowledge is the increased efficiency and precision of the knowledge system it generates. If we know that As are normally Bs, then that may sometimes be good enough. But if we know that all and only As that are Cs are Bs, then the knowledge is more precise, and we have at least the beginnings of a theory of B-ness. Moreover, if we know this, then the fields of evidence for C-ness and B-ness are both increased. For now, any evidence that an A is a B is immediately evidence that it is a C, and conversely. Consequently, the establishment of such a conceptual tie between C-ness and B-ness expands the range of inferences we can draw from the evidence we have, and consequently increases the efficiency of our knowledge system.

I postulate that the desire to know what makes something the case, in the sense of knowing necessary and sufficient conditions for it, is primitive. The interest we have in knowing this is not just the interest of controlling or anticipating nature, although this may help to explain why we have it. For the desire to know the necessary and sufficient conditions for things is manifest even where there is no possibility of control, or the events we are seeking to explain are unlikely to recur. The interest is rather in satisfying our intellectual curiosity, our desire to understand what makes things so.

This desire is partly satisfied by the discovery of conditions which are either necessary or sufficient, for such discoveries also increase the range of inferences we are able to draw. But conditions which are *both* necessary and sufficient appear to be especially significant to us, and we are often willing to sacrifice content, and to modify or refine our concepts to establish such connections, as Lakatos' history of Euler's theorem amply demonstrates (ibid.). If all As are Bs, but some Bs are not As, then A-ness does not adequately account for B-ness. On the other hand, A-ness cannot *by itself* account for B-ness if there are any As that are not Bs. Therefore, we can have an adequate theory of B-ness iff we can find some condition which is both necessary and sufficient for B-ness.

The desire to discover necessary and sufficient conditions for things is thus a very important ingredient of our desire to understand things. So it is not surprising that we should sometimes be willing to modify our concepts, or to reduce the empirical content of our assertions, in order to create such connections. Consider the Lakatosian history of Euler's theorem (ibid.). As the classroom discussion opens, the concepts of polyhedron, polygon, face, edge and vertex are all somewhat amorphous normality concepts. By the end, all of these concepts have been shifted or focused, various conceptual links have been established (provisionally, at least) between them, and Euler's theorem has been embedded in a comprehensive theoretical network.

From a Popperian point of view, the changes which have occurred are content-reducing. For the tighter the conceptual links become in the process of articulating the theory, the more the propositions asserted take on the character of conceptual truths, and the less falsifiable they become. Counter-examples become not only more difficult to find, but more difficult to conceive. We are of course better able to predict the properties of polyhedra, given the theory, than we were before, because we had to learn how to apply the theory in the process of refining and developing it. The theory was improved, however, more as an instrument for conceiving and analysing polyhedra, and so predicting their properties, than as a set of independently testable assertions concerning them. And the scientist, like the carpenter who acquires a better set of tools, finds it more difficult to blame his or her equipment if things go wrong.

The value of connectivity is a basic value in theory development. For the establishment of new conceptual ties inevitably increases our understanding of things. I do not say that this is all that is involved in improving our understanding, but forging new conceptual links is at least an important part of it. The value is one which, more than any other, leads to conceptual innovations, and is therefore a counter to our natural (and proper) epistemic conservatism. It is also a value which is often opposed in its effects to the aim of making our theories more testable. The more tightly our knowledge system is integrated the less vulnerable to empirical refutation many of its elements will become.

8.8 EXPLANATORY POWER

There are ways of increasing our understanding of things other than by establishing conceptual links of the kinds discussed in section 8.7. For there are other sorts of theoretical developments which serve to increase the connectivity of our belief systems, and hence their efficiency for the purposes for which our brains evolved. There are, for example, theories postulating the existence of physical entities which act or interact with each other according to certain principles to produce various effects. Theories of this sort are said to provide *causal explanations* of the effects these entities are supposed to produce. They are what I earlier called *causal process theories*. Other theories seek to explain the characteristics of certain kinds of systems by the contributions these characteristics make to the existence, maintenance, flourishing or well-being of the systems in question. These are what are called *functional* or *teleological theories*. Yet other theories seek to explain the systematic relationships between things by discovering some set of organizational principles from which the more specific relationships can be derived. (Our space-time theories are of this kind.) These are what I have called *systemic theories*.

In general, to explain something is at least this: it is to locate it within a systematic framework of laws, theories, principles, etc., so that whatever is to be explained is linked via these laws, theories, etc. to other items of knowledge, or postulated states of affairs. In other words, it is to *locate epistemically* what is to be explained within what is, or purports to be, an objective knowledge system, so that it is no longer just an isolated belief or item of knowledge, but is integrated with the rest of the system. The main purpose of theorizing, I suppose, is to create the systems of laws, theories, etc. necessary for such integration to be possible. The epistemic value which I would suppose is served by theory construction is again the value of connectivity.

Because we are operating with a values-based epistemology, we should not expect to find any principles of theory construction which have more than the status of epistemic strategies, or rules of thumb. The fact that no one has ever proposed a plausible set of determinative rules for theory construction is in line with this expectation. Moreover, we should expect there to be wide range of different kinds of theories, corresponding to different strategies for establishing epistemic links. Indeed, my expectation would be that new kinds of theories will eventually emerge, establishing new kinds of epistemic connections and creating new opportunities for epistemic location.[12] For I know of no good reason to suppose that there are no ways of establishing epistemic connections other than those that are currently in use.

But, if connectivity is the epistemic value which lies behind theory construction, it is not the only one which is important for the evaluation of theories. For theories become more useful for the purposes of increasing the efficiency of our knowledge systems (which I have supposed to be the biological need served by the value of connectivity) if (1) they depend on a smaller number of postulated entities, or proceed from a smaller number of basic principles, or (2) they establish common links between a larger number, or more diverse range, of phenomena. We should expect, therefore, to find that theories which have these characteristics are generally preferred to those which lack them, or have them to a lesser degree. There can be no doubt that we all have these epistemic preferences. The question is whether the values they reflect are primary (i.e. natural) epistemic values, or acquired ones. Their universality, and their evident functionality clearly suggest that they are natural epistemic values. Let us assume that this is so, and call them the values of *reductiveness* and *comprehensiveness* respectively.

I cannot say more precisely what the values of reductiveness and comprehensiveness are, because they are not precise concepts. Anyone developing the epistemology of theory evaluation may wish to make them more precise, but the precision is not there, as it were, waiting to be discovered. The ideas behind the two concepts are just that a more comprehensive theory explains more, and a more reductive theory explains it more economically in terms of hypotheses or ontological commitments.

The values of *simplicity* and *explanatory power*, which are often appealed to in theory evaluation, are clearly related to the values of reductiveness and comprehensiveness, the more reductive theory usually being judged to be the simpler, and the more comprehensive theory generally being thought to have greater explanatory power. But simplicity and explanatory power are probably not simple epistemic values. For both kinds of considerations often seem to be relevant to judgements of simplicity or explanatory power. For example, if two empirically adequate theories are equally reductive, the more comprehensive theory may sometimes be judged to be both simpler (because it unifies a greater range of phenomena), and more explanatory (for the same reason). On the other hand, if two theories are equally comprehensive, the more reductive theory may be said not only to be simpler (because it is more highly reductive), but also to have greater explanatory power (because its hypotheses are, in a sense, more powerful). Moreover, judgements of simplicity and explanatory power often seem to depend also on other kinds of epistemic evaluation.

The more general evaluative nature of these concepts is most evident in the case of simplicity. For judgements of simplicity, like judgements of truth, often appear to be *overall* judgements based on consideration of a number of different epistemic values. There is, it is true, a principle of simplicity which is directly related to the value of reductiveness, viz. that of not multiplying entities or parameters unnecessarily. This is obviously a rational strategy for constructing theories which are maximally reductive. But the most highly reductive theory, in this sense, is not necessarily the simplest. Considerations, not only of comprehensiveness, but also of theoretical conservatism are also regarded as relevant to judgements of simplicity. As George Schlesinger has pointed out, the simplest curve is not necessarily the simplest planetary orbit (Schlesinger 1963, p. 35). My surmise is that the simplest empirically adequate theory is just the theory which, on current evidence, has the greatest epistemic value. If this surmise is correct, then (1) the justification for choosing the simplest theory is self-evident: the simplest theory is, by definition, epistemically the best available, and (2) simplicity itself is not a value, but, like truth, a concept which can only be understood properly within the framework of an evaluative epistemology.

8.9   SOLVING THE PROBLEM

To solve the problem of induction we need to define a biologically
plausible ideal of rationality on which our inductive practices can
be both explained and justified. I have assumed that, biologically,
we are value-driven decision systems. If this is right, then the
required ideal of rationality will be a natural values-based epistemology. It must refer to an epistemic value system which incorporates our natural epistemic values, and it must describe a set of
optimal strategies for maximizing epistemic value defined with
reference to this system. If the values were not natural human
epistemic values, then the system would lack the intrinsic appeal it
must have to justify the practices it recommends. If the model was
biologically implausible, it would be useless for explaining our
inductive practices. What we must have, to justify our scientific
inductive practices, is a model which is both biologically plausible
and intuitively appealing. The aim of this chapter has been to
sketch an ideal of rationality which meets these requirements.

The list of epistemic values I have given may well be incomplete.
Certainly, there are a great many criteria used for evaluating
theories, and I have made no serious attempt to account for them
all. Also, the epistemic values I have listed may not all be equally
fundamental. Henry Krips, for example, has argued that theoretical conservatism is not an independent virtue (Krips 1982). But
whatever refinements may be necessary or desirable, it is clear that
an ideally rational being at least: is consistent; has a natural
tendency to generalize widely, but is epistemically conservative in
the generalizations it makes; seeks corroboration for its beliefs,
and, other things being equal, believes more strongly in those that
are better corroborated; is driven to seek underlying regularity in
nature, and so conceive of things in terms of norms and exceptions,
or, by extension, in terms of ideal and actual states of affairs; and
finally, strives to increase its understanding by seeking conceptual
connections and comprehensive theoretical reductions. An ideally
rational being must also be supposed to have a belief system which
is perfectly integrated according to its own standards of rationality.

But how might all this solve the problem of induction? Let us suppose that we have at last developed a values-based epistemology which is adequate to explain our scientific inductive practices, i.e. a theory on which our inductive practices either turn out to be rational according to the theory, or not rational, but for reasons we are persuaded are correct. Our inductive practices are now, by hypothesis, embedded in an adequate theory of human rationality. Hence we can now say what makes them rational. They are rational to the extent that they are the practices of an ideally rational being. But then, you may ask, why should we be rational in this sense? Why should we accept the value system of such a being? To this my answer is 'Because you are human'. For these *are* your epistemic values, and you cannot, like a god, step outside your value system to judge whether or not it is rational to have them.

Realism and Epistemic Naturalism

There is a certain tension between the naturalistic theories of truth and rationality I have been developing, and the position of scientific realism which I took as my starting point. The theory of truth and the epistemology at which I have arrived will seem to many philosophers to be basically anti-realist, and hence incompatible with the realist position with which I began. I hope that those who think that this is so will go back to the arguments in Parts I and II of this book, and show me where I have gone wrong. For if this suspicion is well founded, and there is nothing wrong with my arguments, then scientific realism is untenable as a comprehensive world-view. On the other hand, if the suspicion is not well founded, this needs to be shown, and its sources revealed.

The plan of this chapter is to reverse the argument by beginning with the naturalistic theories of truth and rationality developed in chapters 7 and 8, and arguing back to a scientific realist ontology. If I can do this successfully, then I will have shown that a comprehensive and coherent scientific world-view is possible.

The naturalistic epistemology was constructed on the assumption that human rationality is governed by an autonomous system of epistemic values. From a scientific point of view, epistemic values are just basic preferences for certain kinds of concepts, beliefs and belief systems, and for certain ways of preserving, developing and communicating them. To construct the epistemology, I supposed that the most fundamental of our epistemic values are likely to be ones which have contributed significantly to our fitness to survive as members of tribes of social animals, which are in competition with other tribes, and with animals of other species, for scarce resources. I argued that most, if not all, of the epistemic values we need to construct a theoretical ideal of rationality, which is adequate to explain and justify our scientific inductive practices, can be found in this way.

The naturalistic epistemology required is a model theory based on a theoretical ideal of rationality. According to the theory, an ideally rational being is one whose epistemic value system matches the theoretical ideal, and whose belief systems are perfectly constructed, developed and integrated in accordance with just these values. It is a requirement on the model that the theoretical ideal it contains must also be capable of serving as a regulative ideal for ordinary human beings. The values it incorporates must be natural human epistemic values, so that ordinary human beings may naturally aspire to be rational according to the model. The ideal of rationality that is needed turns out to be a high ideal. While human beings may aspire to be ideally rational, they cannot realistically ever hope to be so.

I would argue that the ideal of rationality contained in the model is best exemplified by scientific inquiry. Certainly, the epistemic values postulated as the values of an ideally rational being are all values to which scientists would appeal in appraising theories and evidence about the nature of reality. They would also try, although they can never fully succeed, to allow only their basic epistemic values to influence them in their evaluations of theories and evidence. Of course, there are ethical restrictions on human and animal experimentation which society rightly insists upon. Epistemic values are not our only values, and they can, and often should, be outweighed by other kinds of considerations. But even though scientists must work within such restrictions, they would not, or, at least, should not, allow their moral or political views to influence what they believe about the world. *Qua* scientists, they must rely wholly on epistemic evaluation.

I do not imagine that the theory of rationality developed in chapters 7 and 8 is, as it stands, very satisfactory as an epistemology for scientific inquiry. But if what has been proposed is at least on the right track, then more sophisticated naturalistic epistemologies, more firmly based on scientific research, can be expected to follow, and the ideal of rationality should be refined in the process. In the end, we can envisage an ideal theory of rationality, which is ideal by its own lights, and which is adequate for scientific inquiry, as it ideally should be. If this projected ideal of rationality is based on natural epistemic values, as the proposed theory is, and these values are also weighted in acceptable ways, then it too should be acceptable as a regulative ideal.

Unfortunately, we do not know what is ultimately ideal. We have to work with the best approximation we can currently make to the ideal of rationality we are seeking. Our starting point must be that this is contained in the naturalistic epistemology that has been put forward. Judged by these standards, scientific inquiry is the most rational, and epistemically the most objective, of any inquiry about the nature of things. The scientific view of man and the world is therefore the most rational view to take on these matters.

Scientific realism is a meta-scientific theory about the reality of theoretical entities. This theory relies heavily on a form of argument from the best explanation: if the world behaves *as if* entities of certain kinds exist, then the best explanation of this fact is that they really do exist. It is up to scientists, using the kind of naturalistic epistemology proposed here, to decide what the best explanations are. It is for philosophers to argue about the ontological implications of the explanations scientists accept. We have seen, in chapter 2, that the main argument for scientific realism is limited in its scope, but that when its limitations are understood, and it is properly used, it is a powerful argument for the reality of some kinds of theoretical entities, particularly those postulated in causal process theories. The argument which leads to this ontology is itself well justified on the kind of epistemology I have outlined. For the values of reductiveness, comprehensiveness, and explanatory power used to derive the ontology are basic epistemic values which contribute to the generality and connectivity of human knowledge. Therefore, if one accepts a naturalistic epistemology one should also accept the main argument for scientific realism, and a physicalist ontology like the one derived in chapter 2. Therefore, an epistemic naturalist should also be a scientific realist.

However, scientific realists who have qualms about accepting a naturalistic epistemology and theory of truth are unlikely to be satisfied by this argument. For what they really want is an argument that if you accept this epistemology and theory of truth, you should also believe in an ontologically objective reality, a reality which is not only epistemically objective, as a naturalistic ontology may be, but one which exists independently, and has all of its properties and relationships independently of human epistemic values or evaluation. It has to be possible, and not merely logically possible, that the world is not as even the ideal theory says it is.

We must now face up to this basic issue. What sort of realist should an epistemic naturalist be? We have demonstrated that an epistemic naturalist is committed to scientific realism, and to a physicalist ontology. But what kind of scientific realism goes with epistemic naturalism? Philosophers of many different persuasions would claim to be scientific realists, and it is not clear that a scientific realist needs to be a metaphysical realist, as many would insist. For scientific realism is basically an ontological thesis which appears to be acceptable on almost any theory of truth. Should an epistemic naturalist be an internal realist, perhaps, or a realist of some other kind?

I think most philosophers would say that a scientific realist is committed to metaphysical realism, and that if epistemic naturalism implies scientific realism, then it must also imply metaphysical realism. But it is not clear that this answer is correct. On the contrary, there are good reasons why a scientific realist should not be a metaphysical realist. For this is the form of realism which goes with a correspondence theory of truth, and, as we have seen (in chapters 4 and 5) there is no form of correspondence theory in which a scientific realist can reasonably believe. The theory of truth which a scientific realist should accept is a naturalistic evaluative theory, i.e. a theory which identifies truth with what it is right epistemically to believe, given a certain autonomous system of natural epistemic values. The form of realism which goes with this concept of truth is not metaphysical realism, but a position I call 'naturalistic realism'.

Naturalistic realism might reasonably be said to be a form of internal realism, and I have until recently called myself an internal realist. But there are important differences between the position I wish to defend, and the sorts of positions which usually go by this name. Firstly, it is not my view that truth and reality are theory-relative, as some internal realists hold. That is, I think it makes sense to say that something is true, or exists, without reference to any particular theoretical framework. My concept of truth, and hence of reality, does depend on what I call our *epistemic perspective*. But this is something which is more or less common to mankind. It is not essentially an individual or social product, as a theoretical framework is.

Secondly, I do not rely on the empirical underdetermination thesis, as internal realists usually do, to argue against metaphysical realism, and in favour of some form of ontological relativity. On the contrary, as I argued in chapter 3, I think there are no good arguments for the empirical underdetermination thesis which do not already presuppose metaphysical realism. So internal realists cannot use *these* arguments to support their thesis that ontology is theory-relative. The view I wish to defend is that, for human beings at least, theory is ultimately *determined* by evidence, and by the system of epistemic values with which we are endowed, and if there is any ultimately defensible ontological relativity, it is in relation to the epistemic perspectives of different species of beings. But, as we shall see, even this much ontological relativity is dubious.

Thirdly, I do not argue, as Quine does (in Quine 1960 and 1969) for ontological relativity on the basis of any thesis about the indeterminateness of meaning or translation. Semantic conventionalism of the kind defended by Quine seems to me to be no more defensible than the conventionalism of the early positivists. When Reichenbach argued for conventionalism about length congruence, he distinguished between questions of fact (which can be resolved directly by observation), and questions which require a prior decision before they can be resolved. For example, the question whether two rods placed side by side are equal in length while they are together is a question of fact which can be resolved directly by observation. But the question whether they are the same in length when they are apart is one which requires a prior definition of what is to count as being the same in length under these conditions. The kind of definition required was called a 'co-ordinative definition'. Reichenbach maintained that there is really no truth of the matter whether spatially separated things are or are not the same in length. It depends on what co-ordinative definitions are adopted.

Quine argues, in similar fashion, that there is really no truth of the matter whether a sentence of one language means the same as, or something different from, a sentence of another language. It depends on what system of co-ordinative definitions (in this case, what translation manual) is adopted. Only when a translation manual has been adopted can the question be resolved. But the co-ordinative definitions required for space-time measurement, and for translation from one language to another, are not arbitrary, and it is not evident that in the end there is any room for manoeuvre. The co-ordinative definitions we require have the status of hypotheses in an empirical space-time or linguistic theory.[1] And if the theory is refuted, then these hypotheses can be refuted, and so replaced by other hypotheses within the context of some other, and presumably better, theory. If truth is what it is right to believe, then the true congruence definitions and translations will be those which should ultimately result from this process. There is, therefore, no joy to be found here for those who hold that truth is theory-relative, and hence, no support for the thesis of ontological relativity.

Finally, as Robert Farrell has convincingly argued (in Farrell 1980), there are no good arguments for internal realism which depend on the Löwenheim–Skolem theorem. Nor is the position I wish to defend dependent on any such arguments. Therefore, I should not attempt to defend naturalistic realism in the sort of way that Putnam defends internal realism in Putnam (1977). A theory about the nature of reality is not a formal theory which needs to be interpreted: it is already an interpreted theory. Consequently, the ideal theory about what exists most fundamentally must also be an interpreted theory; and this theory *does* determine the ontology we should believe in, as I argued in chapter 2. It is irrelevant to ontology to show that the abstract formal theory which may be derived from it may be modelled in some other way.

9.1 INTERNAL, PEIRCEAN AND METAPHYSICAL REALISM

It is now fairly generally agreed, and I think it is reasonable to accept, that an item of knowledge is a *true* belief which is *epistemically justified*, and has been *acquired in an appropriate way*. The only important issue about the definition of knowledge which remains to be settled is how beliefs must be acquired if they are to count as items of knowledge. Thus, there are three kinds of conditions for knowledge: one concerns what is true, one is about how our beliefs must be obtained if they are to count as knowledge, and the other concerns the justification of our beliefs. Let us call them the *ontological*, the *epistemigenic* and the *epistemic* conditions respectively. The epistemigenic conditions are needed to rule out some cases of true and justified beliefs which are not knowledge. Fortunately, these need not concern us here.

It would also be widely agreed that satisfaction of the epistemic conditions does not entail satisfaction of the ontological ones, and conversely. We may be justified in believing what is false, and not justified in believing what is true. Philosophers differ about how far this point can be extrapolated beyond the circumstances in which the belief is being evaluated. For one who holds a coherence or pragmatic theory of truth, the truth is something which is at least in principle knowable; for the truth will be just what occurs in some given, or projected, theoretical system. Therefore, for coherence theorists and pragmatists, the ontological conditions for knowledge must be definable somehow in terms of the epistemic ones. Any scientific realist who thinks that this is the case is, in the broadest of senses, an internal realist of some kind.

On a coherence theory of truth, truth, and therefore knowledge, are both considered to be relative to a theoretical perspective, and the question whether a belief is true, absolutely so to speak, makes no sense. On such a theory, the kind of evaluation required to determine whether a belief is true is a determination of whether it properly belongs to some particular knowledge system. Such a theory-dependent concept of truth might, perhaps, be useful in some areas. For example, we might conveniently say, without running much risk of being misunderstood, that Pythagoras' Theorem is true in Euclidean geometry, but not in Riemannian. I should prefer not to use the word 'true' in this way, but I have no strong objection to doing so, because it would not often be misunderstood. I do reject social and cultural relativism about truth, however, and the ways of speaking which go with these positions, because they suggest attitudes of epistemic tolerance which are quite alien to my position.

Pragmatists relate truth, and therefore knowledge, to human interests. Ideal pragmatists, like C. S. Peirce, relate truth and knowledge to our epistemic interests, and, in particular, to those epistemic interests which would be served by the construction of an ideal, or perfect, theory based on total evidence. Let us call any scientific realist who accepts such a theory of truth 'a Peircean realist'.[2] For Peircean realists, then, the two sorts of criteria for knowledge, the epistemic and the ontological, must coincide at the limit of perfect knowledge and understanding. For what is true, they would say, is just what would be justified, given total evidence, and the best possible theory based on it.

For the so-called 'metaphysical realist', on the other hand, the truth remains independent of what would justifiably be believed, even if the evidence were ideally complete, and the theory perfected. Therefore, for the metaphysical realist, the ontological conditions for knowledge must remain independent of the epistemic ones, even up to the point where there is no further evidence which could be, or ever could have been, obtained.

It is important to be clear that Peircean realists do *not* equate truth with *warranted assertability* or *reasonable belief*. For these notions are tied to existing or available evidence, and perhaps also to certain background assumptions and theories which, in the given context, are not in question. No, for Peircean realists, truth is a kind of limit notion of reasonable belief. We all believe that we are limited in what we can know, and that probably some of the things we now believe are false. But we do not, for these reasons, think it unreasonable for us to believe what we do. Circumstances may change what we may reasonably believe. If new evidence is discovered, if a better theory is proposed, if results previously accepted are brought into question, then what we may reasonably believe is affected by such changes. Moreover, we should normally consider these changes to be ones for the better – to be changes which *improve* our knowledge and understanding of the world. Truth, for the ideal pragmatist, and hence for the Peircean realist, is what would result from the completion of this process. It is what we should believe, if our knowledge were perfected, if it were based on total evidence, was internally coherent, and was theoretically integrated in the best possible way.

Metaphysical realists, on the other hand, have a different concept of truth. For them, truth is a relationship between what is true, and what it is true of, which holds independently of our epistemic interests or values. They normally do, and certainly should, admit that we have such values. But truth, they would say, is not dependent on what these values may be. We may, as a matter of fact, have evolved criteria for epistemic evaluation which are well adapted to the goal of discovering what is true. But then again we may not. Even the perfect theory (supposing it existed) might not be true, they would say, though the world, and our systems of epistemic values, might be such that we could never turn up (or have turned up) any evidence which would give us good reason to doubt it.

One's concept of truth need not greatly affect one's beliefs about reality. Consequently, Peircean realists and metaphysical realists may have quite similar ontologies. There is, for example, no reason why a Peircean realist should not be a physicalist. For there is no reason, which is not a reason for anyone else, why a Peircean realist should not consider a physicalist ontology, such as the one outlined in chapter 2, to be the theory it is most rational to believe. Moreover, a Peircean realist can, and indeed should, be a realist in the quite full-blooded sense of believing that there is a reality which exists independently of anyone's knowledge of it, or beliefs about it. For, on the best available theories that we have concerning the nature of the physical world, and our relationship to it, reality would be much the same, even if the human race had never existed.

Of course, there would be no cities, ploughed fields, books, or theories about the world, and maybe some species of animals would not now be extinct, if we had never existed. But overall, the difference would not be very great. The difference would be even less great if we just had different beliefs about the world. It would still be different, of course, because our beliefs are parts of reality, and beliefs have effects; but the basic ontology to which we should subscribe would be unaffected by our having, or coming to have, different beliefs about reality. A Peircean realist should, therefore, believe in the existence of a mind-independent reality. Moreover, the reality he or she should believe in is not a featureless noumenon, but a world of physical objects with physical properties interacting with each other in the usual ways.

Peircean and metaphysical realists have different concepts of truth; and this difference gives rise to another difference. The metaphysical realist is open to a kind of sceptical challenge: if truth is independent of our epistemic values, then we have no good reason to believe that those theories which we should judge to be the best are any nearer to the truth. For, we do not know that our epistemic values are well adapted to discovering what is true. Given the theory of evolution by natural selection, we should, perhaps, expect our epistemic values to be well adapted to our survival; but a metaphysical realist has no good reason to believe that this theory is true either. All he or she knows is that this theory is the best we have, which, according to metaphysical realism, is *not* a good reason to believe that it is true.

Metaphysical realism thus undermines the main argument for realism about theoretical entities in science, and is therefore in tension with scientific realism. For it leaves a gulf between even the best possible theory and reality, a gulf which cannot be bridged by any argument at all. We can investigate nature, and develop a theoretical understanding of the world; but we cannot compare what we think we know with the truth to see how well we are doing. We cannot even be assured that science has made any progress towards its goal of discovering what reality is like. The Peircean realist, on the other hand, is not plagued by these sceptical doubts. Our epistemic values *must* be adapted to the end of discovering what is true, because truth *is* just the culmination of the process of investigating and reasoning about nature in accordance with these values.

Despite the tension between scientific realism, which depends on accepting arguments from the best explanation, and metaphysical realism, which denies the inference from even the best possible explanation, I think most scientific realists would call themselves metaphysical realists. For this is the position associated with the correspondence theory of truth, and this theory has a nice objective ring to it. By contrast, a theory of truth which identifies truth with what it is right epistemically to believe, and would be acceptable to a Peircean realist, sounds too relativistic to be acceptable to a scientific realist. For it threatens to make truth relative to human perceptions and evaluations, and reality a creation of human thought.

However, this is not what Peircean realism entails. For, Peircean realists do not deny that there is a reality which exists independently of anyone's knowledge or understanding of it. On the contrary, since they accept the main argument for realism concerning theoretical entities, they must also accept that most theoretical entities (including all those in the ontology of chapter 2) exist independently of human knowledge and understanding. These entities are not just products of human thought, as an idealist might say, but things involved in various ways in physical causal processes – processes which would take place whether or not there were any humans. For this is what a scientific realist must believe it is right to believe, and hence what a Peircean realist must believe to be true.

9.2 NATURALISTIC REALISM

Naturalistic realism is my own special brand of Peircean realism. It is objective about what exists, in the sense that questions of ontology are assumed to be matters on which non-coercive agreement can in principle be reached. It is naturalistic in the sense that this possibility is supposed to be grounded in our common human nature, and in the fact that we are all responding to the same world. It is realistic in the sense that it assumes that there is an independently existing world to which we are all responding, which is constituted, at least from a human epistemic perspective, in the sort of way envisaged by science.

Naturalistic realism is not a form of idealism. For it is not suggested that the world is our construction, or that there is no independently existing reality. On the contrary, it is assumed that the world out there is the source of the information we receive when we observe it. However, it is also assumed that we obtain and process information about the world in ways which are more or less common to mankind, but may be, for all we know, peculiar to our species. Indeed, it is *a priori* extremely unlikely that intelligent beings throughout the universe gather and process information about the world just as we do. This suggests that our epistemic perspective on reality may be rare, or even unique. It seems implausible, therefore, to suppose that the way the world is for us is the way it is for all other creatures.

We gather information by perception and communication; and we probably have inbuilt mechanisms to serve both these kinds of processes. We reason from beliefs acquired in these ways using various inductive strategies, which may be either primitive or acquired, and seek to rationalize, extend and improve our belief systems the best we can. These processes evidently depend on our having a particular system of epistemic values, and it is in relationship to these values that our judgements of truth and falsity must be made. For these are the values which must determine what it is right or wrong for us to believe, given our perceptual and communicative inputs.

If this picture is basically right, then what it is right or wrong for us to believe must be a function of our perceptual and communicative apparatus, and of the epistemic value system we operate with. To explain the objectivity of science, i.e. the extent of the intersubjective agreement on factual questions and theoretical explanations which is evidently possible, it is not only necessary to suppose that we are perceiving the same world in the same sort of way, it is also necessary to postulate that we have a common system of epistemic values. If this is so, then this common system must have a biological basis, because it is not possible to explain the universality of human rationality on any other assumption.

The evidence that human rationality is everywhere the same comes from linguists and anthropologists. The linguistic evidence is that speakers of any one linguistic community can learn the language of any other community; i.e. that human languages are mutually intelligible, even if the belief systems of different communities are very different. To explain this, we must suppose that ordinary human belief systems all have the same basic structure, and develop in the same sorts of ways. For if the belief systems of different communities had different logical structures from ours, or developed according to different principles of inference, we should expect to find enormous difficulty in making sense of their belief systems, and hence of the languages they use to express them. At least, we should expect there to be some living languages, somewhere in the world, which we cannot understand except on the

assumption that the people who speak them are somehow irrational.

But, in fact, this is not what we find.[3] The belief systems of some
communities may be very strange to us; and the inferences drawn
by people in these communities from evidence presented to them
may often seem bizarre to the uninitiated. But those who work in
these communities always report that when they fully understand
them, and come to appreciate their religions, histories, myth-
ologies, traditions and folklore, the inferences they draw no longer
seem bizarre. Indeed, they are accepted as being the sorts of
inferences that any normal person, believing what the natives
believe, would be expected to draw in the circumstances.

To explain this fact, we must suppose that our belief systems are
similarly structured, and develop in similar ways in the light of
experience. Therefore, we must suppose that there is a common
human epistemic value system which operates at a high level to
determine how we think, and how we structure our belief systems.

We cannot assume, however, that aliens, or beings from other
planets, would naturally think as we do, or share our view of the
nature of reality, although they must be responding to the same
world. For not only may they have quite different ways of perceiving and communicating with each other, they may also have
evolved quite different ways of processing information. From a
scientific point of view, it would, indeed, be extraordinary if this
were not so. It would seem to be possible, therefore, that our
concept of truth, and hence our view of reality, is essentially
different from that of other intelligent beings. Naturalistic realism
thus seems to imply that truth may be species-relative, and hence
that the way the world is for us may be different from the way it is
for other sorts of beings.[4]

9.3　THE HUMAN EPISTEMIC PERSPECTIVE

The complexes which consist of how we perceive and communicate
about the world, and the value systems we use to rationalize,
extend and improve our belief systems, determine what I call our
epistemic perspectives on reality. The epistemic perspectives of people

are not exactly the same. Nevertheless, they would seem to be fairly similar to each other. We perceive the world in the same kind of way; we talk intertranslatable languages; we seek knowledge and understanding in the same sorts of ways; and we all have the same basic epistemic values.

However, it seems that people differ in the *weights* they give to their epistemic values. Some people are more impressed by considerations of connectivity than others; for they are generally very attracted to well-integrated and coherent systems of beliefs. Some people emphasize the value of objectivity more than others, and seek always to depersonalize knowledge and epistemic approval. Many philosophers are attracted to the correspondence theory of truth for this reason. Some people are epistemically more conservative than others, and consequently – although this is a misunderstanding of epistemic conservatism – less willing to explore alternative theoretical frameworks. There is, therefore, no unique epistemic perspective which exists in the community, but a family of closely related epistemic perspectives which differ from each other in the emphases they place on different epistemic values.

To some extent, these differences can be overcome by rational argument, empirical investigation, and discussion, because our epistemic values are not necessarily in harmony with each other, and they sometimes lead to conflicting judgements. Consequently, the weighting we should give to an epistemic value may depend on our experience in using it. The weighting we give to an epistemic value may also depend on factors which have nothing much to do with epistemology, or with what we ought rationally to believe. Some people, for example, enjoy the notoriety of holding outrageous beliefs, or think it is somehow 'deep' to believe a contradiction. Hence the concept of a unique human epistemic perspective, which I need to define the concept of epistemic rightness for human beings, is already something of an idealization of the epistemic perspectives of ordinary people.

It is possible to criticize our epistemic perspectives from within if we demand consistency, because we can consistently give more weight to epistemic considerations of one kind only by giving less weight to epistemic considerations of other kinds. Rationally, we should also insist on some other epistemic values, beside consistency, retaining a primary role in determining what we ought rationally to believe. For the values which are most directly concerned with perception and with testing predictions, viz. empirical certification and corroboration, are intrinsically overriding in human epistemology, and have the greatest weight in deciding what we ought rationally to believe. I call these our *primary epistemic values*. The epistemic values which are concerned more with developing and improving our understanding of the world, e.g. the values of theoretical conservatism and connectivity, while important, have intrinsically less weight in deciding what we should believe. I call these our *secondary epistemic values*. They are secondary in the sense that if considerations based on them all clearly favoured a given hypothesis, the hypothesis would still be rejected if we had good corroboration of a contrary hypothesis, or a demonstration of its inconsistency, or of its incompatibility with some other well-established hypothesis. The primary epistemic values override them.

I speculate that our primary epistemic values are dominant, because our epistemic value system has evolved to serve our interests in interacting with the world; and this has inevitably given greater weight to those epistemic values which are most directly concerned with this process. To interact successfully with the world, it is minimally necessary that we should have quick reliable sources of information about our surroundings, including some knowledge of the causes and their effects, and be able to make successful predictions based on past experience. It is also necessary that we should not hold on to contradictory beliefs. If we go on believing that there are no tigers present when we have come to believe that there is a tiger present, we are not likely to last for long. This would seem to be the biological basis of our primary epistemic values.

What I call *the human epistemic perspective* is an idealization of the epistemic perspectives of ordinary people, in which the weightings given to our epistemic values have not been distorted by any non-rational forces, in which our secondary epistemic values have been appropriately weighted in the ideal limit of experience, using internal criteria to determine their relative epistemic importance, and to bring them into harmony with each other, and which preserves the dominance of our primary epistemic values. Consequently, the question of what it is right for human beings to believe, and hence of what truth is for human beings, does not depend on the epistemic perspective of any particular individual or group in society. For there is a prior question to be settled of what the human epistemic perspective should be.

9.4 ALIEN EPISTEMIC PERSPECTIVES

It is implausible to suppose that the human epistemic perspective is shared by all other intelligent beings. Hence, it seems, there may be many different concepts of truth, possibly as there are species of intelligent aliens. If this is so, then we must ask whether their different perspectives on reality could somehow be synthesized to obtain a truly comprehensive view of the world, one which does not depend on the epistemic perspective of any particular species. The analogy is, of course, with the synthesis of different visual perspectives to obtain a description of an object which is independent of the perspective from which it is viewed. If this analogy holds, then it should be possible to distinguish between how the world is, and how it appears from a given epistemic perspective. Moreover, there should be no question of which epistemic perspective gives the correct view of the nature of reality. Different views from equally powerful epistemic perspectives should be equally valid. How an elephant looks depends on the clarity of one's vision and the standpoint from which it is viewed; and the different viewpoints are equally legitimate.

There are, however, two important ways in which epistemic perspectives differ from visual perspectives. First, when viewing elephants, we can walk around and change our visual perspective without altering the clarity of our vision. But we cannot change our epistemic perspective so easily. It is possible, given our epistemic value system, to improve on our natural perceptual and communicative apparatus, and so improve our knowledge and understanding of reality by improving the analogue of our vision. But we could not change our epistemic value system, even if we knew how technically to do it, without destroying much of the knowledge and understanding we have.

Secondly, in the visual case, there is a way the elephant is, as opposed to how it looks from any particular point of view. So, by analogy, we should expect there to be a way the world is, which is independent of any particular epistemic perspective. However, the way the elephant is an explanatory concept. Among other things, it explains how the elephant looks from various places and angles. So, pursuing the analogy, if there is a way the world is, as opposed to how it looks from any particular epistemic perspective, then it must be capable of explaining, not only how the world looks to us, but also how it looks to other kinds of intelligent beings. However, such a conception of reality would have to be embodied in a general theory of human and alien knowledge; and *this theory* would have to be acceptable *to us*, and so incorporated in our own perspective on reality. Therefore, from our point of view, the way the world is can only be the way it looks from our own epistemic perspective.

What holds for human beings holds *mutatis mutandis* for other sorts of beings. Therefore, no one can make the required distinction between how the world is, and how it appears from their own epistemic perspective, even if they take into account the fact that their particular epistemic perspective may not be unique. Therefore, different epistemic perspectives cannot be synthesized in the kind of way that different visual perspectives can be to construct a global view of the reality which gives rise to them. For any synthesis must be a synthesis made from some particular epistemic perspective, and there can be no *a priori* guarantee that syntheses made from different epistemic perspectives will be the same.

Nevertheless, it is possible that beings with different epistemic perspectives may all, in the end, be able to agree about how the world is, once they have taken their differences into account. For the epistemic values which are primitive in any one system may turn out to be justifiable in any other system in which they do not already occur as primitives. Alternatively, the value systems of the aliens may differ from ours only in the emphases they place on some secondary epistemic values, and we may be able resolve our differences in the sorts of ways people can resolve their differences concerning the relative importance of different kinds of epistemic considerations. In either case, we should be able to speak unambiguously of the way the world is, without reference to any particular species. A universal form of naturalistic realism might therefore be defensible, even if the intrinsic epistemic values of different species are different.

It is also possible that there should be intelligent aliens whose epistemic perspectives we could never grasp; although, if the intelligence displayed by the aliens should prove ultimately to be unintelligible to us, even though they succeeded in doing all sorts of intelligent things, then our capacity to understand the world must be fundamentally flawed. Therefore, if we were to meet such beings, we should be forced eventually to conclude that the world is not the way our best theories say it is.

If we are not thus forced into scepticism, we may yet be pushed into a kind of *species-relativism*. For we may have to admit that there is no way the world is absolutely, only ways it is from different epistemic perspectives, none of which can claim absolute priority. If we did have to admit this, a scientific realist could certainly accept the conclusion – as I once did. Until this century, most philosophers distinguished between absolute and relative motion, believing that absolute motion is required to explain relative. We have learned to do without this distinction, and accept relative motion as the fundamental concept. Similarly, we could abandon the idea that there is a way things are, which is independent of any particular epistemic perspective, and seek only to explain how things appear to be by reference to how they are from our own perspective. The realist's answer to the question: 'Why does the world behave *as if* things of such and such a kind exist?' would then be simply: 'Because this is the way the world is from our perspective'. That is, the main argument for scientific realism could be construed as an argument, not for what exists *absolutely*, but for what exists *from our own epistemic point of view*.

However, these sceptical or relativist conclusions are not yet warranted. For, if an alien epistemology is at all like ours, it must be based on a system of epistemic values. But whether something is an epistemic value is not a question of fact which is independent of how we choose to classify values. It is a question of whether the alien value has a role in the construction of alien belief systems sufficiently like that of our epistemic values in the construction of our belief systems.

Likewise, we must ask whether the alien 'beliefs' are beliefs in our sense, and whether their belief systems have been 'rationally constructed', as we understand this process. For, on the view which has been developed throughout this book, the distinctions between what is a belief and what is not, and what is a rational construction and what is not, are not distinctions of natural kind. The question of what is to be counted as a belief, or as a rationally constructed belief system, is not a question of fact, but of appropriate classification, depending on what family resemblance criteria are satisfied. A given propositional attitude is one of belief iff a person who has this propositional attitude towards a proposition is thereby disposed to behave in sufficiently many ways as if they believed it. A given belief system has been rationally constructed iff it has been constructed using a system of epistemic values sufficiently like our own to b considered adequate for the task.

Therefore, an alien epistemology can be considered to be a *rational* epistemology only if it is basically similar to our own. If the system contains any new values which would not be quickly recognized by us as epistemic values, then we should probably consider those who operated with this value system to construct their belief systems to be irrational. (Why give weight to considerations which have no bearing on what we ought rationally to believe?) To accept the new values as being *epistemic* values, we should need an argument that their roles in constructing alien belief systems are sufficiently like those of our own epistemic values in constructing our belief systems. For if they were not, we should have no good reason to regard them as *epistemic* values, rather than, for example, aesthetic or moral values. Moreover, we should need to be assured that what we are supposing to be the alien's belief systems do actually have the roles characteristic of belief systems in guiding their behaviour, and that they are not, for example, just works of the imagination.

On the third planet of Beta Centauri, there is a race of beings, called 'ents',[5] who live by photosynthesis, and extract moisture and nutrients from the ground like trees. They speak a language, which we may suppose to be like English, but they have very little interest in current events, or in their surroundings, and they use their language mainly for story-telling. Over the centuries – for the ents live for a very long time – they have evolved a wonderful folkloric tradition, and what the ents love to do best of all is to create new story lines, and elaborate on this tradition. However, the ents are very jealous of their tradition, and do not accept any story-developments which are not fully in keeping with it. Normally, to become accepted into folklore, any new story lines must be compatible with the story so far, the actions portrayed must be in character for the actors in these stories, the story development must satisfy various criteria of elegance, dramatic force and simplicity, it must be in keeping with the whole folkloric tradition in which the story is embedded, and it must be able to throw new light on parts of that tradition which were previously left obscure.

These restraints make it difficult for ents to add significantly to the tradition, and even more difficult for them to change it. However, most ents eventually succeed in filling in some details of the stories so far accepted, and once every century or two a genius is born who is able to add a whole new chapter, the story line of which is so compelling that parts of the old tradition have to be rejected to accommodate it.

The ents do not speak of a folkloric tradition, however. They describe it as the 'wisdom of ages', and they speak of the stories they tell as true or false. The stories which they judge to be undoubtedly worthy of inclusion in the folkloric tradition they say are true; those which they would certainly reject they say are false. Some, which are greeted with initial favour, but have not yet been thoroughly tested, are said to be probable; and others, which seem unworthy, and hence unlikely to be included in the tradition, are said to be improbable. The ents evidently operate with a value system for assessing these stories which is, in many ways, like our own epistemic value system. Indeed, the ents' value system includes all of the epistemic values we recognize, except for those which are concerned with grounding beliefs, and generating and testing rational expectations.

Nevertheless, I do not think we should count the entish system as an epistemic value system, or their folkloric tradition as giving us a valid account, from a different epistemic perspective, of the nature of reality. The reason for this has nothing to do with human chauvinism. What the ents are doing in developing their tradition is simply different from what we are doing when we are seeking to discover what exists. And if the ents have concepts of truth or existence, applicable to story lines or things described in their stories, as well they might, then existence for them has a different kind of significance from existence for us. Their concepts of truth and existence are purely intellectual; ours are concepts we have to live by.

In addition to these purely intellectual concepts, the ents would have to have some more practical concepts of truth and existence. For story-telling is presumably not their only activity. For example, they would have to teach young ents to speak the entish language, and induct them into the folkloric tradition. Therefore, they must be able to talk in a metalanguage about the entish language, and about that tradition. If a young ent gets the meaning of a word wrong, or mispronounces it, or makes a mistake about a story line, the older ents would need to be able to correct it. To do so, they would have to be able to say such things as 'That is right' or 'There is a mushroom over there'. That is, they would need to have some much more mundane concepts of truth and existence (signalled by the words 'right' and 'there is') than the ones they use when talking *within* the folkloric tradition. And it is these more mundane concepts of truth and existence which are the most like our own, even though the epistemic value system which governs their use may be a very primitive one by our standards. For these are the concepts the ents have to live by.

For anything to count as a belief system which we should take seriously as providing a different epistemic perspective on reality, it would have to be grounded in experience in the same kind of way as ours, and have the same kind of role in providing rational expectations. It must, therefore, contain epistemic values which are concerned with the grounding of knowledge, and the generation and fulfilment of rational expectations. I do not know that these have to be precisely the same as those of our values which are most directly concerned with these processes, viz. our primary epistemic values of consistency, empirical certification and corroboration, which generally have these roles in our belief systems, but they would have to be capable of replacing them and doing much the same kind of job. What disqualifies the entish system as a rival to ours is that it lacks the value of empirical certification.

Moreover, the weighting of values in an alien system cannot differ too much from our own, if their system is to count as rational.

For example, the beliefs it generates cannot too often be inconsistent with each other, or systematically incompatible with what we are able to certify empirically, if the system is to be counted as a possible rational alternative to our own. At least, we should need a good argument to convince us that it should be. If the aliens seemed to behave rationally, while seeming to hold beliefs which are inconsistent, or manifestly false, then we should need to be convinced that we had understood them properly, and that they really believed what they claimed to believe. If there were any differences at all, therefore, between an alien epistemic value system and a human one, these differences would have to be relatively minor. For, otherwise, the alien system would not count as a rival to ours, and it would not be seen as giving rise to rival concepts of truth and rationality. The two systems might, perhaps, differ in the weightings they give to considerations of elegance or simplicity in the evaluation of theories. But they could not differ much more substantially than this and still be thought to define different epistemic perspectives on reality.

9.5 FULL CIRCLE

We have now come almost full circle. I began by presenting a scientific world-view, and developing the case for scientific realism. I argued that the main argument for scientific realism is not a good argument for the existence of every kind of theoretical entity, but only for those kinds of entities which we have to believe in to accept the causal process theories we do. It is not, for example, a good argument for the existence of numbers, or possible worlds other than the actual world.

I then went on to ask what the ontology of a scientific realist should be, and argued that, given the current state of scientific knowledge, a scientific realist requires a rich and varied ontology in which many different kinds of entities must be supposed to exist fundamentally. But the ontology of scientific realism has no place for abstract ideals, like geometrical points, inertial systems, perfect gases, or perfectly reversible heat engines, and hence no place for such things as propositions or eternal sentences, which have been postulated by philosophers as bearers of truth. These entities are idealized thoughts or beliefs; they are not the ingredients of causal process theories, but of model theories, and the main argument for scientific realism does not require us to believe in them.

Taking this ontology as my starting point, I argued that a scientific realist cannot consistently hold any form of correspondence theory of truth, and that neither correspondence nor redundancy theories are able to account for the *value* of truth. The only kind of theory of truth which a scientific realist can consistently hold, which accounts for the value of truth, is a pragmatic theory which identifies truth with what it is right epistemically to believe. And the epistemology on which this concept of rightness should depend, I argued, is a values-based epistemology, and the theory of truth that is required is an evaluative theory.

However, the truth, so defined, would appear to be only what is true from a human epistemic perspective. It may not be the same for aliens. And, if the epistemic perspectives of different societies or people should be different, then there may not even be a human epistemic perspective. Thus, the epistemology we derived from scientific realism is in danger of leading to a kind of species-relativism, or social relativism, or even subjectivism, about truth. That is, truth may turn out not to be an objective concept.

However, there is good reason to believe that different people, or members of different societies, all have the same basic epistemic values. They may draw very different conclusions from the same evidence, but only because of differences in their beliefs and backgrounds, not because of any inherent differences in their rationality. If different people, or members of different societies, have different epistemic perspectives, then these differences arise more from different weightings being given to the same epistemic values than from any other source; so that some kinds of considerations are seen to weigh more heavily with some than with others. And these differences of emphasis, I argued, are in principle resolvable. For there are some epistemic values, viz. the primary values of consistency, epistemic certification and corroboration, which are intrinsically weightier than others, and in the end must overcome them, and these may be used to monitor the effects of placing too much or too little emphasis on this or that secondary value.

A more serious threat to the objectivity of the naturalistic concept of truth lies with alien belief systems, because there is no reason to suppose that aliens process information as we do, or that their value systems are anything like ours. Moreover, there may be no way of synthesizing the various epistemic perspectives of different intelligent species to obtain a global, species-independent view of the world, because any synthesis of epistemic viewpoints must be a synthesis made from some particular epistemic perspective, and there is no *a priori* guarantee, or even much likelihood, that this synthesis would be acceptable to members of other species. Therefore, we seem to be forced into accepting some kind of species-relativism about truth, and so, presumably, about reality, as being the likely outcome of an encounter with aliens. This is the kind of limited objectivism about truth which I accepted, until recently, as being the probable consequence of accepting a scientific world-view (Ellis 1988b).

However, I no longer think that this conclusion carries the implications for ontology I once thought. Firstly, if beings from other planets have different epistemic perspectives from us, and, consequently, different concepts of truth and existence, then their concepts reflect their interests, not ours. Like the ents, whose case I described in the last section, they are simply engaged in a different kind of evaluation of their beliefs from what would be our epistemic evaluation of them. Secondly, ontology is not just about what it is right to believe. It is about what fundamental categories of things exist, and what their essential natures are. It is about what natural kinds of things must be supposed to exist fundamentally to account for everything we believe in. But if we can come up with an ontology of natural kinds which is adequate, and we can say what the essences of the fundamental categories of things are, then the best explanation of the fact that we can do all this is that these natural kinds really do exist, and have the natures we ascribe to them. If the categories simply reflected our interests, or our particular epistemic perspective, then this would be a remarkable and inexplicable fact.

(1) According to my analysis, the classes of rational agents, epistemic values and true beliefs are not natural kinds. The concepts of rationality, epistemic value and truth are ones we use for our own

purposes, for describing and evaluating our own belief systems and reasoning processes. Consequently, if any aliens have concepts analogous to our concepts of truth and rationality, but are different from ours, we may not have to take them seriously as providing us with different perspectives on reality. The ents, for example, have purely intellectual concepts of truth and existence, since their concepts are not grounded in experience as ours are. Consequently, the entish belief systems are not sufficiently like ours in the relevant respects for us to think of their epistemic perspective as being just a different, but equally valid, perspective on reality. On the contrary, their epistemic perspective is such that they have nothing to teach us about what exists in the real world – although they might, perhaps, have something to teach us about literary creativity or style.

For an alien belief system to be taken seriously for its perspective on reality, we should at least need to be convinced that it is based on alien experience in the sort of way that our belief systems are based on our experience, that it has been developed by careful and systematic investigations of nature, and that it represents a serious attempt to understand and explain the results of these investigations. We should expect the aliens to have arrived at their understanding of nature by recognizably rational means, i.e. by processes of reasoning and theory construction sufficiently like our own to be regarded by us as rational. For example, we should expect them to generalize from the results of their observations in theoretically and conceptually conservative ways, much as we do, to try to discover the underlying principles governing the behaviour of things by constructing idealized models of them, formulating laws with reference to these models, and devising ways and means of testing their adequacy. In short, we should expect them to behave more or less as human scientists do in their quest for knowledge and understanding.

If an alien belief system did not have this kind of dynamic, then we should have no good reason to regard it as being a well-informed and rational system of beliefs about the world, as opposed to, say, a highly speculative or imaginative creation. Therefore, an alien epistemic perspective could not differ very much from our own, and still yield a view of the nature of reality which we should respect. There might be some differences of emphasis here and there on secondary epistemic values, just as there are such differences between the epistemic perspectives of different people. But the range of *possible* epistemic value systems, and weightings of values, which might be considered viable alternatives to our own, is very narrow – much narrower than I used to think. And any differences which do exist are ones we should expect to be able to resolve by appeal to the primary epistemic values which we must be supposed to share.

Aliens could, of course, be very different from us in all sorts of ways. For example, they might have a different perceptual apparatus, and view the world through a different window in the electromagnetic spectrum. They might have very different spatial or spatio-temporal intuitions from us. They might think, for example, that the relatively flat and stable spatial region we inhabit is very boring – not at all like the strongly curved and variable region in the vicinity of that black hole at the centre of the Milky Way where they originated – and find our inability to visualize non-Euclidean geometries somewhat quaint. They might process information very differently from the ways we do. They might, for example, not operate with a belief-desire psychology, or have anything we should recognize as a system of beliefs about the world. So, I am not denying that aliens could be very different from us. The point I want to make is just that, however different they might be, they would have to process information about the world in the sorts of ways we do to have a rational system of beliefs about it. For rationality is a concept concerned with *human* interests, not alien ones.

(2) While the classifications we make when describing and evaluating our belief systems do not correspond to natural kinds, the various categories of things, which should be supposed by scientific realists to exist fundamentally, *are natural kinds*. Whether or not something is a physical entity is a question concerning its essential nature. It is not a question which depends on any decision or convention concerning how things should be classified. Nor does it depend on what our interests or epistemic values may be. If beings elsewhere denied the existence of any of the physical entities we believe in, or postulated the existence of any physical entities we

did not believe in, there would be a real question of who is right. It would be like the question whether what is called 'water' on Twin Earth is water. The answer does not depend on the manifest properties of the stuff the beings on Twin Earth call 'water', or on its functional role in Twin Earth society. It depends on what its chemical composition is. Similarly, the question whether something is a physical entity does not depend on how people, or aliens, classify it; it depends on whether it has mass or energy. For the possession of energy is the *essence* of physical existence. If the thing in question has mass or energy, then it is a physical entity; if it does not, then it is not a physical entity. And that is normally the end of the matter.

Next, it is not a question which depends on a convention whether something is a physical event. If a change in the distribution of energy in a system has occurred, then a physical event has occurred in that system, and not otherwise. Physical events just *are* changes in the distribution of energy. This is their essence. Consequently, if an alien, or a dualist, claims that there are events which are not physical events, then this has a perfectly clear meaning, and if we had to admit that events occurred, which were not changes in distribution of energy, we should have to allow that there are at least two fundamental categories of events, physical and non-physical.

Again, it is not a matter of arbitrary stipulation whether something is a physical property or relationship, or what it is a property of, or relationship between. If there are beings on other planets who have different ideas about which properties are physical, or what things have which physical properties, then this is a difference of opinion which should in principle be able to be settled by empirical investigation. It is a question of what properties or relationships make a difference in physical causal processes, and which physical entities are affected. If the properties or relationships in question do make such a difference, then they are physical properties or relationships; if they do not, then they are not physical properties or relationships. Likewise, if a property makes no physical difference to how a thing behaves, then it is not a physical property of that thing.

Presumably, causal relationships are also natural kinds. It is not clear that we fully understand what causal relationships are, but certainly forces must somehow be involved. It will not do to say that forces are involved as occult intermediate causes connecting manifest physical causes and effects, because then we should want to know what causes the forces to be produced, and how they in turn produce their effects. In my view, and that of my colleagues, John Bigelow and Robert Pargetter, forces are not themselves causes, but are primitive causal relationships – relationships which hold between physical causes and their effects (Bigelow, Ellis and Pargetter 1988). If this is right, then the question: 'What makes a relationship a causal one?' reduces to 'What is it for one thing to exert a force on another?' I do not think we know the answer to this question yet, but we do know something about the virtual particle exchange processes involved in causal interactions, and we are able to distinguish several different kinds of forces, according to the kinds of particles exchanged. It would seem to be part of the essence of a causal interaction that it should involve some such exchange of particles.

Numerical relationships are fairly obviously natural kinds, although it would be hard to say precisely what their essences are. And the same is true of at least some spatio-temporal relationships, e.g. those determining the topology of space-time. It is not so clear that the kinds of metrics we use to measure space, or space-time, or other quantities for that matter, can be said to give correct or incorrect measures of the quantities concerned. And many philosophers have argued that scales of measurement must ultimately be chosen on grounds of simplicity or convenience. However, I do not wish to go into these questions here.

The point should be fairly clear: the ontological categories are generally natural kinds. They are not just similarity classes or groups of things which bear some family resemblances to each other. Therefore, the question whether something belongs to a given ontological category is generally one which has a definite answer (even though we may not know what it is). It depends on whether it has the essential nature of things in this category. If it has, then it belongs to the category; if it has not, then it does not. It is not a question of how well it *resembles* other, or paradigm, cases of things in this category. Therefore, if agreement exists concerning the essential nature of things in a given ontological category, the question whether something does or does not belong to that category should in principle be resolvable by determining whether it has this nature.

But what is most significant is the fact that we have been able to construct an ontology of fundamental natural kinds at all, particularly an ontology which is as economical, comprehensive and explanatory as the ontology of science, and that we have been able to identify the essential natures of things in most of the fundamental categories of this ontology. For it is a remarkable fact that we have been able to explain so much of the diversity of nature in this way. Now the best explanation we have for this fact is that the ontological categories are not just of our own making, but reflect categorical differences of kind in nature. Therefore, by the main argument for scientific realism, we should believe in the ontology of science.

Thus we complete the circle. Scientific realism leads to a theory of truth and an epistemology which lead us back to scientific realism. If the best possible causal explanation of an event or state of affairs postulates or requires the existence of various kinds of things, then it is epistemically right to believe that things of these kinds exist, and, therefore, that it is true that they exist. The best possible causal explanation of the fact that we are able to construct an ontology of natural kinds adequate to account for the wide variety of things we believe to exist, and, in most cases, to identify the real essences of these natural kinds, is that these natural kinds exist and have the essential natures they are postulated by our theories as having. Therefore, by the main argument for scientific realism, we should believe in them. That is, we should believe that the distinctions between the ontological categories are naturally grounded distinctions, and that the things in these categories have the real essences they are postulated by our theories as having.

There is an important difference between questions of truth and reality. The question whether something, e.g. that fundamental particles exist, is true is an epistemic question; it calls for an epistemic evaluation. The ontological question, whether they exist as elements of reality, is not the same kind of question at all; it is a question of what explains the judgement, i.e. what makes it right to believe, that these entities exist. Do they exist as objectively distinct kinds of things, as parts of nature? Did we invent them, as Eddington once claimed we invented electrons? Or, did we have to distinguish them from other kinds of things (e.g. resonances) in a more or less arbitrary way? The ontological question is thus a demand for an explanation of an existential judgement. It is a question of what kind of judgement it is, and what makes it right to believe it.

The question 'What is true?' is a question of what it is right to believe. The question of what exists in reality is a question posed at a different level of inquiry. To answer the first question, we must investigate nature in all the sorts of ways that scientists, mathematicians, sociologists and historians do. To answer the second, we must try to come to grips with fundamental ontological questions, to identify the fundamental categories of things, and their essential natures. These two levels of inquiry are normally distinct. But the two kinds of inquiries merge in fundamental physics. For, at this level, the attempt to discover what is true, and the attempt to discover what exists most fundamentally, become indistinguishable. Therefore, the ontology we should believe in is just the ontology of science with which we started.

Notes

Introduction

1 Recent developments in unified field theory make it look as though there may ultimately be just the one kind of force responsible for all causal interactions. On the other hand, a fifth fundamental force has been mooted.

Chapter 1 The Scientific Point of View

1 It is true that scientists often quantify over the abstract ideals which are the constituents of their model-theoretic explanations. But this only shows that the ontology of science cannot be derived, in any naive way, just by looking to see what scientists quantify over. Being is not, as W. V. Quine says in his essay 'Existence and Quantification' (Quine 1969, pp. 91–113), just a matter of being the value of a variable.

2 This argument is more fully elaborated and discussed in Ellis (1975).

3 It is possible, I suppose, that the laws of nature could turn out to be determinative of the spatio-temporal distribution of things in the universe. If this should happen to be the case, then the fact that the world is a law-determined world would be a basic fact, itself incapable of explanation.

4 This is the view elaborated and criticized in my paper 'Physical Monism' (1967). The only scientifically tenable view, I argued, is a form of physical monism.

5 The concept of verisimilitude is elaborated in Popper (1963), pp. 228–31.

6 These arguments are reviewed and criticized in Ellis (1965b). The following criticisms of their approach are based on those developed in that paper.

7 An ideally rational community might, however, be something different from a community of ideally rational beings. See Sarkar (1983), pp. 178–98, for a good discussion of the concept of group rationality.

Chapter 2 The Ontology of Science

1 This chapter draws heavily on 'The Ontology of Scientific Realism' (Ellis 1987a).
2 See Smart's response to my paper in Pettit, Sylvan and Norman (eds) (1987), pp. 181–4.
3 There are systems, such as electron holes in solid state conduction bands, which are able to interact with other systems, but which have only negative energy. It is also at least possible that a system, which would generally be regarded as a physical system, should exist in a zero energy state. (I am grateful to Mark Zangari for drawing my attention to these points.) There is no intention to exclude such systems from the domain of the physical. A system possesses energy, in the sense here intended, if it exists in an energy state of any kind. It is a question of whether it belongs to the linear order of energetic systems. (See Ellis 1966, ch. 2 for a discussion of the criteria for saying that a system S possesses a quantity q.)
4 This conception of force has been elaborated and defended in Bigelow, Ellis and Pargetter (1988).
5 See my response to Swoyer in J. Forge (ed.) (1987), pp. 319–26.
6 This conception of laws is developed in Dretske (1977), Tooley (1977) and Armstrong (1983).
7 Nancy Cartwright has made much of this point in her excellent book *How the Laws of Physics Lie* (Cartwright 1983).

Chapter 3 Scientific Realism and Empiricism

1 This chapter makes extensive use of material published in 'What Science Aims to Do' (Ellis 1985).
2 See Ellis and Bowman (1967) for a demonstration that clocks can be synchronized by a method of slow clock transport which is logically independent of any assumptions about the one-way velocity of light.
3 See Carnap's essay 'Testability and Meaning' (1953) for an elaboration of this programme.
4 The example is elaborated and discussed in Ellis (1957).

5 This case has been argued in Grunbaum (1969), Salmon (1969), van Fraassen (1969) and Winnie (1970). My reply to Grunbaum, Salmon and van Fraassen is to be found in Ellis (1971).

Chapter 4 The Programme of Analysis

1 This is argued at length in Quine (1960).
2 I argued against the indicative–subjunctive distinction in Ellis (1979) pp. 61–8, claiming that the difference of mood is unimportant.
3 Indeed, according to Dudman (1983) the difference *is* just a difference of tense.
4 Tarski made this point in Tarski (1943–4): ' . . . we may accept the semantic conception of truth without giving up any epistemological attitude we may have had; we may remain naive realists, critical realists, empiricists or metaphysicians – whatever we were before. The semantic conception of truth is completely neutral toward all these issues' (p. 362).
5 Price (1988, ch. 6) distinguishes between what he calls *analytic* and *explanatory* accounts of truth: analytic accounts attempt to say what truth is; explanatory accounts seek to explain why ordinary language users should have come to use such a notion. We shall consider some explanatory accounts in chapters 6 and 7. My own account of truth, developed in chapter 7, is intended to be both analytic and explanatory.

Chapter 5 The Bearers of Truth

1 Davidson (1967), p. 16. Davidson settled, however, for the view that a truth bearer is a sentence as (potentially) spoken by a person at a time.

Chapter 6 Redundancy Theories

1 Michael Devitt makes a similar point in Devitt (1984), but his answer to the question of why we need a concept of truth is very different from mine.
2 The conditional '$p \ \Box \rightarrow q$' is true, according to Lewis, iff there is no possible world in which 'p' is true and 'q' is false which is nearer to the actual world than any in which 'p' and 'q' are both true (Lewis 1973). The two conditionals we are considering are both false, on Lewis'

semantics, because the sets of nearest worlds to the actual world in which the coin was tossed an hour ago always include both worlds in which the coin landed heads and worlds in which it landed tails.

3 The conditional '$p > q$' is true, on Stalnaker's theory, iff the nearest possible world in which 'p' is true is a world in which 'q' is true (Stalnaker 1968). See Stalnaker (1981) for his defence of conditional excluded middle, i.e. the thesis

$$(p > q) \text{ v } (p > \sim q)$$

which is the characteristic thesis of Stalnaker's system.

4 A manuscript entitled 'Probability Logic' was in fact completed in 1969.

5 I refer to an unpublished manuscript dated March 1971, entitled 'Epistemological Foundations of Logic'. The system I was trying to develop was based upon what has become known as the Stalnaker thesis, identifying $p \Rightarrow q$ with q/p, and using an epistemological semantics. It was also based on the assumption that if $P(YZ)0$, then $P(X/YZ) = P(Y \Rightarrow X/Z)$. The manuscript was never published, partly because Stalnaker succeeded (in his 1968 and 1970 publications) in doing what I had been trying to do rather better than I had been able to, but mainly because David Lewis convinced me, in a letter dated 2 June 1972, that one of my main theses was ultimately untenable. What he demonstrated in this letter is that if we have a 'probability conditional $\Rightarrow$' such that whenever $P(YZ)$ is non-zero, $P(Y \Rightarrow X/Z) = P(X/YZ)$, then P is *at most* 4-valued. I had been able to show that the systems I had been working with were consistent with models which were *at least* 4-valued, and I had hoped that they would turn out to be consistent with models which admitted infinitely many values. It came as something of a shock, however, to discover that this was not so, and I shelved the project.

Chapter 7 Naturalistic Truth and Epistemic Evaluation

1 On this point, I agree with Putnam (see Putnam 1981, p. 7).

2 NB. The predicates 'T' and 'F' are predicates of the metalanguage that is being used to evaluate the beliefs expressed in the object language; they are not the truth and falsity predicates of L.

Chapter 8 The Problem of Induction

1 This chapter is a slightly modified version of 'Solving the Problem of Induction Using a Values-based Epistemology' (Ellis 1988a).

2 In Goodman (1954), Nelson Goodman argued for the importance of *theoretical conservatism* as an epistemic value, and claimed that our inductive rules must be applied in theoretically conservative ways if their use is to be rational. I argued something similar in Ellis (1965b). More recently, John Clendinnen (1982) and Wesley Salmon (1982) have argued that *simplicity* and *non-arbitrariness* are the main considerations in determining whether an inductive rule, such as the straight rule, has been rationally applied – thus giving these epistemic values a central role in their theory.

3 For a summary of the major findings on the shortcomings of intuitive reasoning, and an excellent discussion of them, see Nisbett and Ross (1980).

4 Good discussions of the varieties of intuitionism in meta-epistemology are to be found in Alston (1978) and especially Dancy (1982).

5 The case for this has been argued by George Pugh (see Pugh 1978).

6 How consistency may be defined epistemologically is explained in Ellis (1979).

7 Recent empirical work on theory maintenance supports these general conclusions. See Nisbett and Ross (1980) ch. 8 for an excellent review of the psychological literature on this topic.

8 I do not deny the relevance of negative-negative cases to the analysis of correlations. Indeed, our natural disposition to ignore such cases is not always rational. (See Nisbett and Ross 1980, ch. 5.) What is irrational is to treat such cases as reflecting correlations between kinds, and so base an inductive argument on them.

9 I should, in fact, be willing to accept a more general thesis of epistemic conservatism than this ontological one – something very close to Sklar's 'methodological' conservatism. For he argues, as I do, that 'Stability of belief is itself a desirable state of affairs and an end to be sought' (Sklar 1975, p. 389).

10 I have argued in detail for this as a measure of degree of positive support in Ellis (1970). The normalizing factor required is $1/(1 - P(h))$.

11 This striking result is a convincing demonstration of the importance of test variety; and reflects favourably on the normalized scale of evidential support, since the chain rule does not hold for other measures of support.

12 Those, like Stephen Hawking, who are exploring the possibilities of theories using the anthropic principle (Hawking 1988) are evidently envisaging the emergence of new kinds of theories.

Chapter 9 Realism and Epistemic Naturalism

1 The case for regarding the definition of distant simultaneity in this way was argued in Ellis and Bowman (1967) and in Ellis (1971).
2 The term 'Peircean realism' was used by Putnam in this way in Putnam (1977).
3 For a discussion and comparison of patterns of thought in Africa and the West, see Robin Horton's 'Tradition and Modernity Revisited' in Hollis and Lukes (1982). See also the papers by Dan Sperber, Ernest Gellner and Steven Lukes in this same volume.
4 This is a conclusion which I accepted until quite recently (cf. Ellis 1988b); and it is for this reason that I called myself an internal realist. I did not think that truth or reality were relative to a *theoretical* perspective, because I thought that ultimately we could always choose rationally between rival theories, and so determine what it is right to believe. But I did think that our concepts of truth and reality had to be relative to the common human epistemic perspective, which determines what kinds of theories we can construct, and how we should evaluate them. However, for reasons to be explained in the following sections, I no longer find the argument for species-relativism in epistemology very convincing.
5 J. R. R. Tolkien talks about them in *Lord of the Rings*.

Bibliography

Alston, W. P. (1978): 'Meta-ethics and Meta-epistemology', in A. I. Goldman and J. Kim (eds) *Values and Morals*. Dordrecht: Reidel, 275–97.

Armstrong, D. M. (1961): *Perception and the Physical World*. London: Routledge and Kegan Paul.

Armstrong, D. M. (1968): *A Materialist Theory of the Mind*. London: Routledge and Kegan Paul.

Armstrong, D. M. (1978): *Universals and Scientific Realism* (2 vols). Cambridge: Cambridge University Press.

Armstrong, D. M. (1983): *What is a Law of Nature?* Cambridge: Cambridge University Press.

Armstrong, D. M. (1987): 'Comments on Forge and Swoyer', in J. Forge (ed.) *Measurement, Realism and Objectivity*. Dordrecht: Reidel, 311–18.

Austin, J. L. (1950): 'Truth', *Proceedings of the Aristotelian Society, Supp. Vol. XXIV*. Reprinted in G. Pitcher (ed.) (1964) *Truth*. Englewood Cliffs, N. J.: Prentice Hall, 18–31.

Barnes, B. and Bloor, D. (1982): 'Relativism, Rationalism and the Sociology of Knowledge', in M. Hollis and S. Lukes (eds) *Rationality and Relativism*. Oxford: Blackwell, 21–47.

Bigelow, J. C. (1988): *The Reality of Numbers*. Oxford: Clarendon Press.

Bigelow, J. C., Ellis, B. D. and Pargetter, R. G. (1988): 'Forces', *Philosophy of Science* 55, 614–30.

Bigelow, J. C. and Pargetter, R. G. (1988): 'Quantities', *Philosophical Studies* 54, 75–92.

Borges, J. L. (1962): 'Tlon, Uqbar, Orbus Tertius', in *Labyrinths*. New York: New Directions Publishing Company, 3–18.

Boyd, R. (1973): 'Realism, Underdetermination and a Causal Theory of Evidence', *Nous* 7, 1–12.

Boyd, R. (1981): 'Scientific Realism and Naturalistic Epistemology', in P. D. Asquith and R. N. Giere (eds) *PSA, 1980*. East Lansing: Philosophy of Science Association, 613–62.

Boyd, R. (1984): 'The Current State of Scientific Realism', in J. Leplin (ed.) *Scientific Realism*. Berkeley and Los Angeles: University of California Press, 41–82.

Boyd, R. (1985): 'Lex Orandi est Lex Credendi', in P. M. Churchland and C. A. Hooker (eds) *Images of Science*. Chicago: Chicago University Press, 1–34.

Bradley, F. H. (1914): *Essays on Truth and Reality*. Oxford: Clarendon Press.

Brandom, R. (1976): 'Truth and Assertibility', *The Journal of Philosophy* 73, 137–49.

Bridgman, P. W. (1954): *The Logic of Modern Physics*. London: Macmillan.

Byerly, H. C. and Lazara, V. A. (1973): 'Realist Foundations of Measurement', *Philosophy of Science* 40, 10–28.

Campbell, D. T. (1959): 'Methodological Suggestions from a Comparative Psychology of Knowledge Processes', *Inquiry* 2, 152–82.

Campbell, N. R. (1957): *Foundations of Science*. New York: Dover.

Carnap, R. (1953): 'Testability and Meaning', in H. Feigl and M. Brodbeck (eds) *Readings in the Philosophy of Science*. New York: Appleton, Century, Crofts, 47–92.

Cartwright, N. (1983): *How the Laws of Physics Lie*. Oxford: Oxford University Press.

Churchland, P. M. (1979): *Scientific Realism and the Plasticity of Mind*. Cambridge: Cambridge University Press.

Churchland, P. M. (1985): 'The Ontological Status of Observables', in P. M. Churchland and C. A. Hooker (eds) *Images of Science*. Chicago: Chicago University Press, 35–47.

Clendinnen, F. J. (1982): 'Rational Expectation and Simplicity', in R. McLaughlin (ed.) *What? Where? When? Why?*. Dordrecht: Reidel, 1–25.

Cohen, L. J. (1981): 'Can Human Irrationality be Experimentally Demonstrated?' plus 'Open Peer Commentary', *Behavioural and Brain Sciences* 4, 317–70.

Cohen, L. J. (1986): *The Dialogue of Reason: An Analysis of Analytical Philosophy*. Oxford: Clarendon Press.

Conee, E. and Feldman, R. (1983): 'Stich and Nisbett on Justifying Inference Rules', *Philosophy of Science* 50, 326–31.

Copi, I. M. (1977): 'Essence and Accident', in S. P. Schwartz (ed.) *Naming, Necessity, and Natural Kinds*. Ithaca and London: Cornell University Press, 176–91.

Dancy, J. (1982): 'Intuitionism in Meta-epistemology', *Philosophical Studies* 42, 395–408.

Dancy, J. (1985): *An Introduction to Contemporary Epistemology*. Oxford: Blackwell.

Darmstadter, H. (1974): 'Can Beliefs Correspond to Reality?', *Journal of Philosophy* 71, 302–14.

Davidson, D. (1967): 'Truth and Meaning', *Synthese* 17, 304–23. Reprinted in J. W. Davis, D. J. Hockney and W. K. Wilson (eds) (1969), *Philosophical Logic*. New York: Humanities Press, 1–20.

Davidson, D. (1969): 'On Saying That', in D. Davidson and J. Hintikka (eds) *Words and Objections*. Dordrecht: Reidel, 158–74.

Davidson, D. (1984): *Inquiries into Truth and Interpretation*. Oxford: Oxford University Press.

Devitt, M. (1984): *Realism and Truth*. Oxford: Blackwell.

Dretske, F. I. (1977): 'Laws of Nature', *Philosophy of Science* 44, 248–68.

Dretske, F. I. (1981): *Knowledge and the Flow of Information*. Oxford: Blackwell.

Dudman, V. H. (1983): 'Tense and Time in English Verb Clusters of the Primary Pattern', *Australasian Journal of Linguistics* 3, 25–44.

Dudman, V. H. (1984): 'Parsing "If"-Sentences', *Analysis* 44, 145–53.

Dummett, M. (1958–9): 'Truth', *Proceedings of the Aristotelian Society* LIX. Reprinted in G. Pitcher (ed.) (1964) *Truth*. Englewood Cliffs, N. J.: Prentice Hall, 93–111.

Dummett, M. (1973): *Frege: Philosophy of Language*. London: Duckworth.

Dummett, M. (1978): *Truth and Other Enigmas*. London: Duckworth.

Dummett, M. (1981): *The Interpretation of Frege's Philosophy*. Cambridge, Mass.: Harvard University Press.

Ellis, B. D. (1957): 'A Comparison of Process and Non-process Theories in the Physical Sciences', *British Journal for the Philosophy of Science* 8, 45–56.

Ellis, B. D. (1965a): 'The Origin and Nature of Newton's Laws of Motion', in R. G. Colodny (ed.) *Beyond the Edge of Certainty*. Englewood Cliffs, N. J.: Prentice Hall, 29–68.

Ellis, B. D. (1965b): 'A Vindication of Scientific Inductive Practices', *American Philosophical Quarterly* 2, 296–304.

Ellis, B. D. (1966): *Basic Concepts of Measurement*. Cambridge: Cambridge University Press.

Ellis, B. D. (1967): 'Physical Monism', *Synthese* 17, 141–61.

Ellis, B. D. (1969): 'An Epistemological Concept of Truth', in R. Brown and C. D. Rollins (eds) *Contemporary Philosophy in Australia*. London: Allen and Unwin, 52–72.

Ellis, B. D. (1970): 'Explanation and the Logic of Support', *Australasian Journal of Philosophy* 48, 177–89.

Ellis, B. D. (1971): 'On Conventionality and Simultaneity: A Reply', *Australasian Journal of Philosophy* 49, 177–203.

Ellis, B. D. (1973): 'The Logic of Subjective Probability', *British Journal for the Philosophy of Science* 24, 125–52.

Ellis, B. D. (1975): 'Physicalism and the Contents of Sense Experience', in Chung-ying Chen (ed.) *Philosophical Aspects of the Mind–Body Problem.* Honolulu: University Press of Hawaii, 64–77.

Ellis, B. D. (1976): 'The Existence of Forces', *Studies in the History and Philosophy of Science* 7, 171–85.

Ellis, B. D. (1978): 'A Unified Theory of Conditionals', *Journal of Philosophical Logic* 7, 107–24.

Ellis, B. D. (1979): *Rational Belief Systems.* Oxford; Blackwell.

Ellis, B. D. (1980): 'Truth as a Mode of Evaluation', *Pacific Philosophical Quarterly* 1, 85–99.

Ellis, B. D. (1982): 'Reply to Sorensen', *Journal of Philosophical Logic* 11, 460–2.

Ellis, B. D. (1985): 'What Science Aims to Do', in P. M. Churchland and C. A. Hooker (eds) *Images of Science.* Chicago: Chicago University Press, 48–74.

Ellis, B. D. (1987a): 'The Ontology of Scientific Realism', in P. Pettit, R. Sylvan and J. Norman (eds) *Metaphysics and Morality: Essays in Honour of J. J. C. Smart.* Oxford: Blackwell, 50–70.

Ellis, B. D. (1987b): 'Comments on Forge and Swoyer', in J. Forge (ed.) *Measurement, Realism and Objectivity.* Dordrecht: Reidel, 319–26.

Ellis, B. D. (1988a): 'Solving the Problem of Induction Using a Values-based Epistemology', *British Journal for the Philosophy of Science* 39, 141–60.

Ellis, B. D. (1988b): 'Internal Realism', *Synthese* 76, 409–34.

Ellis, B. D. (1990): 'Conventionalism in Measurement Theory', in C. Wade Savage and P. Ehrlich (eds) *Philosophical and Foundational Issues in Measurement Theory.* Hillsdale, New Jersey: Lawrence Erlbaum.

Ellis, B. D. and Bowman, P. (1967): 'Conventionality in Distant Simultaneity', *Philosophy of Science* 34, 116–36.

Evans, G. and McDowell, J. (eds) (1976): *Truth and Meaning: Essays in Semantics.* Oxford: Oxford University Press.

Farrell, R. (1980): 'Blanket Skolemism', a paper presented at the annual conference of the Australasian Association of Philosophy, Sydney, N.S.W.

Field, H. (1972): 'Tarski's Theory of Truth', *Journal Of Philosophy* 69, 347–75.

Fodor, J. A. (1975): *The Language of Thought.* New York: Crowell.

Fodor, J. A. (1983): *Modularity of Mind: An Essay on Faculty Psychology.* Cambridge, Mass.: MIT Press.

Fodor, J. A. (1987): *Psychosemantics: The Problem of Meaning in the Philosophy of Mind.* Cambridge, Mass.: MIT Press.

Forge, J. (1987): 'On Ellis' Theory of Quantities', in J. Forge (ed.) *Measurement, Realism and Objectivity.* Dordrecht: Reidel, 291–310.

Forge, J. (ed.) (1987): *Measurement, Realism and Objectivity.* Dordrecht: Reidel.

Forrest, P. (1986): *The Dynamics of Belief: A Normative Logic.* Oxford: Blackwell.

Freedman, D. Z. and van Nieuwenhuizen, P. (1978): 'Supergravity and the Unification of the Laws of Physics', *Scientific American* 239, 126–43.

Frege, G. (1918): 'Thoughts', translated by P. T. Geach and R. H. Stoothoff, in P. T. Geach (ed.) *Logical Investigations.* Oxford: Blackwell, 1–30.

Gardenfors, P. (1988): *Modeling the Dynamics of Epistemic States.* Cambridge, Mass.: MIT Press.

Gellner, E. (1981): 'Relativism and Universals', in B. Lloyd and J. Gay (eds) *Universals of Human Thought: Some African Evidence.* Cambridge: Cambridge University Press, reprinted in M. Hollis and S. Lukes (eds) (1982): *Rationality and Relativism.* Oxford: Blackwell, 181–200.

Giere, R. N. (1985): 'Constructive Realism', in P. M. Churchland and C. A. Hooker (eds) *Images of Science.* Chicago: Chicago University Press, 75–98.

Goldman, A. I. (1985): 'The Relation between Epistemology and Psychology', *Synthese* 64, 29–68.

Goodman, N. (1954): *Fact, Fiction and Forecast.* London: Athlone Press.

Grover, D. L., Camp, J. and Belnap, N. (1975): 'A Prosentential Theory of Truth', *Philosophical Studies* 27, 73–125.

Grunbaum, A. (1969): 'Simultaneity by Slow Clock Transport in the Special and General Theories of Relativity', *Philosophy of Science* 36, 5–43.

Hacking, I. (1984): 'Experimentation and Scientific Realism', in J. Leplin (ed.) *Scientific Realism.* Berkeley and Los Angeles: University of California Press, 154–72.

Harman, G. (1965): 'The Inference to the Best Explanation', *The Philosophical Review* LXXIV, 88–95.

Harre, R. and Madden, E. H. (1975): *Causal Powers.* Oxford: Blackwell.

Hawking, S. (1988): *A Brief History of Time.* New York: Bantam Books.

Heathcote, A. (1984): *Causal Theories of Space and Time.* Melbourne, La Trobe University, Ph.D. Thesis (unpublished).

Heidelberger, H. (1968): 'The Indispensability of Truth', *American Philosophical Quarterly* 5, 212–17.

Hesse, M. (1974): *The Structure of Scientific Inference*. London: Macmillan (p. 290 for material on scientific realism).

Hesse, M. (1978): 'Habermas' Consensus Theory of Truth', *Proceedings of the Philosophy of Science Association 1978*, 2, 373–96.

Hilpinen, R. (ed.) (1980): *Rationality in Science*. Dordrecht: Reidel.

Hilpinen, R. (1980): 'Scientific Rationality and the Ethics of Belief', in R. Hilpinen (ed.) *Rationality in Science*. Dordrecht: Reidel, 13–28.

Hollis, M. and Lukes, S. (eds) (1982): *Rationality and Relativism*. Oxford: Blackwell.

Hooker, C. A. (1987): *A Realistic Theory of Science*. Albany, N.Y.: State University of New York Press.

Horton, R. (1982): 'Tradition and Modernity Revisited', in M. Hollis and S. Lukes (eds) *Rationality and Relativism*. Oxford: Blackwell, 201–60.

Horwich, P. (1982): 'Three Forms of Realism', *Synthese* 51, 181–201.

Hume, D. (1740): 'An Abstract of a Book Lately Published, Entitled, *A Treatise of Human Nature*', in D. G. C. Macnabb (ed.) *A Treatise of Human Nature, Book One* by David Hume. London and Glasgow: Fontana, Appendix A.

Hume, D. (1777): *Inquiries Concerning the Human Understanding and Concerning the Principles of Morals*, edited by L. A. Selby-Bigge (2nd edn). Oxford: Clarendon Press, 1902.

James, W. (1885): 'The Meaning of Truth'. Republished in *Pragmatism and the Meaning of Truth*, Harvard University Press, 1977.

James, W. (1897): *The Will to Believe*. New York: Longmans Green and Co., 17.

Kahneman, D. and Tversky, A. (1973): 'On the Psychology of Prediction', *Psychological Review* 80, 237–51.

Kaplan, B. (1971): 'Genetic Psychology, Genetic Epistemology, and the Theory of Knowledge', in T. Mischel (ed.) *Cognitive Development and Epistemology*, New York: Academic Press.

Kripke, S. (1972): 'Naming and Necessity', in D. Davidson and G. Harman (eds) *Semantics of Natural Language*. Dordrecht: Reidel.

Kripke, S. (1977): 'Identity and Necessity', in S. P. Schwartz (ed.) *Naming, Necessity, and Natural Kinds*. Ithaca and London: Cornell University Press, 66–101.

Krips, H. (1982): 'Epistemological Holism', *Studies in the History and Philosophy of Science* 13, 251–64.

Kuhn, T. S. (1962): 'The Structure of Scientific Revolutions', *International Encyclopedia of Unified Science II*, No. 2.

Kyburg, H. E. (1983): 'Rational Belief', *The Behavioral and Brain Sciences* 6, 231–45, with commentaries by J. E. Adler; M. Bar-Hillel and A.

Margalit; L. J. Cohen; J. Dorling; J. St. B. T. Evans; G. Harman; W. L. Harper, P. N. Johnson-Laird; D. Kahneman; I. Levi; L. L. Lopes; D. Miller; R. Nisbett and P. Thagard; P. Pollard; R. Revlin; T. Seidenfeld; S. Spielman; R. D. Tweney, M. E. Doherty and C. R. Mynatt, pp. 245–63, and reply by H. E. Kyburg, pp. 263–73.

Lakatos, I. (1963): 'Proofs and Refutations', *British Journal for the Philosophy of Science* 14, 1–25, 120–39, 221–45, 296–342.

Laudan, L. (1984): 'A Confutation of Convergent Realism', in J. Leplin (ed.) *Scientific Realism*. Berkeley and Los Angeles: University of California Press, 218–49.

Leeds, S. (1978): 'Theories of Reference and Truth', *Erkenntnis* 13, 111–29.

Leplin, J. (ed.) (1984): *Scientific Realism*. Berkeley and Los Angeles: University of California Press.

Levi, I. (1967a): *Gambling with Truth*. London: Routledge and Kegan Paul.

Levi, I. (1967b): 'Information and Inference', *Synthese* 17, 369–91.

Levi, I. (1976): 'Truth, Fallibility and the Growth of Knowledge' and 'Acceptance Revisited', in R. J. Bogdan (ed.) *Local Induction*. Dordrecht: Reidel, 1–71.

Levi, I. (1977): 'Epistemic Utility and the Evaluation of Experiments', *Philosophy of Science* 44, 368–86.

Levi, I. (1980): *The Enterprise of knowledge*. Cambridge, Mass.: MIT Press.

Lewis, D. K. (1973): *Counterfactuals*. Cambridge Mass.: Harvard University Press.

Lewis, D. K. (1979): 'Attitudes De Dicto and De Se', *The Philosophical Review* 87, 513–43.

Lewis, D. K. (1986): *On the Plurality of Worlds*. Oxford: Blackwell.

Lukes, S. (1982): 'Relativism in its Place', in M. Hollis and S. Lukes (eds) *Rationality and Relativism*. Oxford: Blackwell, 261–305.

Lycan, W. G. (1985): 'Epistemic Value', *Synthese* 64, 137–64.

Mackie, J. L. (1962): 'Counterfactuals and Causal Laws', in R. J. Butler (ed.) *Analytical Philosophy*. Oxford: Blackwell, 66–80.

Mackie, J. L. (1974): *The Cement of the Universe*. Oxford: Clarendon Press.

Markovic, M. (1980): 'Scientific and Ethical Rationality', in R. Hilpinen (ed.) *Rationality in Science*. Dordrecht: Reidel, 79–90.

Maxwell, G. (1962): 'The Ontological Status of Theoretical Entities', in H. Feigl and G. Maxwell (eds) *Minnesota Studies in the Philosophy of Science III*. Minneapolis: University of Minnesota Press, 3–27.

Maxwell, G. (1970a): 'Structural Realism and the Meaning of Theoretical Terms', in M. Radnor and S. Winakur (eds) *Minnesota Studies in the Philosophy of Science IV*. Minneapolis: University of Minnesota Press, 181–92.

Maxwell, G. (1970b): 'Theories, Perception and Structural Realism', in R. G. Colodny (ed.) *The Nature and Function of Scientific Theories: Essays in Contemporary Science and Philosophy*, University of Pittsburgh Press, 3–34.

Maxwell, J. C. (1881): *Elementary Treatise on Electricity*. W. Garnett (ed.), Oxford: Clarendon Press.

Mayer, J. R. (1842): 'Remarks on the Forces of Inorganic Nature', *Philosophical Magazine* Series 4, 24, tr. by G. C. Foster from the original paper in *Annalen der Chemie und Pharmacie* 42, p. 233. Reprinted in W. F. Magie (ed.) *Source Book in Physics*. New York and London: McGraw-Hill, 197–203.

Merrill, G. H. (1980): 'Three Forms of Realism', *American Philosophical Quarterly* 17, 229–35.

Misner, C. W., Thorne, K. S. and Wheeler, J. A. (1973): *Gravitation*. San Francisco: Freeman.

Musgrave, A. (1985): 'Realism versus Constructive Empiricism', in P. M. Churchland and C. A. Hooker (eds) *Images of Science*. Chicago: Chicago University Press, 197–221.

Nagel, E. (1961): *The Structure of Science*. London: Routledge and Kegan Paul (pp. 141–50 for reality criteria).

Newton-Smith, W. (1980): 'The Underdetermination of Theory by Data', in R. Hilpenin (ed.) *Rationality in Science*. Dordrecht: Reidel.

Newton-Smith, W. (1982): 'Relativism and the Possibility of Interpretation', in M. Hollis and S. Lukes (eds) *Rationality and Relativism*. Oxford: Blackwell, 106–22.

Nisbett, R. and Ross, L. (1980): *Human Inference: Strategies and Shortcomings of Social Judgement*. Englewood Cliffs, N. J.: Prentice Hall.

Nisbett, R. E. and Stich, S. P. (1985): 'Could Man be an Irrational Animal?', *Synthese* 64, 115–35.

Nola, R. (1987): 'Nietzsche's Theory of Truth and Belief', *Philosophy and Phenomenological Research* 47, 525–62.

Peirce, C. S. (1878): 'How to Make Our Ideas Clear', *Popular Science Monthly* 12, 286–302, reprinted in V. Tomas (ed.) (1957) *Charles S. Peirce: Essays in the Philosophy of Science*. New York: Liberal Arts Press, 31–56.

Pettit, P. (1982): 'Habermas on Truth and Justice', in G. Parkinson (ed.) *Marx and Marxisms*. Cambridge: Cambridge University Press, 207–28.

Pettit, P., Sylvan, R. and Norman, J. (eds) (1987): *Metaphysics and Morality: Essays in Honour of J. J. C. Smart*. Oxford: Blackwell.

Pitcher, G. (ed.) (1964): *Truth*. Englewood Cliffs, N. J.: Prentice Hall.

Plantinga, A. (1974): *The Nature of Necessity*. Oxford: Oxford University Press.

Popper, K. R. (1959): *The Logic of Scientific Discovery*. London: Hutchinson.

Popper, K. R. (1963): *Conjectures and Refutations*. London: Routledge and Kegan Paul.

Popper, K. R. (1972): *Objective Knowledge: An Evolutionary Approach*. Oxford: Clarendon Press.

Price, H. (1987): 'Truth and the Nature of Assertion', *Mind* 96, 202–20.

Price, H. (1988): *Facts and the Function of Truth*. Oxford: Blackwell.

Pugh, G. (1978): *The Biological Origin of Human Values*. London: Routledge and Kegan Paul.

Putnam, H. (1975): 'The Meaning of "Meaning"', in K. Gunderson (ed.) *Language, Mind, and Knowledge*. Minneapolis: University of Minnesota Press.

Putnam, H. (1977): 'Realism and Reason', *Proceedings and Addresses of the American Philosophical Association* 50, 483–98. Reprinted in Putnam (1978). 123–40.

Putnam, H. (1978): *Meaning and the Moral Sciences*. London: Routledge and Kegan Paul.

Putnam, H. (1980): 'How to be an Internal Realist and a Transcendental Idealist (at the same time)', in *Language, Logic and Philosophy: Proceedings of the Fourth International Wittgenstein Symposium*. Vienna: Holder-Pichler-Tempsky, 100–8.

Putnam, H. (1981): *Reason, Truth and History*. Cambridge: Cambridge University Press.

Putnam, H. (1982): 'Three Kinds of Scientific Realism', *Philosophical Quarterly* 32, 195–200.

Putnam, H. (1983): *Realism and Reason: Philosophical Papers, Vol. 3*. Cambridge: Cambridge University Press.

Quine, W. V. (1935): 'Truth By Convention'. Reprinted in *The Ways of Paradox and Other Essays*. New York: Random House, 70–99.

Quine, W. V. (1960): *Word and Object*. Massachusetts Institute of Technology: The Technology Press; and New York and London: J. Wiley & Sons.

Quine, W. V. (1966): 'The Scope and Language of Science', in his *Ways of Paradox and Other Essays*. New York: Random House, 215–32.

Quine, W. V. (1969): *Ontological Relativity and Other Essays*. New York and London: Columbia University Press.

Quine, W. V. (1970): *Philosophy of Logic*. Englewood Cliffs, N. J.: Prentice Hall.

Quine, W. V. (1977): 'Natural Kinds', in S. P. Schwartz (ed.) *Naming, Necessity, and Natural Kinds*. Ithaca and London: Cornell University Press, 155–75.

Ramsey, F. P. (1927): 'Facts and Propositions', *Proceedings of the Aristotelian Society, Supp.* VII. Reprinted in *The Foundations of Mathematics*, London: Routledge and Kegan Paul; New York: The Humanities Press, 1931. Partially reprinted in Pitcher (ed.) (1964), *Truth*, 16–17.

Reichenbach, H. (1927): *Philosophie der Raum-Zeit-Lehre*, tr. by M. Reichenbach and J. Freund as *The Philosophy of Space and Time* (1958). New York: Dover.

Ross, W. D. (1939): *Foundations of Ethics*. Oxford: Clarendon Press.

Russell, B. (1918): 'The Philosophy of Logical Atomism', reprinted in R. C. Marsh (ed.) (1956) *Logic and Knowledge*. London: Allen and Unwin, 177–281 (see especially Lectures I–III).

Russell, B. (1940): *An Inquiry into Meaning and Truth*. London: Allen and Unwin; republished as a Pelican Book in 1962.

Ryle, G. (1950): '"If", "So" and "Because"', in M. Black (ed.) *Philosophical Analysis*. Ithaca, N. Y.: Cornell University Press, 323–40.

Salmon, W. C. (1969): 'The Conventionality of Simultaneity', *Philosophy of Science* 36, 44–63.

Salmon, W. C. (1982): 'Further Reflections', in R. McLaughlin (ed.) *What? Where? When? Why?* Dordrecht: Reidel, 231–80.

Sarkar, H. (1983): *A Theory of Method*. Berkeley and Los Angeles: University of California Press.

Schlesinger, G. (1963): *Method in the Physical Sciences*. London: Routledge and Kegan Paul.

Schwartz, S. P. (ed.) (1977): *Naming, Necessity, and Natural Kinds*. Ithaca and London: Cornell University Press.

Sklar, L. (1975): 'Methodological Conservatism', *Philosophical Review* 84, 374–400.

Smart, J. J. C. (1963): *Philosophy and Scientific Realism*. London: Routledge and Kegan Paul.

Smart, J. J. C. (1982): 'Difficulties for Realism in the Philosophy of Science', in L. J. Cohen, J. Los, H. Pfeiffer and K.-P. Podewski (eds) *Logic, Methodology and Philosophy of Science* VI. Amsterdam: North Holland, 363–75.

Sober, E. (1975): *Simplicity*. Oxford: Clarendon Press.

Sober, E. (1978): 'Psychologism', *Journal of the Theory of Social Behaviour* 8, 165–91.

Sober, E. (1981): 'The Evolution of Rationality', *Synthese* 46, 95–120.

Sorensen, R. A. (1982): 'Epistemic and Classic Validity', *Journal of Philosophical Logic* 11, 458–9.

Sorensen, R. A. (1988): *Blindspots*. Oxford: Clarendon Press.

Sosa, E. (1985): 'The Coherence of Virtue and the Virtue of Coherence:

Justification in Epistemology', *Synthese* 64, 3–28.

Sperber, D. (1982): 'Apparently Irrational Beliefs', in M. Hollis and S. Lukes (eds) *Rationality and Relativism*. Oxford: Blackwell, 149–80.

Stalnaker, R. C. (1968): 'A Theory of Conditionals', in N. Rescher (ed.) *Studies in Logical Theory*. Oxford: Blackwell, 98–112.

Stalnaker, R. C. (1970): 'Probability and Conditionals', *Philosophy of Science* 37, 64–80.

Stalnaker, R. C. (1981): 'A Defense of Conditional Excluded Middle', in W. L. Harper, R. Stalnaker and G. Pearce (eds) *Ifs*. Dordrecht, Boston and London: Reidel, 87–104.

Stich, S. P. (1980): 'Justification and the Psychology of Human Reasoning', *Philosophy of Science* 47, 188–202.

Stich, S. P. (1983): *From Folk Psychology to Cognitive Science: The Case against Belief*. Cambridge, Mass.: MIT Press.

Strawson, P. F. (1950): 'Truth', *Proceedings of the Aristotelian Society, Supp. Vol.* XXIV. Reprinted in G. Pitcher (ed.) (1964) *Truth*. Englewood Cliffs, N. J.: Prentice Hall, 32–53.

Swoyer, C. (1987): 'The Metaphysics of Measurement', in J. Forge (ed.) *Measurement, Realism and Objectivity*. Dordrecht: Reidel, 235–90.

Tarski, A. (1936): 'The Concept of Truth in Formalised Languages', tr. by J. H. Woodger, in *Logic Semantics and Metamathematics*. Oxford: Clarendon Press, 152–278.

Tarski, A. (1943–4): 'The Semantic Conception of Truth', *Philosophy and Phenomenological Research* IV, 341–75.

Taylor, C. (1982): 'Rationality', in M. Hollis and S. Lukes (eds) *Rationality and Relativism*. Oxford: Blackwell, 87–105.

Thagard, P. (1978): 'The Best Explanation: Criteria for Theory Choice', *Journal of Philosophy* 75, 76–92.

Thayer, H. S. (ed.) (1953): *Newton's Philosophy of Nature*. New York: Hafner.

Tooley, M. (1977): 'The Nature of Laws', *Canadian Journal of Philosophy* 7, 667–98.

Tranoy, K. E. (1980): 'Norms of Inquiry: Rationality, Consistency Requirements and Normative Conflict', in R. Hilpinen (ed.) *Rationality in Science*. Dordrecht: Reidel, 191–202.

van Fraassen, B. C. (1969): 'Conventionality in the Axiomatic Foundations of the Special Theory of Relativity', *Philosophy of Science* 36, 64–73.

van Fraassen, B. C. (1977): 'The Pragmatics of Explanation', *American Philosophical Quarterly* 14, 143–50.

van Fraassen, B. C. (1980): *The Scientific Image*. Oxford: Clarendon Press.

van Fraassen, B. C. (1982): 'Epistemic Semantics Defended', *Journal of Philosophical Logic* 11, 463–4.

van Fraassen, B. C. (1984): 'To Save the Phenomena', in J. Leplin (ed.) *Scientific Realism*. Berkeley and Los Angeles: University of California Press, 250–9.

van Fraassen, B. C. (1985): 'Replies to His Critics', in P. M. Churchland and C. A. Hooker (eds) *Images of Science*. Chicago: Chicago University Press, 245–309.

Walsh, D. (1979): 'Occam's Razor: A Principle of Intellectual Elegance', *American Philosophical Quarterly* 16, 241–4.

Weingartner, P. (1980): 'Normative Characteristics of Scientific Activity', in R. Hilpinen (ed.) *Rationality in Science*. Dordrecht: Reidel, 209–30.

Wheeler, J. A. (1962): *Geometrodynamics*. New York: Academic Press.

White, A. R. (1957): 'Truth as Appraisal', *Mind* 66, 318–30.

Wiggins, D. (1980): 'What would be a Substantial Theory of Truth?', in Z. van Staaten (ed.) *Philosophical Subjects: Essays Presented to P. F. Strawson*. Oxford: Oxford University Press, 189–221.

Williams, D. (1963): *The Ground of Induction*. New York: Russell and Russell.

Wilson, M. (1985): 'What Can Theory Tell Us About Observation?' in P. M. Churchland and C. A. Hooker (eds) *Images of Science*. Chicago: Chicago University Press, 222–42.

Winnie, J. (1970): 'Special Relativity without One-Way Velocity Assumptions', *Philosophy of Science* 37, 81–99 and 223–38.

Index